Understanding Ethical Failures in Leadership

Why do leaders fail ethically? In *Understanding Ethical Failures in Leadership*, Terry L. Price uses a multidisciplinary approach to understand leader immorality in the public, private, and non-profit sectors. He argues that leaders often know that a certain kind of behavior is generally required by morality but are nonetheless mistaken as to whether the relevant moral requirement applies to them in a particular situation and whether others are protected by this requirement.

Price shows how leaders make exceptions of themselves, explains how the justificatory force of leadership gives rise to such exception making, and develops normative prescriptions that leaders should adopt as a response to this feature of their moral psychology.

Terry L. Price is Associate Professor of Leadership Studies at the Jepson School of Leadership Studies, University of Richmond. He has a PhD in philosophy from the University of Arizona and degrees in philosophy, psychology, and politics from the University of North Carolina at Chapel Hill and the University of Oxford. He has contributed to *American Philosophical Quarterly*, the *Encyclopedia of Leadership*, and the *Journal of Political Philosophy*, and he is editor, with J. Thomas Wren and Douglas A. Hicks, of the three-volume reference set *The International Library of Leadership*.

Cambridge Studies in Philosophy and Public Policy

General editor: Douglas MacLean, *University of North Carolina at Chapel Hill*

Other books in series

David Boonin: *A Defense of Abortion*

Dan Brock: *Life and Death*

Deen K. Chatterjee and Don E. Scheid (eds.): *Ethics and Foreign Intervention*

Norman Daniels: *Justice and Justification*

Elaine Draper: *Risky Business*

R. G. Frey and Christopher W. Morris: *Violence, Terrorism, and Justice*

Robert K. Fullinwider (ed.): *Public Education in a Multicultural Society*

William Galston: *Liberal Purposes*

Robert Goodin: *Utilitarianism as a Public Philosophy*

Douglas Husak: *Drugs and Rights*

John Kleinig: *The Ethics of Policing*

Steven Lee: *Morality, Prudence, and Nuclear Weapons*

Judith Lichtenberg (ed.): *Democracy and the Mass Media*

Erik Nord: *Cost-Value Analysis in Health Care*

Bernard Rollin: *The Frankenstein Syndrome*

Mark Sagoff: *The Economy of the Earth*

Ferdinand Schoeman: *Privacy and Social Freedom*

Henry Shue (ed.): *Nuclear Deterrence and Moral Restraint*

James P. Sterba: *Justice for Here and Now*

Paul B. Thompson: *The Ethics of Aid and Trade*

Jeremy Waldron: *Liberal Rights*

David Wasserman and Robert Wachbroit (eds.): *Genetics and Criminal Behavior*

Ajume H. Wingo: *Veil Politics in Liberal Democratic States*

Understanding Ethical Failures in Leadership

TERRY L. PRICE

University of Richmond

CAMBRIDGE
UNIVERSITY PRESS

CAMBRIDGE UNIVERSITY PRESS
Cambridge, New York, Melbourne, Madrid, Cape Town, Singapore, São Paulo

Cambridge University Press
40 West 20th Street, New York, NY 10011-4211, USA

www.cambridge.org
Information on this title: www.cambridge.org/9780521837248

First published 2006

Printed in the United States of America

A catalog record for this publication is available from the British Library.

Library of Congress Cataloging in Publication Data

Price, Terry L., 1966–
Understanding ethical failures in leadership / Terry L. Price.
p.   cm. – (Cambridge studies in philosophy and public policy)
Includes bibliographical references and index.
ISBN 0-521-83724-3 (hardcover) – ISBN 0-521-54597-8 (pbk.)
1. Business ethics.   2. Leadership – Moral and ethical aspects.
I. Title.   II. Series.
HF5387.P736 2005
174′.4–dc22   2004030867

ISBN-13   978-0-521-83724-8 hardback
ISBN-10   0-521-83724-3 hardback

ISBN-13   978-0-521-54597-6 paperback
ISBN-10   0-521-54597-8 paperback

In Memory of Joel Feinberg (1926–2004)

Contents

Acknowledgments   *page* xi

    Introduction   1

1   Volitional and Cognitive Accounts of Ethical Failures
    in Leadership   12

2   The Nature of Exception Making   28

3   Making Exceptions for Leaders   59

4   Justifying Leadership   91

5   The Ethics of Authentic Transformational Leadership   123

6   Change and Responsibility   147

7   Ignorance, History, and Moral Membership   179

Works Cited   201

Index   213

Acknowledgments

Several chapters of this book have been presented, in part or in whole, at professional conferences and university colloquia. I would like to thank commentators and audience participants at meetings of the American Philosophical Association, the Association for Practical and Professional Ethics, the European Business Ethics Network, and the International Leadership Association. I am also grateful for the opportunity I had to get crucial feedback on my work at Agnes Scott College, the College of William and Mary, Georgetown University, James Madison University, St. Edward's University, the University of Delaware, and the University of Richmond.

I want to acknowledge that parts of the Introduction draw on my "Ethics" entry in George R. Goethals, Georgia Sorenson, James MacGregor Burns (eds.), *Encyclopedia of Leadership* (copyright © 2004 Berkshire Publishing Group), and that two chapters of the book are revised versions of previously published articles. An earlier incarnation of Chapter 1 was originally published as "Explaining Ethical Failures of Leadership" in *Leadership and Organization Development Journal: Special Issue on Ethics and Leadership* (copyright © 2000 Emerald Group Publishing Limited). Chapter 5 is an extended treatment of the content of "The Ethics of Authentic Transformational Leadership," which appeared in *Leadership Quarterly* (copyright © 2003 Elsevier). I wish to express my appreciation to Berkshire Publishing Group, Emerald Group Publishing Limited, and Elsevier, respectively, for their kind permission to use this material.

This book could not have been written without the financial resources and intellectual community at the Jepson School of Leadership Studies at the University of Richmond. A junior research leave in 2002 gave me uninterrupted time to work on this project, and funding for conference travel and research assistance helped me to finish it. Moreover, I owe a dept of gratitude to my colleagues at the Jepson School, each of whom has contributed greatly to my thinking about leadership. If this book achieves any of its interdisciplinary objectives, then it is primarily because I am surrounded by very gifted scholars from anthropology, history, law, management, philosophy, political science, psychology, public administration, and religion.

Elizabeth Faier, George Goethals, Gill Hickman, Crystal Hoyt, Fredric Jablin, Tiffany Keller, Gary McDowell, John Rosenblum, and Kenneth Ruscio went out of their way to direct me to the relevant literature within their disciplines.

Several chapters benefited greatly from careful comments by James MacGregor Burns, Joanne Ciulla, David Jones, Andrew Lewis, and J. Thomas Wren, as well as from readings by my students in Ethics and Leadership, especially Janice Baab.

My friend and colleague Douglas Hicks deserves special mention for working through the entire manuscript, many chapters for the second or third time, just weeks after the birth of his first child.

The time and effort Cassie King spent researching and proofreading the manuscript is second only to the time and effort I spent writing it. No one I have ever worked with is more committed to getting things right, and I certainly owe a lot to Cassie. I am also indebted to my student assistants, Michael Clements and Alison Smith; our administrative assistant, Nancy Nock; and the University of Richmond Library staff – in particular, Lucretia McCulley, Nancy Vick, and Noreen Cullen.

Douglas MacLean, series editor for *Cambridge Studies in Philosophy and Public Policy*, and Terence Moore, Publishing Director for Humanities at Cambridge University Press, strongly supported this project from the beginning, and I am grateful to them for their confidence in me and for their solid advice. Sadly, Terence Moore died before the manuscript was finished.

Beatrice Rehl, Senior Editor for Humanities at Cambridge University Press, ably picked up the project and saw it through to completion.

Ronald Cohen edited the manuscript with care and attention. The book is much improved as a result of his recommendations and corrections.

Finally, my deepest appreciation is reserved for Lori Speagle and Harper Speagle-Price. They cared for and accepted a partner and father who was at times inseparable from his laptop. Philosophical argument aside, the writing process itself gave me a very good sense of how readily I overestimate the importance of my own projects. I am fortunate still to be loved by them despite the exceptions I make of myself.

Introduction

I. THE MAIN ARGUMENT

This book articulates the intuition behind the charge that leaders think that they are special, that ordinary rules do not apply to them, and that followers should be expected to do as the leader says, not as the leader does. My central thesis is that ethical failures in leadership are fundamentally cognitive, not volitional. In arguing for this thesis, I reject the standard view that leaders behave unethically simply because they are selfish. Leader immorality is more a matter of belief and knowledge than a matter of desire and will. As such, the unethical behavior of leaders cannot be fully understood in terms of self-interest and the choices leaders make to put self-interest ahead of what they know to be the requirements of morality. So, for example, leadership ethics is not just about adjudicating between the interests of leaders and followers. An account of ethical failures in leadership must assign a primary role to mistaken moral beliefs.

The argument for the cognitive account of ethical failures in leadership appeals directly to the beliefs leaders hold about the importance of their ends. Of course, we all believe that our ends are important; otherwise we would not have them as ends. Leaders are no different in this respect, but the collective nature of the ends to which leaders are committed gives added justification to these ends. This is what makes leadership ethics distinctive. Leaders can believe, based on the importance of the collective ends they seek to achieve, that they are justified in making exceptions of themselves and in excluding others from the protections of morality. On the account offered in this book, ethical failure is a straightforward consequence of the

1

way we think about leadership and the way leaders think about themselves.[1]

It might be expected that a book on ethical failures in leadership would begin with a moral theory to work from. Relying on an explicit statement of the requirements of morality, I could then infer what constitutes an ethical failure in leadership, thereby putting myself in a position to discern its causes. It is not my aim, however, to offer a direct specification of moral leadership, let alone to begin with one. In fact, this book is better characterized as an analysis of the challenges to determining what morality demands of leaders, especially as this determination is made from the distinctive perspective of leaders. If I am right, such cognitive challenges to morality preclude any kind of foundationalist analysis of ethical failures in leadership. Ultimately, the book seeks to address the question of how leaders ought to act given that they do not always know what morality requires of them. To this end, I offer practical normative responses to the fact that justification is not always transparent to leaders.[2] Leaders should, among other responses, restrict the exceptions they make of themselves to the pursuit of inclusive ends, and publicize their reasons for deviating from the requirements of morality.

In the chapters that follow, I show why, given the nature of leadership itself, leaders are especially likely to face cognitive challenges to ethical behavior. For now, it is enough to point out that leadership is not only goal oriented but privileges the goals of the parties to the relationship. In other words, leadership is characterized by both consequentialism and partiality. Accordingly, it encourages preoccupation with collective ends, sometimes to the neglect of other important moral considerations.

---

[1] My approach is consistent with that of Howard Gardner, who writes, "Our understanding of the nature and processes of leadership is most likely to be enhanced as we come to understand better the arena in which leadership necessarily occurs – namely, the *human mind*. Perhaps this characterization should be pluralized as *human minds*, since I am concerned equally with the mind of the leader and the minds of the followers ... By focusing on the mind and invoking the word *cognitive*, I make deliberate contact with an approach to the study of mind that has developed rapidly in the last few decades. In contrast to the behaviorists, who have focused only on overt actions, and the psychoanalysts, whose interest has been directed chiefly at personality and motivation, cognitive psychologists examine how ideas (or thoughts or images or mental representations) develop and how they are stored, accessed, combined, remembered, and (all too often) rearranged or distorted by the operations of the human mental apparatus" (*Leading Minds: An Anatomy of Leadership* [New York: BasicBooks, 1995], pp. 15–16).

[2] See Allen E. Buchanan, "Social Moral Epistemology," *Social Philosophy and Policy* 19 (2002): 126–152.

First among these considerations is that there are ethical constraints on the means used to achieve group, organizational, or societal goals, even when goal achievement is in the interests of followers.[3] Second, there are other parties in the moral universe besides those individuals in the leader-follower relationship. So, even if it is true that leaders should always put their interests second to the interests of followers, we cannot conclude that so doing is sufficient for ethical success in leadership. Given these two considerations, volitional pressures on leaders to privilege self-interest are a much smaller part of the story than cognitive pressures on leaders to put the interests of the group ahead of the interests of individual followers and the interests of outsiders.

II. THE "HITLER PROBLEM"

One approach to ethics in leadership has been to use normative considerations to delimit the subject matter itself. On this approach, since leadership is moral by definition, unethical behavior by those in power must be something other than leadership. The temptation to resort to definitions has been particularly strong in leadership studies, in part because of basic epistemological commitments that characterize standard social scientific research in this field.[4] But the definitional approach to ethics in leadership goes back at least to Plato, who argues that "every kind of rule, insofar as it rules, doesn't seek anything other than what is best for the things it rules and cares for, and this is true both of public and private kinds of rule."[5] Plato's view that *true* leadership is concerned with the good of the led, not the good of the leader himself, finds twentieth-century expression in the work of James MacGregor

---

[3] For example, adherents of Immanuel Kant's moral philosophy would hardly be impressed by deception and manipulation by a leader whose goal was to advance the interests of followers. Though this kind of behavior can be perfectly altruistic, it can nevertheless fail to show morally appropriate respect for follower agency. In other words, the claim that a leader's deceptive and manipulative behavior was for the good of followers does not answer the charge that he did not engage properly their rational agency.

[4] Given the empiricist assumption that, as David Hume puts it, all knowledge is about "relations of ideas" or "existence and matter of fact," ethics quickly becomes a matter of definition for social scientists (*A Treatise of Human Nature*, 2nd edition, ed. L. A. Selby-Bigge [Oxford: Oxford University Press, 1978], p. 458). After all, no amount of empirical data will give us the ethical facts, as opposed to people's ethical perceptions.

[5] Plato, *Republic*, trans. G. M. A. Grube (Indianapolis: Hackett Publishing Company, 1992), p. 21 [345d–e].

Burns, who goes so far as to deny that Adolf Hitler was a leader because "[l]eadership, unlike naked power-wielding, is . . . inseparable from followers' needs and goals," and Hitler was "an absolute wielder of brutal power."[6]

Must leadership be ethical to be leadership at all? This question is important to consider at the beginning of a book on understanding ethical failures in leadership. If the definitional approach to leadership is defensible, then there would seem to be no ethical failures in *leadership* for us to understand! I think we can admit that normative considerations help to mark off the domain of inquiry in leadership studies without undermining the book's purpose. Consider, for instance, that completely coercive relationships hardly count as leadership. Because the behavior of coerced agents is involuntary, the relationship between the coercer and the coerced is closer to the relationship between master and slave than that between leader and follower. Still, there is a large gap in reasoning between recognition of this conceptual point and the conclusion that behavior that deviates from morality is not leadership at all. Even if we assume that the relationship of leadership implies minimal agency on the part of followers, it would not follow that leadership always shows sufficient respect for the agency of followers or, for that matter, their well-being. Nor would it follow that leadership always puts the agency of followers to work in the service of ethical ends. Accordingly, we are left with many important moral problems that cannot be easily assumed away.

Joanne Ciulla contends that definitional approaches to leadership conceal particular normative commitments regarding the nature of the relationship between leaders and followers.[7] In effect, the definitions are misguided attempts to specify what constitutes good leadership, where *good* means both "morally good and technically good or effective."[8] This

---

[6] James MacGregor Burns, *Leadership* (New York: Harper and Row Publishers, 1978), pp. 19, 27.

[7] This paragraph and the one that follows it draw from Terry L. Price, "Ethics," in George R. Goethals, Georgia Sorenson, James MacGregor Burns, eds., *Encyclopedia of Leadership* (Thousand Oaks, CA: Sage Publications, 2004), pp. 462–470, copyright © 2004 Berkshire Publishing Group. Reprinted with permission of Berkshire Publishing Group.

[8] Joanne B. Ciulla, "Leadership Ethics: Mapping the Territory," in Joanne B. Ciulla, ed., *Ethics, the Heart of Leadership* (Westport, CT: Praeger, 1998), p. 13. See also James O'Toole, *Leading Change: The Argument for Values-Based Leadership* (New York: Ballantine Books, 1996); and John W. Gardner, *On Leadership* (New York: Free Press, 1990), ch. 7. O'Toole writes, "But that necessary factor of effectiveness turns out to be

distinction helps us understand what Ciulla calls the "Hitler problem."[9] Burns and others who contend that Hitler was not a leader exploit the ambiguity in the question of whether he was a *good* leader. Since Hitler was at most technically good or effective, he can have been a good leader in only one sense of the term. Understanding the Hitler problem is therefore a prerequisite to beginning work in leadership ethics. Articulating particular normative commitments about leadership is the real task ethicists have faced all along. Simply calling some individuals *leaders* and others by a different name does not get around the fact that people in power sometimes engage in unethical behavior. Regardless of what we call these people, we want to be able to understand their behavior and help them to avoid it.

Commentators who make their normative commitments explicit by offering recommendations for how leaders ought to behave most often identify morally good leadership with what the definitional approach holds is necessary for leadership itself – namely, concern for the good of followers. It is on these grounds that thinkers from Aristotle to Machiavelli separate good and bad rule.[10] Contemporary observers of leadership have been no less inclined to make the opposition between concern for self and concern for others the defining distinction in

insufficient . . . The values-based leadership advocated in these pages is different, therefore, from the prevailing modes in that its calculus includes the factors of *morality*"(p. xii).

[9] Ciulla, "Mapping the Territory," p. 12. According to John Gardner, "We say that we want effective leadership; but Hitler was effective. Criteria beyond effectiveness are needed" (*On Leadership*, p. 67).

[10] Aristotle distinguishes correct from deviated constitutions, claiming that "[w]henever the one, the few, or the many rule with a view to the common good, these constitutions must be correct; but if they look to the private advantage, be it of the one or the few or the mass, they are deviations" (*The Politics*, trans. T. A. Sinclair [New York: Penguin Books, 1981], pp. 189–190 [1279a28–1279a30]). Aquinas, appealing to God's exhortation in Ezekiel 34:2, "Woe to the shepherds of Israel who have fed themselves," similarly makes concern for the good of followers both sufficient and necessary for good leadership: "[I]f a ruler should direct a community of free persons for the common good of the people, there will be a right and just regime, as befits free persons. And if the governance of a ruler be ordained for the private good of the ruler and not for the common good of the people, there will be an unjust and wicked regime" (*On Kingship, To the King of Cyprus*, in Michael L. Morgan, ed., *Classics of Moral and Political Theory*, 3rd edition [Indianapolis: Hackett Publishing Company, 2001], p. 398). Even Machiavelli, who is known for the amoralism of *The Prince*, defends a historical cycling between good and bad leadership in his *Discourses*, with the former being characterized by leaders who "[put] their own interests second and the public good first" (*The Prince*, eds. Quentin Skinner and Russell Price

leadership ethics.[11] This commitment to a volitional understanding of ethical failures in leadership makes for a sharp contrast with the cognitive account. Although it is not my aim to offer a direct specification of what morality requires of leaders, my argument for the cognitive account of ethical failures in leadership directly challenges the ascendancy of the view that it is enough that leaders forgo the claims of self-interest so that they might serve group, organizational, or societal goals. Service to these goals can promote mistaken beliefs by leaders that they are justified in making exceptions of themselves and in excluding others from the protection of morality's requirements. In these cases, their ethical failures are primarily cognitive, not volitional, in nature.

III. THE STRUCTURE OF THE BOOK

Chapter 1 introduces the cognitive account of ethical failures in leadership as a viable alternative to the volitional account, and identifies what I argue is the conceptual source of the cognitive limitations to which leaders are particularly susceptible. I suggest that ready acceptance of the volitional account of ethical failure misses an important distinction

[Cambridge: Cambridge University Press, 1988]; and *Discourses on the First Ten Books of Titius Livius*, in Michael L.Morgan, ed., *Classics of Moral and Political Theory*, 3rd edition [Indianapolis: Hackett Publishing Company, 2001], p. 472.)

[11] Robert K. Greenleaf recommends a form of leadership on which the leader "*is* servant first . . . That person is sharply different from one who is *leader* first, perhaps because of the need to assuage an unusual power drive or to acquire material possessions" (*Servant Leadership: A Journey into the Nature of Legitimate Power and Greatness* [New York: Paulist Press, 1977] p. 13). Jane Howell and Bruce Avolio come to this same conclusion about the ethical use of power by way of an appeal to David McClelland's distinction between *personalized* and *socialized* power motives, suggesting that leaders should be motivated by a concern for the common good. (See Jane M. Howell and Bruce J. Avolio, "The Ethics of Charismatic Leadership: Submission or Liberation?" *Academy of Management Executive* 6, 2 [1992]: 43–54; and David C. McClelland, *Human Motivation* [Glenview, IL: Scott, Foresman and Company, 1985].) Indeed, some leadership scholars believe that altruism makes a leader's behavior both ethical and effective and thus that the Hitler problem is not so problematic after all. According to Rabindra N. Kanungo and Manuel Mendonca, "Because the 'other' – that is, the organization and its members – is the raison d'être of the leader's efforts, the altruistic motive becomes the only consistent motive for the leader's role" (*Ethical Dimensions of Leadership* [Thousand Oaks, CA: Sage Publications, 1996], p. 35). On this view, "[L]eadership effectiveness is ensured only by altruistic acts that reflect the leader's incessant desire and concern to benefit others despite the risk of personal cost inherent in such acts" (Kanungo and Mendonca, *Ethical Dimensions of Leadership*, p. 35).

leadership have been noted among men, perhaps simply because men are more likely to be in positions of leadership, I consistently refer to the male gender when discussing ethically failed leaders. My hope is that this book will make some contribution to gender equality in this area by reducing the kind of ethical failures in leadership we have become used to seeing.

Chapter 1

Volitional and Cognitive Accounts of Ethical Failures in Leadership

I. INTRODUCTION

One surprising feature of ethical failures in leadership is that, very often, the immorality of the relevant decision, action, or policy was never in doubt.[1] Unfortunately, this is true across leadership contexts: in public, private, and non-profit sectors. For example, when Senator Trent Lott waxed nostalgic recently over our segregationist past, there was little debate about the immorality of his remarks, which ultimately resulted in his resignation as Senate majority leader. Similarly, we hardly needed sophisticated moral theory to determine whether Enron executives were wrong to engage in accounting irregularities in order to inflate profits. Finally, lest we think that high-profile leaders outside of politics and business are immune to straightforward ethical failure, recall that William Aramony was forced to step down as president of the United Way under allegations that "he lived lavishly and romanced women with thousands of dollars of the charity's money."[2] In these cases and others like them, when ethical failures in leadership are exposed, we look for an *explanation* of the leader's behavior, not a *moral analysis* of the moral status of what was done.

Much of moral theory, however, is preoccupied with questions about how to figure out what morality requires. In an effort to answer these

Reprinted with revisions from Terry L. Price, "Explaining Ethical Failures of Leadership," *Leadership and Organization Development Journal: Special Issue on Ethics and Leadership* 21 (2000): 177–184, Copyright © 2000 Emerald Group Publishing Limited. Reprinted with permission from Emerald Group Publishing Limited.

[1] Dean C. Ludwig and Clinton O. Longenecker, "The Bathsheba Syndrome: The Ethical Failure of Successful Leaders," *Journal of Business Ethics* 12 (1993): 265–273.

[2] Sam Fulwood III, "Former Head of United Way is Convicted," *Los Angeles Times* (April 4, 1995).

questions, moral theorists work to locate those features of decisions, actions, and policies that make them morally good or morally right. This focus seems to imply that a more complete characterization of ethical success would put leaders in a better position to behave morally. But the central question raised by the cases cited here seems to be not so much one about *how* leaders should act but, rather, one about *why* they act as they do. *Why* do leaders fail ethically when it is so obvious to the rest of us *how* they should act? This question has its home in the general area of moral psychology. So located, it is closely related to questions about ethical failure more generally. In fact, one might think that the moral psychology behind ethical failures in leadership is part and parcel of a basic truth about human nature – namely, that our behavior, especially in its immoral varieties, is largely self-interested.

The standard argument in moral theory and applied ethics relies on this view of human nature, holding that ethical failures are essentially *volitional*, not *cognitive*. On this argument, we behave immorally because we are moved to do something other than what morality requires, not because we lack access to morality's requirements. Initially, at least, the volitional account would seem to fit well with the examples given of ethical failures in leadership. We are often inclined to say of morally tainted leaders that they *knew* that what they were doing was morally wrong but, nevertheless, that they were *motivated* to do it anyway.[3] I will argue, however, that the volitional account of human immorality is not sufficient for an understanding of ethical failures in leadership. Simply applying the volitional account to leadership contexts ignores the fact that leadership exaggerates cognitive challenges that can lead to ethical failure. More than most agents, leaders may have reason to believe that they are not bound by the requirements of morality. As a consequence, what constitutes an ethical failure in leadership may not be so obvious to leaders after all.

The primary purpose of this chapter is to introduce these cognitive challenges and to suggest that leaders might be particularly susceptible to them. Section II lays out the volitional account of ethical failures in leadership as it is articulated in the work of Dean Ludwig and Clinton Longenecker.[4] These authors appeal to the volitional account to make

---

[3] In Chapter 5, I appeal to Aristotle's distinction between *baseness* and *incontinence* to articulate two different motivational accounts of why leaders do what they know is wrong.

[4] Ludwig and Longenecker, "The Bathsheba Syndrome."

sense of the fact that "many of the ethics violations we have witnessed in recent years result from a ready willingness to abandon personal principle – not so much a matter of ethics as of virtue and lack of fortitude and courage."[5] Section III distinguishes between two kinds of cognitive challenges to moral behavior: mistakes about the *content* of morality and mistakes about its *scope*. This distinction is important because the initial plausibility of the volitional account turns on the weaknesses of only one version of cognitive account, the version on which ethically fallen leaders are said to be mistaken about morality's content. If the cognitive account of ethical failures in leadership is ultimately richer than the argument for the volitional account makes out, then perhaps this argument is not so forceful after all. Section IV further articulates the cognitive account of ethical failures in leadership. It does so by highlighting the peculiarities of leadership that make this account well suited to analyses of wrongdoing by leaders. The section concludes by indicating some of the main normative implications of the cognitive account for the way we think about leadership and the privileges that typically accompany it.

II. THE VOLITIONAL ACCOUNT OF ETHICAL FAILURES IN LEADERSHIP

The volitional account of ethical failure implicitly assumes that much of human behavior is egoistic. On this view of human motivation, morality competes not with ignorance but, rather, with self-interest. Compliance with moral principles thus depends greatly on the extent to which agents can reasonably expect that immoral behavior will be found out and, upon being found out, that agents will face unwanted consequences for engaging in it. Fortunately, society provides many effective mechanisms for making sure that the demands of self-interest parallel the requirements of morality. It is typically in our interests to conform our behavior to these requirements because, when we do not, others withhold their cooperation or, worse still, work in concert to punish us. As people sometimes say in corporate contexts, "good ethics is good business." Still, there will sometimes be reasons for agents to think that their interest in behaving morally has run out. If the egoistic view of human motivation is correct, agents will be inclined to behave immorally when they have these reasons.

[5] Ludwig and Longenecker, "The Bathsheba Syndrome," pp. 267–268.

A character in Plato's *Republic* well illustrates the strongest version of this view with the story of the shepherd Gyges.

The story goes that he was a shepherd in the service of the ruler of Lydia. There was a violent thunderstorm, and an earthquake broke open the ground and created a chasm at the place where he was tending his sheep. Seeing this, he was filled with amazement and went down into it. And there, in addition to many other wonders of which we're told, he saw a hollow bronze horse. There were windowlike openings in it, and, peeping in, he saw a corpse, which seemed to be of more than human size, wearing nothing but a gold ring on its finger. He took the ring and came out of the chasm. He wore the ring at the usual monthly meeting that reported to the king on the state of the flocks. And as he was sitting among the others, he happened to turn the setting of the ring towards himself to the inside of his hand. When he did this, he became invisible to those sitting near him, and they went on talking as if he had gone . . . When he realized this, he at once arranged to become one of the messengers sent to report to the king. And when he arrived there, he seduced the king's wife, attacked the king with her help, killed him, and took over the kingdom.[6]

The point of Plato's interlocutor is that Gyges' behavior does not set him apart from the rest of us: With nothing to fear from behaving immorally, each of us would behave just as Gyges did. This argument from egoism has important implications for thinking about the ethical challenges of leadership. The most important is that power can insulate leaders from the contingencies that force self-interest and morality together. That is, individuals in leadership positions may think they have less reason to expect the setbacks to self-interest that most of us associate with immoral behavior. Herein lies one of the moral perils of leadership: Leaders, we might say, have too many rings.

For good reason, many readers will be unwilling to accept this strong version of the volitional account. A weaker version of this account finds insightful expression in Ludwig and Longenecker's articulation of "the Bathsheba Syndrome." These authors draw upon the biblical story of David and Bathsheba to argue that success brings with it formidable motivational challenges. In this story, David seduces Bathsheba, the wife of Uriah, and Bathsheba becomes pregnant with David's child. In an attempt to create the impression that Bathsheba is pregnant with Uriah's child, David hastens to have Uriah returned home from battle. To the surprise of David, however, Uriah's loyalty to his fellow combatants

---

[6] Plato, *Republic*, trans. G. M. A. Grube (Indianapolis: Hackett Publishing Company, 1992), pp. 35–36 [359d–360b].

makes him unwilling to sleep with Bathsheba. David finally resorts to a more serious breach of faith: David has Uriah sent to the battlefront to guarantee that he will lose his life. Uriah is indeed killed, and upon learning of his death, David takes Bathsheba as his wife. On Ludwig and Longenecker's view, the essential features of David's ethical failing are no different from that of the contemporary ethical failures in leadership. These authors tell us that "David clearly knew the gravity of the violation he was engaging in and clearly knew the penalty if exposed."[7] Not unlike ethically fallen leaders of today, that is, David simply lacked motivation to do what was morally right, even though he well knew what morality required.

Ludwig and Longenecker locate the source of ethical failures in leadership in success itself. On their analysis, the by-products of success can seriously strain a leader's motivational ties to morality. First, successful leadership can make for complacency and loss of strategic focus. Second, it is commonplace for a leader's success to be accompanied by privileged access to information, people, or objects. Third, successful leaders frequently have unrestrained control of organizational resources. Fourth, a leader's success can inflate his belief in his own ability to control outcomes. In combination, according to these authors, these by-products are especially liable to spawn unethical behavior. They make mention of two such "explosive combination[s]."[8] Complacency frees up a leader to act on temptations that privileged access brings with it, and unrestrained control of resources feeds a leader's inflated belief that he can conceal his actions and their effects when these temptations have gotten the best of him. On either combination, then, leaders succumb to challenges that are essentially volitional in nature.

Admittedly, as with all volitional understandings of immorality, Ludwig and Longenecker's explanation of ethical failures in leadership must draw upon the cognitive considerations surrounding the transgression. In other words, in addition to pointing out the temptations that give rise to ethical failure, the explanation must also appeal to the fact that leaders believe both that immorality is in their interests and that it is within their power to carry out a successful cover-up. These explanations of ethical failure are nonetheless best characterized as volitional because the beliefs in question are factual ones that become

---

[7] Ludwig and Longenecker, "The Bathsheba Syndrome," p. 266.
[8] Ludwig and Longenecker, "The Bathsheba Syndrome," p. 269.

morally problematic only when coupled with the egoistic assumption that their possessor will be motivated to act on them. Volitional understandings of immorality, that is, do not claim that an explanation of unethical behavior will make no appeal to the beliefs of immoral agents, just that mistaken moral beliefs play no part in this explanation. The assumptions of egoism come out most clearly in Ludwig and Longenecker's proposed solutions to the Bathsheba Syndrome. The ultimate aim of these solutions is to force morality and self-interest back together again, to get leaders to see that "[e]ven kings who fail to provide ethical leadership are eventually found out."[9] By way of advice to individual leaders, the authors propose strategies for maintaining an accurate view of what constitutes one's self-interest. They suggest, for example, that leaders would do well to "read the papers for constant reminders that the chances of being caught have never been greater."[10]

Ludwig and Longenecker also recommend that leaders anticipate opportunities for immorality and create conditions under which it will be difficult to act solely upon self-interest. They advise leaders, for instance, to engage in a form of self-binding by surrounding themselves with "ethical team[s] of managers,"[11] much as Homer's Odysseus made use of ropes for his body and wax for his men's ears to fend off the temptations of the sirens' song.[12] The advice for boards of directors is no different on this score. Since "[d]etection is the primary factor that deters unethical behavior," organizations should "make prudent use of such devices as regularly scheduled audits" and "consider the use of ombudsmen."[13] Here, as with all the recommendations, the goal is to institute transformative checks, checks that remake self-interest so that it is expressed in morally acceptable ways. By significantly increasing the chances that unethical behavior will be detected, the purpose of these checks is to guarantee that it is no longer in a leader's self-interest to behave immorally. The underlying assumption behind all these solutions, then, is that the problems themselves are primarily egoistic in nature. Given that self-interest routinely drives ethical failures of leadership, egoistic solutions are necessary to make certain that leaders

---

[9] Ludwig and Longenecker, "The Bathsheba Syndrome," p. 271.
[10] Ludwig and Longenecker, "The Bathsheba Syndrome," p. 272.
[11] Ludwig and Longenecker, "The Bathsheba Syndrome," p. 272.
[12] Homer, *The Odyssey*, trans. Robert Fitzgerald (Garden City, NY: Anchor Books, 1963), pp. 214–215.
[13] Ludwig and Longenecker, "The Bathsheba Syndrome," p. 272.

perceive their self-interest as being bound up with the requirements of morality.

It can hardly be disputed that leaders sometimes fail ethically because they are willing to sacrifice common morality for self-interest. Ludwig and Longenecker are to be commended for reminding us of the temptations that leadership brings with it and, in particular, that leadership often provides opportunities to think that acting on these temptations might make this kind of sacrifice worthwhile. My claim, however, is that the egoistic assumptions at the heart of this view do not do justice to the moral psychology of leaders. For the volitional account assumes that leadership does little more than alter the contingencies associated with normal human motivation. In other words, it assumes that leadership does not effect changes in the way that leaders think about morality. On this assumption, the ethical challenges of leadership are no different in kind from the motivational challenges that we all face. It is just that leaders must face them on a much grander scale because the circumstances of success often ease the tensions between self-interest and immorality. I propose the notion that there is something cognitive about ethical failures in leadership. The argument for this claim turns on showing that there is a plausible alternative to the volitional account.[14]

III. THE COGNITIVE ACCOUNT OF ETHICAL FAILURES IN LEADERSHIP

Much of the strength of the volitional account rests on the apparent weaknesses of the cognitive account of ethical failures in leadership. What leader is ignorant, for example, of the immorality of deceptive and manipulative behavior? Plainly stated, since leaders can typically be expected to know the moral status of their behavior, it is hard to see what we might appeal to – aside from motivation – to explain those instances in which they fail ethically. This inference assumes, though, that all relevant cognitive challenges to moral behavior are connected to mistakes about what kinds of behavior are required or prohibited by morality. On a first reading, this assumption seems acceptable enough.

---

[14] Richard Nisbett and Lee Ross write, "[L]ike many contemporary psychologists, we believe that motivational constructs have been too readily and indiscriminately invoked to explain failings that are at the least importantly aided, and perhaps even largely determined, by cognitive shortcomings" (*Human Inference: Strategies and Shortcomings of Social Judgment* [Englewood Cliffs, NJ: Prentice Hall, 1980], p. 229).

After all, it is a small step from knowing that particular behaviors are morally required or prohibited to knowing what one ought to do. But, in this section, I want to draw attention to a second kind of cognitive challenge to moral behavior, one to which leaders are particularly susceptible. On this line of argument, we cannot infer from the fact that a leader knows what kinds of behaviors are required or prohibited by morality that he is not morally mistaken in a way that vindicates the cognitive account of ethical failures in leadership.

Cognitive mistakes about morality come in two basic varieties: mistakes about its *content* and mistakes about its *scope*. Mistakes of content are indexed to beliefs about the moral status of *act-types*, most commonly to beliefs about what types of actions are morally permissible or right. For instance, a leader might mistakenly believe that lying is a morally permissible means of getting follower compliance or that it is morally right to seek revenge for disloyalty. Content mistakes can also be indexed to failures to see why certain kinds of action are wrong – that is, to ignorance of what features make them wrong. In contrast, mistakes of scope are indexed to beliefs about the moral status of *individuals*, specifically to beliefs about their place within the moral community and the extent to which these individuals are subject to the rights and responsibilities that membership implies. Scope mistakes are thus errors about the application of morality's strictures. In their most straightforward form, questions of scope endeavor to fix the domain of individuals to whom moral obligations are owed. A central scope question for business leaders might be whether they have moral obligations to the general public or to the international community, in addition to any moral obligations that they have to stockholders, employees, and customers. For example, we might ask what responsibilities the CEO of Wal-Mart has to the owners of small, local stores that are often put out of business when Wal-Mart enters a community.

Ethicists and philosophers spend a lot of time thinking about questions of moral content. This alone should give us reason to question the ascendancy of the volitional account of ethical failures in leadership. If morality is as difficult as these thinkers make it out to be, then it would seem to follow that people can behave immorally because they are sometimes ignorant of what actions are morally right or good. That said, it is worth noting that much of our history's most morally reprehensible behavior has been connected to questions about the scope of morality, not its content. Here, we need only reflect upon the institution of slavery in the United States, the treatment of Jews and others in Nazi Germany, and the policy of apartheid in South Africa. Even Trent Lott's racially offensive remarks, which were mentioned in the introduction of this chapter, can be understood in terms of a mistake about morality's scope. We might also think about our own society's treatment of women. Suffice it to say that we have a long history of ignoring the moral status of particular individuals in our society.

For our purposes, the primary point of relevance of these examples is that mistakes about the scope of morality's requirements make for a second way in which ethical failures can be grounded in how we think about morality. Simply put, cognitive challenges to moral behavior are not limited to mistakes about the content of morality. The most commonplace scope mistakes are represented by the extension of morality's *protections* to particular individuals and not to others. But questions about the scope of morality are not exhausted by this particular concern. In a less straightforward – yet equally significant – form, scope questions endeavor to fix the domain of individuals who have these obligations in the first place. Scope mistakes, that is, can also take the form of cognitive errors about which individuals are *bound* by morality's requirements.[15] An individual of moderate income, for instance, might mistakenly believe that he, unlike the wealthy, is not subject to a moral requirement to help the poor. This latter kind of mistake about the scope of morality is equally relevant for understanding ethical failures in leadership.

As an impetus to my argument for this claim, let us reconsider Ludwig and Longenecker's rejection of a cognitive understanding of David's ethical failure. The authors claim that "David clearly knew the gravity of the violation he was engaging in . . . " and that it was "the prophet Nathan (who was in this case the equivalent of a modern day whistleblower) who led David to realize that his cover-up had been a failure."[16] Since David knew that what he did was wrong, Nathan's role was simply to convey to David that he had been found out and to expose his wrongs to all of Israel. It is significant, though, that the biblical text itself gives a much larger role to Nathan.

And the Lord sent Nathan to David. He came to him, and said to him, 'There were two men in a certain city, the one rich and the other poor. The rich man had very many flocks and herds; but the poor man had nothing but one little ewe lamb, which he had bought. And he brought it up, and it grew up with him and

[15] Jean Hampton, "The Nature of Immorality," *Social Philosophy and Policy* 7, 1 (1989): 22–44.
[16] Ludwig and Longenecker, "The Bathsheba Syndrome," pp. 266, 271.

with his children; it used to eat of his morsel, and drink from his cup, and lie in his bosom, and it was like a daughter to him. Now there came a traveler to the rich man, and he was unwilling to take one of his own flock or herd to prepare for the wayfarer who had come to him, but he took the poor man's lamb, and prepared it for the man who had come to him.' Then David's anger was greatly kindled against the man; and he said to Nathan, 'As the Lord lives, the man who has done this deserves to die; and he shall restore the lamb fourfold, because he did this thing, and because he had no pity.' Nathan said to David, 'You are that man.'[17]

To be sure, Nathan does inform David that his wrongs have been discovered. But this passage reveals an additional task for Nathan. What exactly was Nathan trying to do? The answer to this question must focus on the purpose of the parable. Why, for example, does Nathan appeal to the wrongs of another to make his point? My answer is that Nathan's use of the parable is educative: The story addresses peculiar cognitive challenges to ethical leadership. In the end, David was mistaken about the scope of morality, and this mistake comes to bear on our understanding of his behavior.

The main argument for this claim is that the parable is out of place on alternative analyses of David's ethical failure. On the assumption that David's moral challenge was volitional and that Nathan's task was essentially that of a whistle-blower, the parable is unnecessary to the task set for Nathan. If David knows what morality demands of him, then he does not require a story from Nathan to get him to see its force. The volitional account thus makes Nathan's parable redundant since this explanation rests on the assumption that David already knew what the parable conveys. Nathan's story is similarly unmotivated on the view that David was mistaken about the content of morality. This application of the cognitive account to David's ethical failure makes the parable not redundant but, nonetheless, unhelpful in a different way. For the parable makes moral sense to David only if he recognizes that it is generally wrong for the privileged to take advantage of the less privileged. Put another way, if Nathan's story is to have any purchase with David, we must assume that David was not mistaken about the general moral status of the actions attributed to the rich man. This means that David must have had some basic understanding of the content of the relevant

---

[17] *New Oxford Annotated Bible with the Apocrypha: Revised Standard Version*, eds. Herbert G. May and Bruce M. Metzger (New York: Oxford University Press, 1977), 2 Samuel 12:1–7.

moral requirement. The parable is educative in character, then, in precisely this sense: It was meant to show David the universality of a moral requirement that he already accepts. David, it seems, failed to see that this requirement also applied to him. The purpose of the parable was to teach him that he too is bound by morality, that success did not remove him from its scope.

What should we make of the fact that David instigated an intricate scheme to cover up his actions? Would not this fact imply that David knew that what he was doing was wrong? We should first note that David's scheme implies only that he believed that others – in particular, Uriah – would object to his seduction of Bathsheba.[18] While this belief may be relevant to an assessment of David's culpability for his ignorance, it would be a mistake to infer from David's awareness of potential objections to his behavior that he himself accepted that what he was doing was wrong.[19] Here, the inference is no more valid than the argument for the claim that the "closet racist" really knows that his views are wrong. Notice, too, that even though children are prone to cover-ups of immoral behavior, we generally reject the view that they have a proper understanding of morality's requirements. The cognitive predicaments of childhood come to bear on our attributions of responsibility to them, and this is true regardless of whether children are able to apply the labels of morality with a good degree of success. My suggestion is that David's cognitive predicament was importantly similar to that faced by others who know only enough to keep their thoughts and actions from pubic view. The difference is that whereas some adults and children have yet to see what morality requires, David had lost sight of it.

A second point of response on behalf of the cognitive account appeals to what David must have believed about the nature of morality. One belief that we can safely attribute to David is that his actions could not be

---

[18] According to Jonathan Glover, "Some of the [Nazi] motives for concealment were linked to the furtherance of Nazi aims...It mattered that a future generation 'might not understand.' It probably mattered that some of their family and friends also might 'not understand'" (*Humanity: A Moral History of the Twentieth Century* [New Haven: Yale University Press, 2000], p. 354). Kurt Eichenwald, commenting on Enron and other corporate scandals, claims that "'You don't understand' is a phrase that has emerged in every single one of these cases where you would see people raising warning signals, raising flags early on, and the response of senior management is, 'You don't understand'" ("Kurt Eichenwald discusses the collapse of energy giant Enron," *Fresh Air* [January 17, 2002]).

[19] See, for example, Holly Smith, "Culpable Ignorance," *Philosophical Review* 92 (1983): 543–571.

hidden from God, who was for David the source of morality's authority. Given David's commitment to this view of morality, his cover-up cannot be understood as an effort to evade the authority of moral requirements that he took to be binding on him. Again, moral judgment for David was essentially judgment from God. So locating the authority behind David's morality therefore undermines much of the plausibility of Ludwig and Longenecker's explanation of his ethical failure. Unlike the successes of leaders not committed to theologically based moralities, David's success could not have made him any more able to circumvent genuine moral judgment. As a consequence, we cannot accept a view on which it is assumed that David believed that he could get away with behavior that was immoral before God. A more plausible explanation of David's ethical failure, then, appeals to the distinction between the content and scope of moral requirements. Although David believed that what he did was generally wrong, he did not believe that these prohibitions applied to him.[20]

IV. NORMATIVE IMPLICATIONS OF THE COGNITIVE ACCOUNT

My argument to this point, of course, is not intended as an exercise in biblical exegesis. Rather, it is offered as an alternative account of why leaders are particularly susceptible to ethical failure. According to the account on offer, ethical failures in leadership are closely connected to mistaken beliefs about morality's scope. Leadership can induce and maintain a leader's belief that he is somehow excepted from moral requirements that apply to the rest of us. The purpose of the final section of this chapter is to begin to fill out the cognitive account of ethical failures in leadership. In particular, it aims to underscore the peculiar features of leadership that effect this cognitive transformation. My claim is that the way we think about leadership is bound up with the notion of *justification*. It is this conceptual link that structures the moral psychology of leaders, sometimes with ethical failure as a result.

---

[20] The cognitive account also lends itself to an explanation of why so many cover-ups seem rather half-hearted. Contrary to what the volitional account might predict, it seems that leaders frequently make little or no effort to conceal their ethical failings. When there is no intricate scheme of deception to be found, we are often struck not by the rational use of the resources at the disposal of leaders but rather by the seemingly irrational fashion in which these resources were neglected. An appeal to mistakes of scope thus explains the near-flaunting nature of many ethical failures in leadership.

An individual's action is *justified* when he did what is right or, at least, permissible. For instance, if an employee misses a staff meeting because only he can complete a time-sensitive task that has materialized at the last minute, then his absence was justified on the grounds that what he did was appropriate to the circumstances. Justification differs from *excuse* in the following way: To say that an individual's action is excused means that even though the behavior in question is in some sense inappropriate, we do not hold the individual accountable because of the presence of responsibility-undermining factors. If the employee missed the meeting, say, having been inadvertently locked in his office by the housekeeping staff, then his absence is excused because it was due to factors beyond his control. Although he did what he should not have done, he is not to blame for his inappropriate behavior. The distinction between justification and excuse thus marks two basic ways in which individuals can elude attributions of blameworthiness for behavior that is typically subject to disapprobation. In the case of justified behavior, the actor is not bound by a requirement that normally applies since this requirement has been undercut by an alternative one that better suits the circumstances. This means that the actor's behavior falls outside of the scope of the normal requirement. With respect to excused behavior, the actor is no less bound by the requirement in question than any of the rest of us. But, in this case, the individual eludes an attribution of blameworthiness because we cannot reasonably expect satisfaction of the requirement in the circumstances, not because the requirement itself has been undercut.[21]

For our purposes, this distinction is important because it lends itself to an accurate understanding of the moral psychology of leaders. Leadership purportedly brings with it justification for doing myriad things that others are not permitted to do. In other words, a leader's position very often supports the assumption that its occupant is removed from the scope of requirements that apply in full force to the rest of us. To take a tragic example in New York City, "Councilman James E. Davis was shot to death on a City Hall balcony by a political rival" as a result of a policy according to which "elected officials did not have to walk through [metal] detectors."[22] A more ordinary example is that leaders

---

[21] Terry L. Price, "Faultless Mistake of Fact: Justification or Excuse?" *Criminal Justice Ethics* 12, 2 (1993): 14–28.

[22] Winnie Hu, "Bloomberg Says He Has Improved Security at City Hall," *New York Times* (July 26, 2003).

routinely give little notice to standard expectations of promptness. Even when he was governor of Arkansas, Bill Clinton often showed up as much as two hours late for scheduled events.[23] Here, of course, the idea is that leaders are justified in being late, as the requirements of promptness are subordinate in force to the other requirements to which leaders are subject. Simply put, leaders sometimes have more important matters to which they must attend. As a consequence, the inclination of followers is often to say that this kind of leadership behavior is justified.

When leaders elude attributions of blameworthiness in this way, it is not quite right to classify what they have done as excused. This is because the presence of legitimating reasons for their behavior implies that the relevant requirement fails to apply to them in the circumstances. In these particular circumstances, the claim is that they have done what is permissible or, more strongly, required of them by their positions of leadership. There is a sense, then, in which leadership has removed them from the scope of the requirement. But if leaders are regularly removed from the scope of such requirements, then this feature of leadership makes for a formidable cognitive task. Explicitly stated, leaders must differentiate between those requirements that apply to them and those with respect to which a deviation would be justified. We can expect ethical failure to occur when leaders do not heed the fact that their behavior is well within the scope of a moral requirement that applies to the rest of us.

Perhaps it is just this kind of disregard that made Vaclav Havel, then president of the Czech Republic, vulnerable to criticism for "driving [a model car] about 100 miles an hour, far above the posted speed limit."[24] Similarly, before becoming governor of Massachusetts, Lieutenant

---

[23] David Maraniss, *First in His Class: The Biography of Bill Clinton* (New York: Simon and Schuster, 1995), p. 363.

[24] Steven Erlanger, "Havel Finds His Role Turning From Czech Hero to Has-Been," *New York Times* (November 4, 1999). Former South Dakota Congressman Bill Janklow, who was convicted of second-degree manslaughter for running a stop sign and killing a motorcyclist, told the judge, "While I was governor, I drove fast – really fast. I had a lot of places to go and things to do" (Carson Walker, "Former congressman gets jail time for traffic crash," Associated Press State and Local Wire [January 22, 2004]). According to later accounts, Janklow "was stopped 16 times by state troopers during his last term as governor but was never ticketed ... Troopers felt they should not ticket Janklow out of respect for his authority or fear of retribution, said the report by the patrol superintendent, Col. Dan Mosteller, for Gov. Mike Rounds" ("Janklow stopped 16 times as governor, not ticketed," *Richmond Times-Dispatch* [July 1, 2004]).

Governor Jane Swift was called before the state Ethics Commission for using a state police helicopter to travel home for Thanksgiving and for using "staff members to take in her dry-cleaning and watch 'adorable' Elizabeth [Swift's daughter] in the office."[25] Justifying this behavior by appeal to her leadership position, Swift said, "I have stated on numerous occasions that I face many of the same challenges as other working parents but I also have some differences because of my schedule."[26] A potentially more serious case of using leadership to justify exception-making behavior was the George W. Bush administration's decision to show pictures of the dead bodies of former Iraqi president Saddam Hussein's sons, Odai and Qusai. Defense Secretary Rumsfeld justified the decision this way: "It is not a practice that the United States engages in on a normal basis . . . I honestly believe that these two are particularly bad characters, and that it's important for the Iraqi people to see them, to know they're gone, to know they're dead and to know they're not coming back."[27]

Unfortunately, negotiating these scope questions in an effort to avoid ethical failure is not an easy task, especially in environments in which the justificatory force of leadership is at its strongest. Generally, when there are great disparities between what is required of leaders and what is required of others, we might well expect leaders to come to see themselves as outside of the scope of morality altogether. It should come as no surprise to us, I think, that the backdrop for David's ethical failing was an environment apparently rich in such disparities. Nathan reminds David, for example, that God "gave [him his] master's house, and [his] master's wives into [his] bosom, and gave [him] the house of Israel and of Judah; and if this were too little, [God] would add to [him] as much more."[28] With this consideration in mind, there is reason to suspect that indulgence might have been part of the cause of David's ethical failure,

---

[25] "Ms Swift's dilemma," *Economist* (January 29, 2000).

[26] Michael Rezendes, "Swift Defends Aides' Help in Personal Life," *Boston Globe* (January 6, 2000). Swift was also widely criticized for being almost one hour late to a reading program ceremony at which she was to hand out certificates to schoolchildren: "Finally, at about 11:20 a.m., Swift appeared, offering thanks for the audience's patience, but no explanation" (Michael Crowley, Stephanie Ebbert, Anthony Flint, Frank Phillips, Michael Rezendes, and Arist Frangules, "Political Capital; Net-Surfing Beacon Hill Watchers Now Able to Read Budgets, Bills Online," *Boston Globe* [April 9, 2000]).

[27] Robert Burns, "Rumsfeld says American forces had no chance of taking Saddam's sons alive," Associated Press (July 24, 2003).

[28] *New Oxford Annotated Bible*, 2 Samuel 12:8.

not its solution. To extend the critique of God's treatment of David, notice that David's punishment was no different in this respect: "[D]ivine judgment fell upon the child [born to David by Bathsheba], according to the ideas of the day, *as a special favor to David*."[29] The justificatory force of leadership in David's particular circumstances, it seems, aggravated the cognitive challenges to which he was exposed as a leader of the Israelites.

The main challenge in leadership ethics is to clarify and to give precision to the justificatory force of leadership. Leaders are excepted from moral requirements only on the condition that there be some reason or set of reasons that legitimates the exceptions. The practical aspect of this challenge, of course, is to create and sustain an environment in which the justificatory force of leadership cannot be reduced to a set of assumptions that simply accompany a leader's position. Perhaps the most important feature of this model environment is the expectation that leaders make explicit appeal to the reasons that legitimate deviations from moral requirements by which the rest of us are bound. This expectation is one that groups, organizations, and societies must make of leaders and leaders must make of themselves if we are to accommodate the cognitive challenges that leadership brings with it. At the very least, so clarifying the justificatory force of leadership would entail an examination of the normative foundations of the powers and privileges of leadership. As I have argued, the greatest threat embodied in these powers and privileges comes from their contributions to the moral psychology of leaders. An appeal to the cognitive account of ethical failures in leadership thus draws our attention to a prima facie reason against the exceptions we make for leaders, a reason that stands to be outweighed by legitimating reasons for these exceptions. Interestingly enough, an analysis of the justificatory force of leadership involves precisely the kind of moral theorizing that initially seemed irrelevant to our understanding of ethical failures in leadership.

---

[29] *New Oxford Annotated Bible*, p. 390, emphasis mine.

Chapter 2

The Nature of Exception Making

I. INTRODUCTION

The volitional account of ethical failures in leadership holds that leaders know what morality requires yet fail to act ethically out of a concern for self-interest. In essence, their unethical behavior is the motivational up-shot of desires and preferences that compete with morality. Of course, proponents of this account allow that leaders who engage in immoral-ity can be mistaken as to whether it is all-things-considered in their interests to act on these desires and preferences. For example, acting immorally to satisfy current desires and preferences sometimes leads to the dissatisfaction of future, perhaps weightier, desires and preferences. The claim of the volitional account, then, is that ethically failed leaders put their desires and preferences ahead of morality, knowing that it is wrong to do so but believing that it will make an all-things-considered contribution to the advancement of their interests. As such, there is no place for an appeal to mistaken moral beliefs in an analysis of ethical failures in leadership. Although leaders are sometimes ignorant of the effects that unethical behavior will have on their own interests, they are not ignorant of the immorality of engaging in it.

In Chapter 1, I introduced a competing account of ethical failures in leadership. On the cognitive account, these failures are the result of mistaken moral beliefs, specifically about the scope of morality. Lead-ers sometimes understand the content of moral requirements, thereby recognizing that certain actions are wrong, but fail to see that the re-quirements prohibiting these actions apply to their behavior. Leaders can be mistaken as to whether they are bound by these requirements as well as to whether these requirements protect outsiders. However, showing that the cognitive account provides an alternative explanation of why leaders behave unethically does not prove that we should generally favor it over the volitional account. To this more controversial end, I take up much of this chapter to develop the notion of *exception making*, arguing that volitional understandings of this notion underestimate the complexity of the moral psychology of agents. I make this argument by way of an appeal to the perceived costs and benefits of immorality. One of the main claims of this chapter is that an analysis of how immoral agents think about the costs and benefits of unethical behavior will incorporate the very causes of ethical failure that advocates of volitional understandings seek to exclude.

The final two sections of the chapter show why volitional understandings of exception making are especially lacking when it comes to a characterization of the moral psychology of leaders. It is commonplace for such characterizations to identify the benefits of immorality with what advances the interests of leaders and its costs with the effects that immorality has on the achievement of group ends. Advocates of the volitional account who rely on this identification thus pit leader self-interest against the interests of the group to explain exception-making behavior by leaders. But the general plausibility of this understanding of the costs and benefits of immorality will depend on the nature of the relationship between leader self-interest and the achievement of group ends.

A second main claim of this chapter is that an examination of leader motivation seriously questions the claim that conflicts between leader self-interest and group interests exhaust the causes of ethical failures in leadership, particularly for leaders who value group ends for their own sake. As I shall argue, a better way to frame the moral reasoning of such leaders focuses on conflicts between the value of group ends and broader costs of immorality. Leaders committed to the intrinsic value of group ends can believe that goal achievement justifies moral costs to followers as well as outsiders and, therefore, that it justifies exception-making behavior.

II. MORAL MOTIVATION

Perhaps the most rigorous defense of a volitional understanding of immorality is that offered by Jean Hampton.[1] On her view, immorality is the result of improper motivation, not mistaken moral belief: "[K]nowing

---

[1] Jean Hampton, "The Nature of Immorality," *Social Philosophy and Policy* 7, 1 (1989): 22–44, and Jean Hampton, "*Mens Rea*," *Social Philosophy and Policy* 7, 2 (1990): 1–28.

the better and doing the worse," the immoral agent "chooses to defy what she knows to be an authoritative moral command in the name of the satisfaction of one or more of her wishes, whose satisfaction the command forbids."[2] In this respect, the behavior of immoral agents parallels that of irrational agents: "Those who defy reason do not merely rebel against its directives, but attempt to install another authority in its place which will endorse the action they wish to perform . . . What is the new authority? Normally, it will be whatever desire motivates the interest in performing the action."[3] In other words, neither immoral nor irrational agents are mistaken about what they ought to do; rather, they forgo the requirements of morality and reason for the sake of their own desires and preferences.

Advocates of volitional understandings recognize that if this kind of analysis of the nature of immorality is to be convincing, it must also tell us why people choose to put their desires and preferences ahead of morality. After all, we sometimes abide by moral requirements even though we strongly desire to do otherwise. The explanation Hampton offers seems simple enough. When agents act on desires to engage in immoral action, it is because they think that they can get away with it. "Rebels reject the rulership of commanders," she writes, "not only when they perceive the commander to be directing them to act in a way that harms their interests but also when they think they can 'get away' with the rebellion . . ."[4] In other words, immoral agents defy the requirements of morality because they believe "it is possible to evade the bad consequences of rebellion, or because they believe its costs will be outweighed by its benefits."[5] Here too, for Hampton, there is a close connection between cases of immorality and cases of irrationality. Irrational agents "believe that they are permitted to try a forbidden activity because they are exempted from the sorts of problems that normally plague those who engage in it."[6] They tell themselves that they are "special enough to have [their] desires prevail."[7]

In its appeal to perceived costs and benefits, this understanding of ethical failure grants that immorality can indeed be a matter of

[2] Hampton, "*Mens Rea*," p. 15.
[3] Hampton, "*Mens Rea*," p. 5.
[4] Hampton, "The Nature of Immorality," p. 40.
[5] Hampton, "The Nature of Immorality," p. 40.
[6] Hampton, "*Mens Rea*," p. 7.
[7] Hampton, "*Mens Rea*," p. 8.

mistaken belief.[8] Although immoral agents do not lack cognitive access to the requirements of morality, they hold mistaken factual beliefs about whether they can avoid the consequences of flouting these requirements. Hampton is not specific about the exact nature of these consequences. Instead, she opts to be intentionally "vague about what 'costs' and 'benefits' refer to here, because different moral philosophers committed to the objective authority of morality will have different ways of cashing out what they are (for example, Aristotle would talk of human flourishing, Kant would talk of the persistent indictment of reason one would feel following the defiance)."[9] However, Hampton clearly rejects the Socratic view on which morality is always in one's best interest, claiming that moral requirements "can and frequently do *conflict* with one's self-interest . . . Immorality is simply a rebellion against a kind of authority which one may very well dislike, given the way it often opposes one's interests."[10]

Despite Hampton's proposal that we "choose [our] favorite way of cashing out these terms," a lot depends on how we understand the costs and benefits of immorality and, specifically, the perspective that immoral agents take on its costs.[11] The claim that immoral agents believe they can get away with their behavior is particularly well suited, for example, to an explanation of the ethical failures of agents who see the costs of immorality exclusively in terms of instrumental effects on self-interest. Such individuals are held morally at bay only by external constraints, constraints meant to give motivational force to moral requirements by creating the expectation that immoral behavior will result in significant costs being imposed upon them by others. Unfortunately, since these constraints are external in nature, immoral agents will sometimes believe that the promised costs can be avoided, in which case unethical behavior would seem worthwhile. Calculations of self-interest can surely be incorrect, based either on mistaken probability assignments or on an underestimation of the seriousness of the potential

---

[8] Hampton seems to think that it is always a mistake to believe that one can get away with immorality: "Now are moral rebels right to think they can get away with their rebellion and escape without paying any significant costs? Presumably any moral theorist committed to the authority of morality would argue that they cannot do so in any situation over which the moral authority is sovereign" ("*Mens Rea*," p. 23).

[9] Hampton, "*Mens Rea*," pp. 22–23.

[10] Hampton, "The Nature of Immorality," pp. 40–41.

[11] Hampton, "*Mens Rea*," p. 23.

costs. Rightly or wrongly, though, agents who understand the costs of immorality exclusively in terms of self-interest will sometimes be motivated to engage in unethical behavior in the belief that they can avoid these costs.

Although this perspective on the costs of immorality fits well with at least one view of moral motivation, it risks undermining the claim that immoral agents who adopt this perspective believe that it really is wrong *for them* to do what they are doing.[12] For example, as ethical egoists understand the costs of immorality, the normative force of moral requirements rests solely on the connection between these requirements and individual self-interest. In other words, these agents believe that moral requirements apply to them in exactly those cases in which their interests are advanced by behavioral conformity to the requirements. But, given their adherence to this view, they cannot believe that they should do anything other than deviate from what is generally taken to be a moral requirement when they conclude that conformity to it would be all-things-considered against their interests. Since these agents believe, mistakenly perhaps, that self-interest demands a deviation, they reject the normative force of the moral requirement. Of course, if we assume that they believe that a deviation from this requirement makes only some contribution to self-interest, not an all-things-considered contribution, then we could attribute to them the view that it has normative force for them after all. However, because ethical egoists understand moral costs exclusively in terms of self-interest, the assumption that they fully expect such costs to be associated with their behavior undermines the claim that they believe they can ultimately get away with it.[13]

Not all agents understand the costs of immorality exclusively in terms of self-interest.[14] With this consideration in mind, we might broaden the perspective that agents take on the costs of immorality to accommodate internal constraints on behavior, locating moral motivation in

---

[12] Here, I ignore the debate about whether moral reasons must be motivational. Rather, my claim is that particular views of moral motivation fit better with particular assumptions that agents might hold about the normative force of moral requirements.

[13] Since this would reduce immorality to irrationality, the way to prevent ethical failure would be to get immoral agents to be more rational.

[14] In fact, Hampton puts it more strongly than this: In some cases, "no such connection is made between moral actions and a person's good" ("The Nature of Immorality," p. 40).

everything from feelings of shame and guilt to pains of remorse and the pangs of conscience. Initially at least, even these consequences of immorality look egoistic in nature, and so would seem to support the view that agents behave morally only because they want to avoid the internal costs of immorality and to experience the counterpart benefits of pride, rectitude, and conscientiousness. In *The Theory of Moral Sentiments*, Adam Smith attributes this view to his mentor Frances Hutcheson:

Dr. Hutcheson was so far from allowing self-love to be in any case a motive of virtuous actions, that even a regard to the pleasure of self-approbation, to the comfortable applause of our own consciences, according to him, diminished the merit of a benevolent action. This was a selfish motive, he thought, which, so far as it contributed to any action, demonstrated the weakness of that pure and disinterested benevolence which could alone stamp upon the conduct of man the character of virtue.[15]

Hutcheson's view, according to Smith, stands in opposition to "the common judgments of mankind," on which "this regard to the approbation of our own minds is so far from being considered as what can in any respect diminish the virtue of any action, that it is rather looked upon as the sole motive which deserves the appellation of virtuous."[16]

A view of moral motivation that accommodates internal constraints on behavior must ultimately make an appeal to motives other than agent self-interest. Joseph Butler, in his sermon "On the Love of our Neighbour," writes:

Self-love never seeks anything external for its own sake, but only as a means to some further end; the particular affections seek external things for their own sakes. And this latter point is evident from the fact, that the pleasure arising from them could not exist, were there not a prior suitableness between the passion and its object. Now all affections are our own as much as self-love: and if the gratification of our passions be mere self-love, then the affections must be mere self-love also, and all our affections must be resolvable into this one principle; but this clearly is untrue; for in the one case the principle is a love of one's ownself, in the other, the love of another. Self-love, then, and these particular

---

[15] Adam Smith, *The Theory of Moral Sentiments*, eds. D. D. Raphael and A. L. Macfie (Oxford: Clarendon Press, 1976), p. 303 [VII.ii.3.13].

[16] Smith, *The Theory of Moral Sentiments*, p. 303 [VII.ii.3.13]. Smith concludes that both Hutcheson's view and the common view should be rejected as extreme: "[I]t does not follow that a regard to the welfare of society should be the sole virtuous motive of action, but only that, in any competition, it ought to cast the balance against all other motives" (pp. 304–305 [VII.ii.3.17]).

affections, are distinct. Further, self-love is concerned with our own happiness alone, but public affections tend towards external things.[17]

Joel Feinberg makes what is essentially the same point: "Not only is the presence of pleasure (satisfaction) as a by-product of an action no proof that the action was selfish; in some special cases it provides rather conclusive proof that the action was *unselfish*. For in those special cases the fact that we get pleasure from a particular action *presupposes that we desired something else* – something other than our own pleasure – as an end in itself and not merely as a means to our own pleasant state of mind."[18] Similarly, in standard cases of ethical behavior, anticipated feelings that accompany immoral action are linked to other costs of immorality, costs that make such action wrong independently of its effects on self-interest. If agents do not believe that these costs will be associated with unethical behavior, then why would they expect to experience shame and guilt for engaging in it? This means that selfish desires to avoid the costs of immorality will not fill out an explanation of why agents do what morality requires.

There is no denying that there can be cases in which we cannot locate feelings of remorse or hurt conscience in a current cognitive commitment about the costs of immorality. I might experience these reactions after engaging in behavior that I no longer believe to be morally prohibited – for instance, having sex before marriage or, despite my atheism, missing church on Sunday. In cases of this kind, however, the corresponding costs of our behavior seem quite foreign to us as moral agents. It is precisely because these consequences are disconnected from our beliefs about morality that we do not claim them as *moral* costs that we must bear. In fact, understanding their non-cognitive origins, say, by tracing them to the way we were reared as children, or to social pressures from our peer group, is sometimes sufficient to shake the feelings altogether or, at least, to reduce them to a kind of embarrassment. In this respect, feelings of remorse or hurt conscience are similar to desires that we have but do not endorse.[19] When we act on such desires, we do not think that

---

[17] Joseph Butler, "Sermon XI: On the Love of our Neighbor," in his *The Analogy of Religion, Natural and Revealed, to the Constitution and Course of Nature; To Which Are Added, Two Brief Dissertations: On Personal Identity, and On the Nature of Virtue; and Fifteen Sermons* (London: Henry G. Bohn, 1852), p. 361.

[18] Joel Feinberg, "Psychological Egoism," in Joel Feinberg and Russ Shafer-Landau, eds., *Reason and Responsibility: Readings in Some Basic Problems of Philosophy*, 10th edition (Belmont, CA: Wadsworth Publishing Company, 1999), pp. 496–497.

[19] See my discussion of Harry Frankfurt's and Gary Watson's views in Chapter 5.

self-interest demands it any more than we think that morality demands that we yield to obsessive "moral" feelings. To the contrary, our lack of identification with the desires implies that their satisfaction will often conflict with self-interest as we understand it.

The importance of these structural connections within our moral psychology exposes the root of the problem with volitional understandings of immorality. If agents are motivated to act morally by internal constraints on their behavior, and these constraints regularly presuppose explicit beliefs about what makes conduct morally wrong, then it is hard to see how volitional understandings would work. How, for example, could internally motivated agents come to believe that they can get away with unethical behavior? After all, unlike agents for whom the costs of immorality are imposed by others, these agents are paradigms of moral efficiency, consistently imposing moral costs on themselves. Given the nature of the constraints on their behavior, they have direct access to the consequences of unethical behavior when they do what they believe is morally wrong. In short, on this view of moral motivation, we cannot make sense of the claim that internally motivated agents believe they can avoid the consequences of their behavior. Because they hold that what they are doing is wrong, they cannot help but recognize that there is no escaping the feelings associated with immorality.

Perhaps agents motivated by internal constraints on their behavior do not believe that they can get away with immorality altogether but, rather, that "its costs will be outweighed by its benefits."[20] Accordingly, when they engage in conduct that they take to be morally wrong, they fully expect to feel guilty or remorseful for what they have done. It is just that they believe that these feelings are ultimately worth it. What is a little moral regret, these agents might think to themselves, if it gets one a night of pleasure or a life of luxury? But, as we have seen, internally motivated agents must be concerned with more than the "costs *they pay* because of their defiant action."[21] In other words, costs in terms of guilt, remorse, and regret cannot be all that matter to them. The origins of the feelings they associate with immorality require that these agents also be concerned with independent costs that make their behavior wrong, and this concern will preclude their understanding the costs of immorality simply in terms of the costs they pay. Internally motivated

[20] Hampton, "The Nature of Immorality," p. 40.
[21] Hampton, "*Mens Rea*," p. 22, emphasis added.

agents have a significantly broader understanding of what these costs will be.

Even if agents take a broadened perspective on the costs of immorality, they can nonetheless believe that the benefits they themselves receive will ultimately be greater than all anticipated costs, including the costs they impose on others, say, in the form of disrespect or suffering. Whether this particular rendering of what it means to get away with unethical behavior captures the complexity of our moral psychology, especially the moral psychology of those of us motivated by internal constraints on our behavior, is essentially a matter of how true it is to the processes by which we weigh the costs and benefits of immorality. However, once we allow that our calculations can include considerations that are unconnected to self-interest, it follows that these processes are quite complex indeed. One aspect of this complexity stems from the fact that a determination of the costs and benefits of immorality juxtaposes the value of satisfying our desires against the value of behaving morally, and the requisite comparison ultimately involves an appeal to beliefs about the relative normative force of these two sets of action-guiding considerations. As I shall argue, so understanding the moral psychology behind ethical failure makes room for fundamental mistakes about the scope of morality on the part of agents who engage in the relevant weighing processes.

III. MAKING EXCEPTIONS OF OURSELVES

What it means to have a desire is not so different from what it means to have a moral commitment. On Joseph Raz's argument, for example, desires – by their very nature – are closely connected to beliefs about value.[22] As Raz puts it, "we have [desires] only if we hold their objects to be worthwhile and ... [they] disappear once the belief disappears."[23] This claim should not be taken to suggest that we always think it best to satisfy our desires, just that "[w]e cannot want what we have no reason to want."[24] So when an agent acts on a desire, it is because "there is something in the way he sees the action – in his beliefs about it, its circumstances, and consequences – that makes it appear a sensible action

---

[22] Joseph Raz, *Engaging Reason: On the Theory of Value and Action* (Oxford: Oxford University Press, 1999).
[23] Raz, *Engaging Reason*, p. 53.
[24] Raz, *Engaging Reason*, p. 53.

to him."[25] Likewise, an action is judged sensible from the perspective of our moral commitments when there is something about the action itself or the consequences to which it gives rise that constitutes a reason to engage in it. In effect, both the objects of desire and the ends of morality must be "seen under some aspect of the good."[26]

The agent who deviates from a moral requirement on the grounds that satisfying his desires outweighs the costs of acting immorally does so against a set of beliefs about the importance of the objects of his desires as against the importance of the ends of morality. The conclusion that one is weightier than the other in a particular case is thus a judgment of value. When this judgment is part of an explanation of immorality, it suggests that the good of satisfying a desire is believed to be more worthwhile than avoiding the costs associated with the action taken to satisfy this desire. If the agent believed that there is no greater value in satisfying this desire than in abiding by the relevant moral requirement, then it is hard to see why he might believe that the benefits of a deviation outweigh its costs. So, to say that he believes that his action is all-things-considered beneficial implies that he denies that doing what morality requires is of greater comparative importance. As a result of this comparison, what the agent takes to be the relative normative force of the moral requirement is insufficient to justify his disregarding his own desires.

On this view of the processes by which we weigh the costs and benefits of immorality, agents can come to believe that they are not bound by moral requirements. Such agents need not conclude that they are outside the scope of morality altogether, only that particular moral requirements fail to apply to them or that the normative force with which such requirements apply is comparatively weak in the circumstances in which these agents find themselves. Understanding ethical failure in this way thus assumes that agents are able to see action-guiding considerations as being authoritative in some circumstances but not in others. The assumption that the authority of moral requirements can vary in this way will be uncontroversial to those agents who accept that some actions have greater moral costs than other actions. For example, other things being equal, on the belief that failing to save a life is worse than acting in bad faith, the prohibition on promise breaking lacks authoritativeness when a life is at stake. Behind this kind of variability is the idea that prohibitions against less serious wrongs have relatively less

[25] Raz, *Engaging Reason*, p. 56.
[26] Raz, *Engaging Reason*, p. 56.

normative force and so are more readily subject to variations in authority than are prohibitions against more serious wrongs.[27]

An appeal to the idea that action-guiding considerations can have variable authority fits well with the examples that Hampton understands as cases of irrationality. On her account, irrational agents "mistakenly attribute to themselves a control over reality that they simply do not and cannot have."[28] In an attempt to justify his actions, one of these agents might have said to himself, "'I'm special enough to be able to do something other people can't do.'"[29] So when this agent finally had to face the costs of his behavior, "he learned something. He not only learned what he could plausibly accomplish and what he could not, but he also learned something about himself: His place in the world turned out not to be as high as he thought, and he realized that he was a lot more like other people in power and importance than he thought."[30] But this depiction of the case suggests that the agent did not believe that rationality prohibited the behavior or, at least, that the prohibition was as strong for him as for others. Had he acknowledged the authoritativeness of the requirement, which would imply that the costs of acting against it would exceed the benefits of a deviation, then he could not have believed that he was any more likely to get away with his behavior in the first place.[31]

What we need, then, to understand cases of irrationality as well as cases of immorality is a distinction between two senses of what it means to think that one is special. On the first meaning, the meaning to which Hampton's version of the volitional account is committed, to think that one is special is to acknowledge the authoritativeness of a requirement of rationality or morality in a particular case but to believe, nevertheless, that one can get away with doing what one desires. As we have seen, this sense of what it means to think one is special renders both immoral behavior and irrational behavior incoherent. If we assume that what

[27] The argument here appeals to something akin to W. D. Ross's notion of prima facie duties. See his *The Right and the Good* (Oxford: Clarendon Press, 1930).

[28] Hampton, *"Mens Rea,"* p. 9.

[29] Hampton, *"Mens Rea,"* p. 7.

[30] Hampton, *"Mens Rea,"* p. 9.

[31] This actually undermines Hampton's account of irrationality because the belief, if true, would make the action rational. Irrationality does not rest on mistaken beliefs of this kind, as Hampton herself says (*"Mens Rea,"* p. 2). However, if the agent engages in the behavior despite his belief that he is no different from others, then it looks more like a case of irrationality.

agents believe about the authority of an action-guiding consideration is derived from their understanding of the costs and benefits associated with a deviation from it, then they can hardly expect anything other than an all-things-considered loss in value when they act against a requirement of morality or rationality that they take to be authoritative. On a second meaning, to think that one is special is to believe that a requirement of immorality or irrationality fails to apply in one's particular circumstances. Agents who believe they are special in this sense need not expect an all-things-considered loss in value. In fact, their positive assessment of the overall costs and benefits of their behavior in the situation confirms their beliefs that they are special.

To see the explanatory power of the second sense of what it means to think that one is special, let us consider a case that is central to Hampton's discussion: "the person who is a decent member of our community but who nonetheless decides, while in a great hurry to get her shopping done at the mall, to sneak into a parking space someone else has been patiently waiting for."[32] Hampton claims that the parking-space thief believes that she can get away with taking the parking space in this case "because her own wishes are too important to 'lose' it."[33] Yet this claim actually supports an analysis of the case on which the parking-space thief believes that she is special enough to be excepted from the relevant moral requirement. By virtue of the importance of satisfying her desires and preferences, she holds that she is merely taking possession of something that is rightfully hers. Her belief, that is, is not about whether she is sufficiently special to avoid the consequences of violating the requirement. Rather, her belief is about the authority of this requirement as it applies to her situation. Or, as Hampton herself puts it, the parking-space thief mistakenly believes "that she can and *should* 'get away with it.'"[34]

Volitional and cognitive understandings of immorality thus offer competing views of what it is for an agent to think that he is special. In so doing, each view identifies immorality with the way in which we are inclined to make exceptions of ourselves. Here, both accounts are in good historical company. Immanuel Kant, for example, claims that "[i]f

---

[32] Hampton, "*Mens Rea*," p. 17.
[33] Hampton, "*Mens Rea*," p. 18.
[34] Hampton, "*Mens Rea*," p. 18, emphasis added. Jeffrie Murphy also appeals to the cognitive elements of immorality in his critique of Hampton's work ("Jean Hampton on Immorality, Self-Hatred, and Self-Forgiveness," *Philosophical Studies* 89 [1998]: 227).

we now attend to ourselves whenever we transgress a duty, we find that we in fact do not will that our maxim should become a universal law – since that is impossible for us – but rather that its opposite should remain a law universally: we only take the liberty of making an *exception* to it for ourselves (or even just for this once) to the advantage of our inclination."[35] As Kant readily acknowledges, though, to will that the opposite of our maxim should remain a law universally would seem to make it equally impossible for us to will the transgression. Simply put, universalization rules out the exception itself. In an effort to get around this difficulty, Kant distinguishes between two points of view that we might take on an exception, only one of which he thinks allows the possibility of willing a transgression. From *the point of view of reason,* "if we weighed it all up ... we should find a contradiction in our own will," whereas from *the point of view of will,* it is possible to "permit ourselves a few exceptions which are, as we pretend, inconsiderable and apparently forced upon us."[36]

Kant's appeal to pretense and appearance reflects his commitment to the claim that when we make exceptions of ourselves, "we in fact recognize the validity of the categorical imperative."[37] In order to will a transgression, we have to see the "universality of the principle" in a different way – namely, as "a mere generality."[38] But if we can take this perspective on moral requirements, then why is it impossible for us to believe that it is legitimate to see them in this way? The plausibility of the claim that we can see moral requirements as something short of universal principles actually increases on the assumption that we can believe that this way of thinking about the requirements is part of an acceptable account of the scope of morality. On this understanding of the application of moral requirements, reason itself apparently allows us to draw upon the very considerations to which Kant claims we disingenuously appeal from the point of view of will. Indeed, when the moral costs of an exception seem "inconsiderable" or "forced upon" us by the need to prevent even greater costs, our exceptions do look importantly different from many of the exceptions that others make of themselves. Regardless of whether these differences actually justify our exceptions

---

35 Immanuel Kant, *Groundwork of the Metaphysic of Morals,* trans. H. J. Paton (New York: Harper and Row Publishers, 1964), pp. 91–92 [424].
36 Kant, *Groundwork,* p. 92 [424].
37 Kant, *Groundwork,* p. 92 [424].
38 Kant, *Groundwork,* p. 92 [424].

in the end, we can nevertheless believe that we are special enough to secure this kind of justification.[39]

This is not to suggest that the exceptions immoral agents make of themselves can always be attributed to the idea they are special in this way or, for that matter, in any other way. An agent can violate a requirement of morality not in the belief that he can get away with it according to his own conception of value but, instead, fully expecting that the costs of his behavior will outweigh its benefits. In some cases of this kind, the immoral agent, not unlike the irrational agent, will act to satisfy an impulse or urge with which he does not identify. Perhaps the impulse or urge is so intense that he satisfies it, as we say, "despite himself." The most extreme cases of this kind of behavior might be attributed to addictions to drugs, alcohol, gambling, or sex. Alternatively, the desire that is satisfied can have as its object something that is of value or even great value for the agent and yet be of less value than what he thinks will be lost by his acting on it. In this kind of case, the calculation that potentially justifies satisfaction of the desire comes up short. Here, we must admit that this understanding of immorality makes the failures of such agents a matter of volition. The agents in question choose to engage in immoral behavior, all the time aware of the conflicts with their conceptions of value and, so too, of the consequences of their behavior.

While this rendering of the volitional account makes for a coherent moral psychology, it also creates substantial space for cognitive considerations in an understanding of ethical failure. Unless we assume that agents always begin with an accurate understanding of the costs of immorality, we can expect that the cognitive errors they make will go beyond mistaken factual beliefs about the contribution their behavior will make to what they find valuable. Without this assumption, even if agents are correct about the connection between their behavior and the consequences it would have for their conceptions of value, they can nonetheless arrive at incorrect conclusions about the authority of moral requirements. Just as they can come to recognize that a moral requirement applies to them, which this rendering of the volitional account must assume, they can also fail to recognize that a requirement applies when it does, or believe that it applies when it does not. The fact that agents sometimes begin with incorrect conceptions of value, that

---

[39] This assumption is all the more plausible on the view that we normally desire things for reasons – namely, the reasons for which we believe the objects of desire to be of value.

is, means that they will sometimes end up making incorrect determinations of authoritativeness. When their conceptions of value are incorrect, behavioral conformity to these conceptions will hardly be sufficient for ethical success. In these cases, ethical failure is fundamentally a matter of cognition.[40]

Where the volitional account and cognitive account ultimately differ, then, is in their characterizations of what causes us to make exceptions of ourselves. The volitional account claims that an understanding of immorality need only look to our desires or, at most, to our beliefs about how we might avoid the negative consequences of acting on them. When this account forgoes any appeal to the notion that immoral agents believe that they can get away with their behavior, it traces exception making by these agents to the satisfaction of a desire that they themselves take to be in conflict with their conceptions of value. Since not all exception making by agents is a result of behavioral inconsistency with their values, this version of the volitional account offers an incomplete understanding of immorality. However, when the volitional account concedes that exception making by agents can be the result of behavioral consistency with their conceptions of value and, accordingly, endorses the notion that immoral agents sometimes believe they can get away with their behavior, we must attribute to these agents an understanding of the costs of immorality that can lead them to think they are outside of the scope of moral requirements. The exceptions that such agents make of themselves are the result of mistaken beliefs about the authority of moral requirements as these requirements apply to their situation.

The cognitive account acknowledges that mistaken beliefs about our control over the consequences of immorality will not complete an account of ethical failure. According to this account, our understanding of immorality must also consider the ways in which inaccurate determinations of authoritativeness can lead us to act against moral requirements. Specifically, it must appeal to mistaken beliefs about our own importance and the ways in which this importance comes to bear on the application of morality's requirements to us. According to the cognitive account, we sometimes think that it is permissible for us to engage in behavior that would normally be unacceptable by overestimating our

---

[40] See, for example, Susan Wolf, "Sanity and the Metaphysics of Responsibility," in Ferdinand Schoeman, ed., *Responsibility, Character, and the Emotions: New Essays in Moral Psychology* (Cambridge: Cambridge University Press, 1987), pp. 46–62; and Susan Wolf, *Freedom Within Reason* (Oxford: Oxford University Press, 1990). I discuss Wolf's view in Chapter 7.

own importance and the importance of satisfying our desires in a particular set of circumstances. In these cases, we mistakenly believe that the circumstances justify our making exceptions of ourselves because we underestimate the relative importance of behavioral conformity to the moral requirement. This account thus maintains the idea that immoral agents sometimes believe that they are sufficiently special to get away with doing what other people should not do and what they themselves are normally prohibited from doing. With respect to their particular circumstances, they see themselves as beyond the scope of morality.

IV. LEADER SELF-INTEREST

What are the implications of Sections II and III for thinking about ethical failures in leadership? The claim that these failures can be traced to self-interest typically means that leaders who behave immorally knowingly put their desires and preferences ahead of the good of the group for which they are responsible. There is no denying that such conflicts do arise and that leaders sometimes fail ethically by resolving them in their own favor. But making sense of the role of leader self-interest, not unlike giving a general analysis of moral motivation, requires a more complicated moral psychology than this standard opposition suggests. As we have seen, there is normally a structural connection between an agent's desires and preferences, on the one hand, and his beliefs about value, on the other. We must therefore ask what leaders might believe about the importance of satisfying their own desires and preferences. Answering this question will show that leader self-interest is ultimately linked to group ends in ways that challenge the general applicability of the volitional account of ethical failures in leadership.

The volitional account assumes that leaders who privilege self-interest do so in full knowledge of the wrongness of their behavior. It assumes, that is, that leaders do not believe that the importance of satisfying their own desires and preferences justifies their acting on self-interest. Yet the case for this particular kind of mistaken belief about justification is even stronger with respect to leaders than it is with respect to other moral agents. After all, who has a better claim to importance in our society than our leaders? The conclusion that they are important is confirmed by everyone from educators to investment analysts and social critics, and, based on this conclusion, we readily clear not only parking spaces for our leaders but sometimes entire streets and runways upon recognition of their need. It is little wonder, then, if leaders come to an exaggerated conception of just how special they really are, a conception that cannot but have implications for the perspective they take on the importance of satisfying their desires and preferences.

The argument for the claim that leaders are likely to overestimate the importance of satisfying their desires and preferences is at its strongest when we consider that, for leaders, desire and preference satisfaction is normally related to the achievement of group ends. As Joanne Ciulla puts it, "We want leaders to put the interests of followers first, but most leaders do not pay a price for doing that on a daily basis, nor do most circumstances require them to calculate their interests in relation to the interests of their followers. The practice of leadership is to guide and look after the goals, missions, and aspirations of groups, organizations, countries, or causes."[41] In other words, since leaders have a substantial interest in the achievement of group ends, their self-interested behavior will usually be consistent with the interests of group members or, at least, with what is *perceived* to be the interests of group members. In fact, the possibility of congruent interests is often what brings leaders and followers together in the first place.

To say that leaders and followers typically have congruent interests is not to say that their interests are identical at all levels. In some cases, the pursuit of group ends is simply a means to the attainment of other goods sought after by leaders. Leaders sometimes enter into relationships with followers not because of any commitment to them or to their ends but, rather, because of the instrumental value that goal achievement can have in terms of wealth, power, or fame. Similarly, followers need not be seen as having a commitment to the intrinsic value of goal achievement. Perhaps they are members of the group only to secure a paycheck or to get the esteem from others that pursuit of group ends entails. Nevertheless, these instrumental connections to goal achievement and others like them forge significant bonds of self-interest between leaders and followers, making it difficult to draw sharp lines between leadership behavior that is self-interested and that which is for the good of the group. Even leaders and followers who are in it only for themselves, that is, must recognize that using this relationship to satisfy their desires and preferences is largely dependent upon meeting the interests of other parties to the relationship.

[41] Joanne B. Ciulla, "Ethics and Leadership Effectiveness," in John Antonakis, Anna T. Cianciolo, and Robert J. Sternberg, eds., *The Nature of Leadership* (Thousand Oaks, CA: Sage Publications, 2004), p. 316.

When looked at from the perspective of followers, the connection between leader self-interest and the good of the group puts the desires and preferences of leaders in territory that is increasingly hospitable to the formation of justificatory beliefs. In many cases, satisfying a leader's desires and preferences is itself a practical means to goal achievement. For example, after being forced into bankruptcy by high-profile corporate scandals, Enron and WorldCom nonetheless proposed pay plans to incoming CEOs that overseers rejected as "overreaching and inappropriate"[42] and "grossly excessive."[43] The putative justification for satisfying CEO self-interest, of course, is that anticipated salary increases and deferred compensation packages, so-called "golden handcuffs," give leaders incentives to continue their work toward group ends. Similarly, performance bonuses, promotions, and "golden parachutes" are meant to reflect the past efforts of leaders. Regardless of whether these goods are part of a forward-looking scheme of incentives or based on a backward-looking appeal to desert, the connection between leader self-interest and group ends accounts for much of the perceived importance of satisfying the desires and preferences of leaders.

This means that the importance of leader self-interest does not rest simply on the notion that leaders are special people. It can be derived directly from the relevance that leader self-interest has to the achievement of group goals, the very thing that makes our leaders special to

---

[42] Alison Maitland, "Clearing up after the visionaries," *Financial Times* (January 30, 2003). According to Ben White, a staff writer for the *Washington Post*, "Executive compensation consultants say corporate boards are eager to avoid further revelations of exorbitant pay packages. But the consultants also say board members continue to embrace the cult of the indispensable chief executive and fear that any big cutbacks could reduce their chances of keeping or landing a star" ("Stock Options Becoming Pay-Plan Dinosaurs?; Image-Sensitive Firms Get Creative With Perks," *Washington Post* [January 31, 2003]). Similarly, "Most states think nothing about giving special perks to governors and lieutenant governors. Some state executives are provided with housing (ever heard of governor's mansions?), planes, helicopters, cars, chauffeurs, maids, and other assorted lackeys" (Jack Williams, "Double standard for pols lives," *Boston Herald* [May 19, 2000]).

[43] Reuters News Service, "WorldCom CEO pay plan 'excessive,'" *Houston Chronicle* (December 11, 2002). This case is also interesting because outgoing CEO Bernard J. Ebbers did not take personal advantage of the fraudulent accounting at WorldCom. One explanation is that "[t]here is – or at least many corporate executives used to believe there was – a gray area between flexible accounting and fraud. And that gray area may help answer a perplexing question: Why didn't WorldCom's chief executive sell before the stock collapsed" (Floyd Norris, "If Ebbers Masterminded the Fraud, Why Didn't He Sell More Stock?" *New York Times* [March 5, 2004]).

us. One implication of this connection between group interests and desire and preference satisfaction for leaders is that there is less reason than we might initially think to pit leader self-interest against group interests as part of a general account of ethical failure. For one thing, individuals primarily concerned with acquiring the goods of leadership are particularly unlikely to overlook these straightforward instrumental connections. Given that the motivational constraints on these leaders are primarily external in origin, satisfaction of their desires and preferences calls for behavior that at least mimics what Manuel Mendonca calls *"mutual altruism* – a helping concern for others combined with concern for one's own self-interest."[44] Crudely egoistic behavior, which "involves a concern for self with no concern for others," is unlikely to get a leader very far with followers.[45] Along with the power and privileges of leadership come clear expectations that their use will be reserved for the advancement of group ends.

Still, it would surely be too strong to suggest that it is always in a leader's self-interest to further the interests of followers. Edwin Locke comes very close to making this suggestion in his defense of egoistic leadership.

The rational leader will neither want to sacrifice his or her legitimate interests to the employees nor to sacrifice the [employees'] interests to his or her own . . . To get and keep good employees, the leader will want to appeal to the employees' self-interest, viz. if you come to work here, I will give you mentally challenging work and chance to grow, fair rewards, and competitive benefits, etc. He or she will not think just of the range of the moment (viz., I will work them to the bone and make my results look good to my boss this quarter), but also of the long-range consequences of his or her actions (e.g., what will happen if the best people all quit). His or her goal will be to merge . . . interests of all parties so that everyone gets something out of it and the organization prospers. The ideal relationship is mutual trade to mutual benefit.[46]

As evidenced by Locke's reference to "[t]he ideal," the implied universality of this suggestion is no more plausible than the claim that it is always in an individual's self-interest to be moral. In at least some situations, the interests of leaders and followers diverge. When the egoistic

---

[44] Manuel Mendonca, "Preparing for Ethical Leadership in Organizations," *Canadian Journal of Administrative Sciences* 18 (2001): 268.

[45] Mendonca, "Preparing for Ethical Leadership," p. 268.

[46] Bruce J. Avolio and Edwin A. Locke, "Contrasting Different Philosophies of Leader Motivation: Altruism Versus Egoism," *Leadership Quarterly* 13 (2002): 181.

leader faces the resulting choice between the two, egoism requires that he put his own interests over the interests of others. Although he may take it as an important end to avoid this kind of divergence, the value of achieving group goals is derived from the instrumental connection between these goals and the advancement of his interests and, accordingly, must be seen by him as secondary to self-interest.

Following Ayn Rand, Locke attempts to get around this line of criticism by arguing that "there can be no conflicts of interest between rational men."[47] According to this argument, "desires are not the starting point in deciding how to act or what is good. One first has to identify and validate a proper code of morality."[48] Given the precedence of this code, Locke thinks, "It is not rational to hold a wish based on an invalid premise, e.g., one that is wrong because it contradicts reality, such as wanting something you have no right to."[49] The reason leaders cannot pursue self-interest at the expense of the interests of others, then, is that it cannot be in a leader's interest to engage in behavior that unjustifiably makes others worse off. So, to adjudicate between the claims of leaders and followers in cases in which their interests *appear* to diverge, we need only discover which party wrongfully desires that to which the other party has a right. Clearly, the problem with this claim is that it makes a blatantly circular case for egoistic leadership: How should leaders behave? They should act in their own interests. How do we determine their interests? Their interests are determined by figuring out how they should behave. On Locke's defense of egoistic leadership, notions of morality and self-interest are each defined in terms of the other.

What Locke gets right is that there is indeed a false dichotomy in "[t]he conventional belief that a leader either has to be a self-sacrificing servant of others or a conniving wheeler-dealer."[50] Although respect for the interests of others is not always "critical" or "a tool of success,"[51] it very often is. The weaker, sustainable conclusion, therefore, is that

---

[47] Avolio and Locke, "Contrasting Different Philosophies of Leader Motivation," p. 179. Locke cites Ayn Rand, "The 'Conflicts' of Men's Interests," *Objectivist Newsletter* 1, 8 (1962).

[48] Avolio and Locke, "Contrasting Different Philosophies of Leader Motivation," p. 179.

[49] Avolio and Locke, "Contrasting Different Philosophies of Leader Motivation," p. 179.

[50] Avolio and Locke, "Contrasting Different Philosophies of Leader Motivation," p. 173.

[51] Avolio and Locke, "Contrasting Different Philosophies of Leader Motivation," p. 173.

leader self-interest is regularly connected to group interests by virtue of an expectation central to the practice of leadership – namely, that leaders will act to advance group ends. This conclusion is perfectly consistent with the claim that leaders can get away with doing things the rest of us cannot do. In fact, consistency between the two is a straightforward consequence of the role differentiation that characterizes leadership. This is why Plato's story of the ring of Gyges, a ring that makes its bearer invisible to others, can be read as a metaphor for thinking about the ethical pitfalls of the power and privileges that leadership brings with it.[52] Unlike the shepherd in the story, however, leaders do not ordinarily find these rings. Usually, the rings are given to leaders, and we very quickly take the rings away when leaders do not meet our expectations that the power and privileges be used to serve group ends. In many ways, these expectations make leaders more visible than the rest of us, not less. We might even go so far as to say that some leaders lose as many rings as they gain.[53]

Many Americans suspected that these expectations were not met, for example, when runways at Los Angeles International Airport (LAX) were closed so that President Clinton could get a $200 haircut from a Hollywood stylist.[54] In what became known as "haircutgate," presidential aides were left scrambling to justify Clinton's behavior. George Stephanopoulos, senior advisor to the president, told the press, "As you know, he has a very busy schedule, and he just tries to work it in when he can. That was when we were able to work it in."[55] Underlying this justification is the assumption that Clinton was busy doing very important things for the country. Indeed, Stephanopoulos makes this assumption quite explicit, urging that people "look at his economic package . . . that's designed to turn this around and to really get some real benefits to middle-class Americans. And that's what's *important*."[56] Again, such justificatory beliefs can explain why leaders often make little effort to conceal seemingly self-interested behavior. After all, LAX is

---

[52] Plato, *Republic*, trans. G. M. A. Grube (Indianapolis: Hackett Publishing Company, 1992), pp. 35–36 [359d–360d].

[53] Leaders may have had almost unlimited power in twentieth-century company towns and totalitarian regimes, but this is hardly true for leaders in contemporary corporations and modern democratic states.

[54] The effects of the president's behavior on air traffic were later found to be minimal.

[55] Thomas L. Friedman, "Haircut Grounded Clinton While the Price Took Off," *New York Times* (May 21, 1993).

[56] Friedman, "Haircut Grounded Clinton," emphasis added.

not exactly an inconspicuous place for a president to get a haircut. In a case of much greater extravagance, minutes from meetings of the board of directors show that Tyco CEO Dennis Kozlowski, who allegedly used company money to pay for a Manhattan apartment, furnishings such as a $6,000 shower curtain, and his wife's fortieth birthday party, did not conceal roughly $20 million dollars in loans from the board of directors and its compensation committee, despite early accounts to the contrary.[57] Maybe Kozlowski saw his self-interested behavior as justified and thought that others would as well because of the regular connection between the satisfaction of his desires and preferences and the advancement of goals that reflect group interests.[58]

The volitional account of ethical failures in leadership concedes that leaders are aware of these expectations but holds that leaders willingly defy them in the belief that the power and privileges of leadership insulate them from the negative consequences of unethical behavior. But if self-interest is regularly connected to the advancement of group goals in the ways I have argued it is, then it is more plausible to think that egoistic leaders overestimate the normative force of the connection between self-interest and goal achievement than that they overlook the importance of these connections. To assume otherwise would be to fail to do justice to the motivational assumptions that characterize egoistic forms of leadership. Because of the nature of the goods they seek, egoistic leaders are no more likely than internally motivated leaders to act against perceived expectations of the group. On the assumption that these leaders are externally motivated, they have substantial interests in following the dictates of morality in cases in which they believe that group members see them as being bound by these requirements. No doubt it is just this kind of attention to the expectations of others, disingenuous though it may be, that puts egoistic leaders into positions of leadership in the first place.

This leaves us with the task of explaining the unethical behavior of egoistic leaders without undermining the motivational assumptions we make about them. The cognitive account of ethical failures in leadership holds that immoral leaders can believe they are justified in acting

---

[57] Andrew Ross Sorkin and Jonathan D. Glater, "Some Tyco Board Members Knew of Pay Packages, Records Show," *New York Times* (September 23, 2002).

[58] The notion that leaders are expected to be concerned with the way they look, the clothes they wear, and the cars they drive, and so on, supports my more general point that attributions of selfishness can be very complicated in leadership contexts.

on their desires and preferences precisely because of the connection between self-interest and the advancement of group goals. Perhaps egoistic leaders hold this belief based on all they have done for their group, organization, or society.[59] Alternatively, they may conclude that their self-interested behavior is justified by an appeal to what is necessary to motivate them to do even more good. In either case, these leaders believe not only that they can get away with satisfying their desires and preferences but also that they *should* get away with it. Past successes and the possibility of future success encourage them to think that they are special and, accordingly, to overestimate the normative force of the connection between self-interest and the advancement of group ends. In other words, when leaders come to an exaggerated view of just how special they really are, they can conclude that they are justified in making self-interested exceptions of themselves that would not be justified for others in their group, organization, or society.

V. LEADER VALUES

The goal of the previous section was to show that immoral leaders can believe that they are justified in acting in self-interest. While such a belief may be at odds with prevailing notions of justification, we should not be surprised that some leaders hold it, especially given the lengths to which many thinkers have gone to show that this belief is actually correct. From Thrasymachus's argument in Plato's *Republic* that justice is whatever is in the interest of the stronger[60] to the contemporary egoist's claim that "leaders (and everyone else) should be selfish,"[61] there is a strong tradition in moral theory to support the view that justification can be grounded in leader self-interest. Descriptive analyses in the social sciences parallel these prescriptive arguments, suggesting that people

---

[59] In a *Richmond Times-Dispatch* expos of spending by public officials at the 2003 Virginia Municipal League convention, "Bluefield Mayor William King defended the expenditures as fair compensation for long hours of public service." Harrisonburg Mayor Joseph G. Fitzgerald claimed that "charging taxpayers for spouses' trips ... [is] basically the only fringe benefit this job has besides a parking space at the municipal building." And, Berryville Mayor Richard Sponseller responded, "I put in a lot of hours as mayor and don't get much compensation, so I think it's appropriate" (Bill Geroux, "Public picks up the tab, Officials spend $410,000 at convention," *Richmond Times-Dispatch* [October 5, 2003]).

[60] Plato, *Republic*, p. 14 [338c].

[61] Avolio and Locke, "Contrasting Different Philosophies of Leader Motivation," p. 169.

commonly take an appeal to self-interest to be a socially acceptable way to justify their behavior.[62] Still, we would do well to ask whether all leaders understand their behavior in terms of self-interest. Just as we challenged the general claim that agents understand the costs of immorality only in these terms, we can question the view that external goods associated with goal achievement are sufficient to explain the behavior of leaders. On a broader view of leader motivation, leaders can act on the belief that their exceptions are justified based on the intrinsic value of group ends themselves.

Notice that even Edwin Locke's version of egoistic leadership betrays a commitment to motivating factors beyond the external goods associated with goal achievement. Consistent with Rand's moral theory, Locke's defense of ethical egoism prohibits only self-sacrificial behavior, which is characterized by "the sacrifice of a higher value to a lower one."[63] As a consequence of this characterization, the founding CEO who "loves his job and his company" can agree to "take no salary for 2 years until his company gets off the ground" without facing the objection he engaged in self-sacrifice.[64] Similarly, soldiers who die "for the protection of our country against an aggressor" do not act self-sacrificially, at least on the condition that they "love their country."[65] CEOs and soldiers can be justified in acting on group ends, Locke thinks, because such individuals are ultimately pursuing their highest values. Perhaps it is Locke's own values that are exposed when he criticizes Mother Teresa as someone who "worshipped poverty," holding that we should instead admire those who "worship production, like Bill Gates."[66] A somewhat more plausible criticism of Mother Teresa's behavior, however, would rest on the claim that efforts to serve society are indeed self-sacrificial because society cannot embody values in the way that a company or a country can. Regardless of the ultimate force

---

[62] Dale T. Miller calls these conclusions "prescriptive" because they are about what people believe they ought to do, reserving "descriptive" conclusions for how people actually behave ("The Norm of Self-Interest," *American Psychologist* 54 [1999]: 1053–1060).

[63] Avolio and Locke, "Contrasting Different Philosophies of Leader Motivation," p. 170.

[64] Avolio and Locke, "Contrasting Different Philosophies of Leader Motivation," p. 181.

[65] Avolio and Locke, "Contrasting Different Philosophies of Leader Motivation," p. 182.

[66] Avolio and Locke, "Contrasting Different Philosophies of Leader Motivation," p. 181.

of this claim, Locke clearly endorses the view that leaders should act on their commitments to the intrinsic value of group ends. His version of egoistic leadership must therefore assume that leaders can act on these commitments in the belief that they are justified in doing so.

If leaders can be motivated by the intrinsic value of group ends, then we have another reason to think that they will often behave in ways that respect group interests. In the typical case, internally motivated leaders will have no choice but to show this kind of respect, as group interests are embodied in the ends themselves.[67] Of course, the fact that group interests are often respected when leaders take their ends to be intrinsically valuable does little to resolve conflicts of interests *between* groups. In a response to Locke's argument for egoistic leadership, Bruce Avolio points to the competition between corporate America and the United States military for graduates of West Point. According to Avolio, the selfish interest of corporations is to draw from the pool of well-trained junior officers, but "[t]he selfish interest of our military leaders is to retain cadets to lead the nation's armed forces."[68] On top of this, "the young officer might argue that it is in his or her selfish interest to leave the military to pursue lucrative job offerings."[69] Avolio thus understands these conflicts of interests to be the result of the selfishness of the parties involved in the conflicts. The suggestion that retaining these cadets "is good for our nation" only confirms "[t]he selfish interest of our military leaders."[70] Even the young officer who reasons that leaving the military "can provide a higher quality of life for his or her family" is seen simply as privileging selfish interests.[71]

Why do both Locke and Avolio so readily appeal to selfishness to characterize leadership behavior directed at the intrinsic value of group ends? For Locke, the answer is that a more narrow view of self-interest would severely restrict the claims that can be made about how leaders ought to be motivated. On such a view, whether leadership behavior is

---

[67] There can also be purely instrumental connections between respecting group interests and advancing ends that a leader takes to be intrinsically valuable.

[68] Avolio and Locke, "Contrasting Different Philosophies of Leader Motivation," p. 175.

[69] Avolio and Locke, "Contrasting Different Philosophies of Leader Motivation," p. 175.

[70] Avolio and Locke, "Contrasting Different Philosophies of Leader Motivation," p. 175.

[71] Avolio and Locke, "Contrasting Different Philosophies of Leader Motivation," p. 175.

self-interested depends solely on the instrumental connection between the achievement of group ends and the satisfaction of a leader's desires and preferences. When coupled with a commitment to ethical egoism for leaders, this view of self-interest would mean that intuitively moral behavior, such as giving one's life for a cause, is not moral after all. By instead giving a central place to the intrinsic value of group ends in his assumptions about leader motivation, Locke is in a position to respect the intuition that such behavior sometimes meets the demands of morality. In contrast, the answer for Avolio's defense of altruistic leadership is that a more narrow view of self-interest would severely restrict the claims that can be made about how leaders should *not* be motivated. In order to isolate self-interest as the general cause of leader immorality, Avolio must impute selfishness to a leader's behavior anytime the leader unethically resolves a conflict of interests in favor of the interests of his own group. Characterizing this kind of behavior as selfish, even though it clearly promotes group interests, allows him to say that "it is here where some sacrifice or altruism oftentimes needs to be considered for the good of both groups."[72]

The trouble with a broadened view of self-interest is that it makes too much leadership behavior selfish. In fact, selfishness would be at the root of all leadership behavior based on the intrinsic value of group ends and the interests they reflect. According to Locke, the soldier who gives his life for the sake of his country is no less selfish than the soldier who hides behind him to protect what he values most – namely, his own life. Although both soldiers act on their highest values, it is insufficiently discriminating to describe both kinds of behavior as selfish. Likewise, Avolio claims that "a group, an organization, or even a nation may have at any one point in time equally competing selfish interests."[73] Besides stretching the language of self-interest almost beyond recognition, an attribution of selfishness to these collective bodies does not distinguish the interests in question from non-selfish interests that might be said to compete with each other. Since nothing would be lost by saying "equally competing interests" instead of "equally competing *selfish* interests," an appeal to self-interest does not add anything to our understanding of these conflicts.

---

[72] Avolio and Locke, "Contrasting Different Philosophies of Leader Motivation," p. 175.
[73] Avolio and Locke, "Contrasting Different Philosophies of Leader Motivation," p. 176.

Locke and Avolio are correct, then, that a narrow view of leader motivation is insufficient to explain either moral or immoral leadership behavior. Their mistake is to think that what we need to do to make sense of this behavior is broaden our understanding of self-interest. While making more room for attributions of selfishness is certainly one way to generate a broadened view of leader motivation, it does so at the expense of conceptual clarity. A more discriminating way to understand leader motivation is to say that leaders who act on the intrinsic value of group ends ultimately do so for the sake of the ends themselves and the interests these ends embody, not for the sake of self-interest. Of course, such leaders also have desires and preferences indexed to the attainment of group ends and the fulfillment of group interests. But so do agents who value more general ends such as justice and the promotion of human welfare. The mere fact that values give rise to desires and preferences cannot make behavior in the service of these values self-interested, let alone selfish.[74] What distinguishes the motivation of leaders who act from the intrinsic value of group ends is that these leaders do so independently of any beliefs they have about the contribution that the attainment of these ends would make to the promotion of their interests.

It is little wonder that the behavior of leaders who act on the intrinsic value of group ends is not properly understood as selfish. For one thing, a distinction between the two kinds of leader motivation is necessary for us to make sense of attributions of selfishness to leaders in cases in which their behavior disregards the group interests that these ends reflect. In other words, if the behavior of a leader is selfish even when he acts on the intrinsic value of group ends, then selfishness cannot be what explains his behavior when he sacrifices the interests of the group for the sake of his own interests. This distinction is also necessary to make sense of the claim that a leader's commitment to the intrinsic value of group ends means that he must occasionally sacrifice some of his own interests for the interests of the group. Of course, one might object that it "is not a sacrifice if [the lesser values you give up] are, in fact, less important."[75] But this objection equivocates on what it means to make a sacrifice. While

---

[74] Patricia H. Werhane writes, "I am the subject of my interests, so there is a trivial sense in which all my interests are 'self-interests.' That is, they are interests *of* the self. But I am not always the *object* of those interests" (*Moral Imagination and Management Decision-Making* [Oxford: Oxford University Press, 1999], pp. 18–19).

[75] Avolio and Locke, "Contrasting Different Philosophies of Leader Motivation," p. 181.

it may not be an all-things-considered sacrifice (of value) to forgo the satisfaction of one's own interests for the sake of group ends, it remains a sacrifice just the same. In the best of all possible worlds, group ends could be attained at no cost whatsoever to one's interests. In fact, it is the possibility of getting the benefits without paying any costs that drives many of the collective action problems leaders try to solve. Not enough people are willing to sacrifice their individual interests for the sake of collective goods, and everyone is made worse off for it.

The unselfish nature of commitments to the intrinsic value of group ends can affect the perceived normative force associated with the attainment of these ends. After all, on this understanding of leader motivation, attributions of selfishness are to be reserved for those individuals who stand in the way of the satisfaction of group interests. By putting group interests first, leaders who act on the intrinsic value of group ends are apparently immune to a very forceful line of moral criticism. Unfortunately, this way of thinking about moral motivation may give group ends greater normative force than they deserve, not least of all when the attainment of these ends requires the imposition of moral costs on particular followers. By drawing on beliefs about the intrinsic value of group ends, leaders can think they are justified in showing less than normal respect for follower agency or in demanding inordinate sacrifices from individual followers in terms of well-being. For example, although intimidating and overworking followers is generally understood to be morally wrong, leaders can believe that exceptions are sometimes justified because of the importance of the ends to which they and others are committed. In essence, leaders can act from the belief that the prohibitions against intimidating and overworking followers have relatively less normative force compared with the demands generated by group ends. As a result, leaders come to see themselves as no longer bound by moral requirements that are authoritative for the rest of us.

The moral costs imposed in the name of group ends are certainly not reserved for followers. Since leadership ordinarily assumes giving priority to group members, advancing their ends and satisfying their interests sometimes requires that leaders show significantly less respect for the ends and interests of people outside their own company, country, or social class. While this standard leadership response to conflict between groups need not make leaders susceptible to a charge of selfishness, a leader's giving priority to group members is no less a significant source of immorality than would be his prioritization of himself. Such priority implies a commitment to the importance of their ends and interests not unlike the commitment of the leader who is prone to overestimate the importance of his desires and preferences. Indeed, the belief that group members are special by virtue of their ends and interests can blind a leader to the importance of the ends and interests of others and, as a consequence, cause him to ignore the fact that outsiders too are protected by moral requirements. Based on class interests in Stalin's Russia, wealthy peasants called "kulaks" were relegated to the status of outsiders and eventually subjected to a government policy of liquidation or "dekulakization." Later, China's Mao Zedong defended the cruelty of the Cultural Revolution on the grounds that "the exploitation and oppression . . . by the landlords, capitalists, imperialists, revisionists and their lackeys . . . *fully justi[fy]* any rebellion against the reactionaries."[76] More recently, Nuon Chea, whose authority within the Khmer Rouge was second only to Pol Pot's, admitted "there was a mistake. But I had my ideology. I wanted to free my country. I wanted people to have well-being."[77]

In some cases, we might have reason to question the morality of the costs that leaders willingly impose upon themselves for the sake of group ends. Dogmatic value-commitments can leave little room for real agency on the part of leaders, thereby threatening their physical and psychological well-being when they do what is necessary to live up to these commitments. Minimally, we can point to established linkages between work-related stress, on the one hand, and disease and personal dysfunction, on the other.[78] Some leaders, however, make a more complete sacrifice to group ends. When Marxist theorist and Communist International leader Nikolay Bukharin spoke during the show trials of

---

[76] Jonathan Glover, *Humanity: A Moral History of the Twentieth Century* (New Haven: Yale University Press, 2000), p. 289, emphasis added.

[77] Miranda Leitsinger, "Genocide charge denied," *Richmond Times-Dispatch* (January 19, 2004). Adolf Eichmann went so far as to claim that forced emigration was good for the Jews: "Yes, it was something very positive, and I was strengthened in my opinion by the desire of the Jews to emigrate. I could see that on a daily basis" (*The Trial of Adolf Eichmann*, PBS Home Video [ABC News Productions and Great Projects Film Company, 1997]). Describing the recently captured Saddam Hussein, Adnan Pachachi of the Iraqi Governing Council claimed, "He tried to justify himself by saying he was a just and firm ruler" (Susan Sachs, "The Capture of Hussein: Ex-Dictator; Hussein Caught in Makeshift Hide-Out; Bush Says 'Dark Era' for Iraqis Is Over," *New York Times* [December 15, 2003]).

[78] See, for example, National Institute for Occupational Safety and Health, United States Department of Health and Human Services, "Stress at Work," Publication No. 99-101 (January 7, 1999).

the Stalinist purges, he voiced "a commitment to the Soviet Union" and confessed "as a last *service* to the Party."[79] Bukharin was found guilty and executed. Here it is worth noting that normative theories of leadership such as Robert Greenleaf's *servant leadership*, according to which leaders should be "servant first,"[80] do little to protect leaders from such costs. Because of the close conceptual connection between serving and servility, making service the defining ethical attitude of leadership puts leaders at significant moral risk of getting less than egalitarian respect for their own agency and interests.[81] This form of leadership may be particularly out of place for members of oppressed communities in which serving and servility, not respect for their agency and well-being, are the norm.[82] It seems especially inappropriate to ask that leaders in these situations meet the "unrelenting demand that each of us confront the exacting terms of our own existence, and, like Sisyphus, *accept our rock and find our happiness in dealing with it.*"[83]

The fact that leaders can be motivated by commitments to the intrinsic value of group ends further undermines the general explanatory power of the volitional account of ethical failures in leadership. Although leaders can believe they are justified in making exceptions of themselves because of instrumental connections between self-interest and the advancement of group goals, the behavior of leaders who act from the intrinsic value of group ends is independent of any beliefs they have about the potential contribution of this behavior to their interests. In other words, unlike leadership behavior that can be understood in terms of these instrumental connections, leadership behavior motivated by the intrinsic value of group ends need not make room for an explanatory appeal to self-interest and, specifically, to beliefs about justified self-interest. But an explanation of the behavior of internally motivated leaders must appeal to justificatory beliefs all the same. These leaders can believe that they are justified both in making exceptions of

---

[79] Glover, *Humanity*, pp. 246, 263, emphasis added.

[80] Robert K. Greenleaf, *Servant Leadership: A Journey into the Nature of Legitimate Power and Greatness* (New York: Paulist Press, 1977), p. 13.

[81] See, for example, Thomas E. Hill, Jr., "Servility and Self-Respect," in his *Autonomy and Self-Respect* (Cambridge: Cambridge University Press, 1991), pp. 4–18; and Norman Bowie, "A Kantian Theory of Leadership," *Leadership and Organization Development Journal: Special Issue on Ethics and Leadership* 21 (2000): 185–193.

[82] See, for example, Douglas A. Hicks, "Self-Interest, Deprivation, and Agency: Expanding the Capabilities Approach," *Journal of the Society of Christian Ethics* (in press).

[83] Greenleaf, *Servant Leadership*, p. 11.

themselves and in excluding the interests of outsiders because of the perceived normative force associated with group ends. This means that the satisfaction of desires and preferences that compete with what leaders take to be authoritative moral requirements will not be sufficient to explain the behavior of leaders motivated by the intrinsic value of group ends. An explanation of their immoral behavior, like an explanation of the behavior of leaders who make exceptions of themselves because of normative pressures to privilege self-interest, will include exactly those cognitive causes of ethical failure that advocates of the volitional account seek to exclude.

Chapter 3

Making Exceptions for Leaders

I. INTRODUCTION

Whether in business, government, or non-profits, leaders sometimes act as though generally applicable moral requirements do not apply to their behavior. Generally applicable moral requirements are ethical prescriptions or proscriptions that usually or almost always bind the behavior of actors but can be overridden by other, more weighty moral considerations. In some cases, there will be considerable room for argument as to whether the leaders in question are justified in making exceptions of themselves. Is the CEO justified in breaking a promise if it is the only way to save the company? What about the behavior of the politician who must orchestrate a large-scale deception in order to thwart a terrorist attack? Can the director of a charitable organization justify pandering to a donor on the grounds that it is the most efficient way to garner resources to achieve a worthwhile goal? Other cases, however, will be significantly more straightforward: the executive who condones improper accounting, the state official who authorizes the arrest of political opponents, or the head of the charity who uses fraudulent means to secure a donation. To most of us on the outside, it is reasonably clear that the exceptions these leaders make of themselves are not morally justified.

In this chapter, I am principally concerned with cases in which leaders *mistakenly* believe that they are justified in making exceptions of themselves. The most straightforward explanation of their mistaken beliefs points to an important feature of the first set of cases at the beginning of the chapter. Given the difficulty inherent in many moral decisions, leaders will sometimes think they are justified in deviating from generally applicable moral requirements when, in fact, they are not. On this score, we should not expect leaders' ethical responses to hard cases to be any different from our own. But I want to suggest that an appeal to the nature of morality and our access to it is not sufficient to explain the mistaken beliefs that leaders hold about justification. My claim is that our basic understanding of leadership, especially effective leadership, can give rise to these mistakes. According to this explanation, there is something unique about the moral psychology of leaders. Compared with the rest of us, leaders are more inclined to think about their behavior in ways that purport to ground deviations from generally applicable moral requirements.

II. BEHAVIORAL DISTINCTIVENESS

Why would leaders mistakenly believe they are justified in deviating from generally applicable moral requirements? One answer to this question focuses on the ways in which they might understand their own behavior as part of the leadership process. This way of filling out the moral psychology of leaders considers how they might think about their own characteristics as actors, the situations in which they exercise leadership, and their relationships with followers. If they understand their behavior as being distinctive in one or more of these respects, then this understanding can serve as the foundation for the belief that they are justified in making exceptions of themselves. This does not mean, of course, that a leader's commitment to the distinctiveness of his behavior ever actually justifies an exception. Perhaps there really is no such distinction, or the distinction lacks relevance to a justification for the exception he seeks to make, or the distinction has relevance but is not sufficient to justify this exception. Nevertheless, a leader's good faith attempt to offer a justification of this kind must appeal to the distinctiveness of his behavior as he understands its place in the leadership process.

An appeal to distinctiveness is necessary because justifications for exceptions turn on the presentation of reasons. When it comes to a generally applicable moral requirement, a leader who sincerely believes that he is justified in a deviation must also believe that there is some relevant distinction between his own case and the cases to which the moral requirement typically applies. He could hardly admit that his own case is identical in all relevant respects to that of others and, nevertheless, argue that a generally applicable moral requirement fails to apply to him. Were there nothing distinctive about the leader's case, there would be no reason to which he might appeal to justify the exception. So he must believe there is some such distinction if he is to avoid the charge that his behavior is arbitrary. Furthermore, a leader must believe that the distinction is sufficient to justify the exception. He must believe, that is, that he has reason to deviate from the requirement and, in addition, that he has greater reason to make an exception for himself than to do what is typically required by morality.

To see the place of appeals to distinctiveness in justification, consider the parable of the Good Samaritan. This parable presents the ethical failures of two religious leaders, a priest and his designated lay associate, a Levite, by drawing a sharp contrast between their behavior and that of a Samaritan, a religious outsider.

A man was going down from Jerusalem to Jericho, and fell into the hands of robbers, who stripped him, beat him, and went away, leaving him half dead. Now by chance a priest was going down that road; and when he saw him, he passed by on the other side. So likewise a Levite, when he came to the place and saw him, passed by on the other side. But a Samaritan while traveling came near him; and when he saw him, he was moved with pity. He went to him and bandaged his wounds, having poured oil and wine on them. Then he put him on his own animal, brought him to an inn, and took care of him. The next day he took out two denarii, gave them to the innkeeper, and said, "Take care of him; and when I come back, I will repay you whatever more you spend."[1]

One pertinent question for an exercise in moral psychology asks why the Samaritan was inclined to give aid to the injured man. Unlike the priest and the Levite, foreigners were "not expected to show sympathy to Jews."[2] For present purposes, however, the relevant line of inquiry considers the reasons that the priest and the Levite failed to engage in what was generally expected behavior toward fellow Jews.[3] On the

---

[1] *HarperCollins Study Bible: New Revised Standard Version*, ed. Wayne A. Meeks (London: HarperCollins Publishers, 1989), Luke 10: 30b–35.
[2] *New Oxford Annotated Bible with the Apocrypha: Revised Standard Version*, eds. Herbert G. May and Bruce M. Metzger (New York: Oxford University Press, 1977), p. 1261.
[3] To cut off the questioning, of course, we might simply assume that these leaders were motivated by self-interest and rationally decided that the payoff of helping would not be worth the bother. As Doug Hicks has pointed out to me, this line of explanation would be completely counter to the communal mindset of first-century Jews.

assumption that these leaders believed they were justified in their behavior, what reasons might they have appealed to in order to ground this belief?

Historical examples, much less fictional ones, do not lend themselves to easy epistemic analysis. The most that we can do in this case is to speculate about the beliefs of the priest and the Levite by developing plausible argumentative possibilities. A first possibility is that these religious leaders believed that they were different from followers by virtue of characteristics such as righteousness and, moreover, their possessing these characteristics was sufficient to justify their doing less in these circumstances than what others might have been expected to do. This interpretation fits nicely with an important detail of the parable. The parable is presented in response to the questions of a lawyer who sought to "*[j]ustify himself* . . . by defining the limits of his duty, and showing how he had fulfilled it."[4] According to Hoyer and McDaniel, "[B]y using a priest and a Levite in his story, Jesus is pointing out to the smugly intelligent lawyer that being good in the traditional, legalistic sense" is not being good enough.[5] In other words, the priest and the Levite were wrong to think that they could get by morally on good character and on what they have done to acquire it. On this interpretation of the parable, the lawyer is likewise mistaken about the implications of his own righteousness.

A second argumentative possibility is that the priest and the Levite believed that the importance of avoiding a delay in their journey justified the disregard they showed the victim of the attack. Setting up their famous study of helping behavior called "From Jerusalem to Jericho," Darley and Batson suggest that "[o]ne can imagine the priest and Levite, prominent public figures, hurrying along with little black books full of meetings and appointments, glancing furtively at their sundials."[6] But what exactly were they on their way to do? One provocative answer to this question is consistent with Darley and Batson's suggestion that the priest and the Levite were on their way to carry out important business, but it challenges the claim that we can explain their behavior simply

---

[4] *New Oxford Annotated Bible*, p. 1260.
[5] Stephen Hoyer and Patrice McDaniel, "From Jericho to Jerusalem: The Good Samaritan From a Different Direction," *Journal of Psychology and Theology* 18 (1990): 329.
[6] John M. Darley and C. Daniel Batson, "'From Jerusalem to Jericho': A Study of Situational and Dispositional Variables in Helping Behavior," *Journal of Personality and Social Psychology* 27 (1973): 101.

by appeal to the fact that they were in a hurry to get there. Hoyer and McDaniel claim that

> a careful reading of the text implies that the priest and the Levite were going *from* Jericho *to* Jerusalem, which might very well mean that they were on their way to perform temple duties. If such were the case, it would be impossible for them to stop and render aid because they couldn't be sure whether the victim was alive or not... And knowing the law as they did, the priest and the Levite knew that if they were to come into contact with a corpse (Lev. 21: 1–4), they would be rendered ceremonially unclean and unable to perform their duties.[7]

A third argumentative possibility, then, is that the priest and Levite were "concerned about impurity from contact with a *half dead* person."[8] Assuming they believed that they were bound to the norms of a special relationship that required seemingly neglectful behavior in these circumstances, we cannot infer that they were simply too busy to render aid.

The case of the priest and the Levite highlights three general sources of distinctiveness on which justifications for exceptions might be grounded. Leaders can appeal to personal characteristics, to features of the situation, or to norms of special relationships in order to differentiate their behavior from that of others. For example, leaders may think they are smarter, better motivated, or more virtuous than followers. Alternatively, even if they reject the view that they are different from followers in these or in other ways, they may believe that the situational demands to which they must respond are relevantly dissimilar to the situations in which followers act. Here, the thought is that their behavior is a reaction to objectively important features of the situations in which leaders find themselves. Finally, leaders may hold that the relationships they have with followers give rise to distinct requirements on their behavior. Given the way that norms apply to leaders, it can be permissible – indeed required – for a leader to engage in behavior that would be prohibited for followers.

Again, on each of these possibilities, the force of the claim that a leader makes a justified exception rests on showing that there really is just such a distinction, that the distinction is relevant to the application of a generally applicable moral requirement, and that this distinction is sufficient to justify a deviation from this requirement. Meeting these

---

[7] Hoyer and McDaniel, "From Jericho to Jerusalem," p. 327. Here, they follow T. C. Smith, "The Parable of the Samaritan," *Review and Expositor* 47 (1950): 434–441.

[8] *HarperCollins Study Bible*, p. 1980.

conditions is rarely an easy task. Still, it would be difficult to argue that these sources of distinctiveness never generate acceptable justifications for leaders. Morally relevant differences exist between people, the situations they face, and the norms to which they are subject. It matters morally, for example, whether a bread thief is capable of getting food in other ways, whether the person from whom he stole has plenty, and whether the person for whom he stole was his hungry child. In some cases at least, we might think that these kinds of differences are sufficient to justify deviations from a generally applicable moral requirement – for example, the requirement that we respect the private property of others. Accordingly, leadership ethics must be open to the possibility that a leader's characteristics, the extraordinary situations he faces, or the special norms to which he is subject might similarly justify an exception for him.

What I want to argue, however, is that there is reason to think that leaders will be inclined to overestimate the normative force of these distinctions. I make the argument for this claim by way of an examination of three general approaches to leadership, each of which gives expression to one of the sources of what is distinctive about leadership. On *trait approaches*, leaders are fundamentally different from followers by virtue of their talents, skills, and abilities. *Situational approaches* hold that leadership behavior depends less on the presence or absence of particular characteristics in leaders than on the situations in which leadership is exercised. As these situations vary, so too do the requirements that apply to leaders. *Transactional approaches* take leadership to be relationships of exchange that define role responsibilities for leaders and followers. On this set of approaches, central behavioral expectations are determined by the outcome of exchanges between leaders and followers. As a consequence, expectations on leaders and followers can differ dramatically according to their contributions to the exchange.

These approaches to leadership purport to tell us what leaders are like, how they respond to features of the situation, and why they are freer than followers to negotiate existing normative boundaries. To the extent that any particular approach is correct, it also tells us a lot about what leaders ought to do in order to be effective. Depending on the approach, leaders ought to acquire qualities that ultimately distinguish them from followers, to guide their behavior by accurate appraisals of what effectiveness requires in the situation, or to take appropriate advantage of disparities between what is expected of them and what is expected of followers. Since my examination of these approaches to leadership is not fundamentally empirical in nature, it does not take issue with the central claims they make or even with their implications for leader effectiveness. Rather, as part of an ethical analysis, it considers the moral importance that accepting these approaches might have for leadership processes, especially as these processes are informed by the beliefs leaders hold about the distinctiveness of their behavior. In showing that these approaches can promote ethical failure, my analysis identifies more fundamental moral concerns about the basic understandings of leadership they represent.

III. TRAIT APPROACHES TO LEADERSHIP

Despite America's fascination with corporate family dynasties, and its penchant for electing the offspring of former politicians, few serious students of leadership would ascribe to "the Great Man" view of leadership in its purist form. This is the view that leaders are not made of the same meager material from which the rest of us grow and develop but rather are somehow born to greatness. By virtue of their inherited traits, these leaders have great-making characteristics almost ready at hand. The standard reading of Plato's *Republic*, for example, suggests that he advocates a version of this view, arguing that the philosopher king is "fitted by nature both to engage in philosophy and to rule in a city, while the rest are naturally fitted to leave philosophy alone and follow their leader."[9] But even Plato readily concedes the role of the environment in the development of leaders. For Plato, virtue requires that the natural leader be exposed to "appropriate instruction," lest he "develop in quite the opposite way."[10] Aristotle, who also recognizes that some might be better suited to rule than others,[11] similarly holds that for the soul to be virtuous it "needs to have been prepared by habits for enjoying and hating finely."[12]

The intellectual descendents of these views are the *trait approaches to leadership*. Advocates of these approaches embrace the claim that there

---

[9] Plato, *Republic*, trans. G. M. A. Grube (Indianapolis: Hackett Publishing Company, 1992), p. 149 [474c].
[10] Plato, *Republic*, p. 165 [492a].
[11] Aristotle, *The Politics*, trans. T. A. Sinclair (New York: Penguin Books, 1981), pp. 215–216 [1284b23–1284b34].
[12] Aristotle, *Nicomachean Ethics*, trans. Terence Irwin (Indianapolis: Hackett Publishing Company, 1985), p. 292 [1179b25].

are fundamental differences between leaders and followers. For example, a survey of the research by Kirkpatrick and Locke identified "certain core traits which significantly contribute" to the success of leaders, thus reclaiming the place of these approaches in leadership studies.[13] While some of these "traits" are closely associated with genetic make-up or with relatively stable dispositional properties, others are better understood as skills acquired "through experience and training."[14] The main point, however, is that "[r]egardless of whether leaders are born or made or some combination of both, it is unequivocally clear that *leaders are not like other people.*"[15] When we finally come to terms with what Plato and Aristotle already knew – namely, that leaders are not "ordinary people" – we can use this knowledge "to select and train leaders effectively."[16]

Kirkpatrick and Locke's list of leadership traits gives content to one source of the distinctions upon which leaders might ground a justification for exception making. Broadly construed, the trait differentials they endorse make effective leaders superior to followers in terms of motivation, knowledge, virtue, and self-confidence. First, under the category of motivation, leaders differ from followers in drive, which these authors understand in terms of achievement, ambition, energy, tenacity, and initiative, as well as with respect to leadership motivation or their desire to lead. Second, leaders are more knowledgeable than followers. They have relatively greater cognitive ability, and they use this ability to understand the leadership context in which they act. Third, it turns out that virtue is more readily found in leaders than in followers, at least in their exhibition of integrity and honesty. Finally, compared with followers, leaders have more self-confidence. Not only do they have the requisite characteristics for leadership, but they also hold this belief about themselves.[17]

Taking each trait category in turn, let us consider the claim that effective leaders have a "high desire for achievement" and that they are "very ambitious about their work and careers and have a desire to get ahead."[18] These motivational pressures can be closely connected to

---

[13] Shelley A. Kirkpatrick and Edwin A. Locke, "Leadership: Do Traits Matter?" *Academy of Management Executive* 5, 2 (1991): 49.
[14] Kirkpatrick and Locke, "Do Traits Matter?" p. 58.
[15] Kirkpatrick and Locke, "Do Traits Matter?" p. 59.
[16] Kirkpatrick and Locke, "Do Traits Matter?" p. 59.
[17] Kirkpatrick and Locke, "Do Traits Matter?" pp. 49–56.
[18] Kirkpatrick and Locke, "Do Traits Matter?" pp. 49–50.

mistaken beliefs about justification. The concern is that leaders will find it difficult to embrace the appropriateness of their desires for achievement and their ambition without also holding a set of beliefs about the relative importance of their goals, their work, and their careers. If leaders do not believe that there is something special about the particular goals they seek to achieve, the particular work they are doing, and the particular careers they have chosen to pursue, they will be hard pressed to explain why they care so much about these endeavors in the first place. The easiest way for leaders to avoid the charge that their superior motivation is akin to an irrational obsession is for them to understand their desires for achievement and their ambition as responses to the relative importance of their goals, work, and careers. But this means that they will be inclined to believe that these aspects of their lives are of greater relative importance than corresponding aspects of the lives of others, in which case these leaders will also be susceptible to mistakenly believing that they are justified in making exceptions of themselves.

It does not help that trait approaches combine the desire for achievement and ambition with high levels of energy, tenacity, and initiative. Recent scandals have made us well aware that leaders can draw on the resources of hard work, persistence, and pro-activity to get around requirements that apply generally to others. Enron, a company that relied heavily on these characteristics to fashion an energy-trading market, collapsed as a result of charges that its executives were willing to go to equally great lengths to hide its debts from investors and analysts. Of course, even Kirkpatrick and Locke, who recommend that "leaders must keep pushing themselves and others toward the goal" and not be afraid "to challenge the process," point out that leaders should only "persist in the right things."[19] But when the right things are identified with the business ends to which these authors appeal – namely, "satisfying the customer, growth, cost control, innovation, fast response time, and quality"[20] – such limits on leadership motivation ultimately do little to assuage any ethical worries we might have about the behavior of leaders with exceptional drive.

Perhaps these ethical worries can be addressed by appeal to the second motivational resource that Kirkpatrick and Locke ascribe to leaders: the desire to lead. Here, the authors distinguish between a leader with

[19] Kirkpatrick and Locke, "Do Traits Matter?" pp. 51–52.
[20] Kirkpatrick and Locke, "Do Traits Matter?" p. 51.

a *personalized power motive* and a leader with a *socialized power motive*.[21] The former "seeks power as an end in itself," whereas the latter "uses power as a means to achieve desired goals, or a vision."[22] The problem with an appeal to this distinction is that it does not do justice to the full moral value of generally applicable requirements, specifically that they can prevent leaders from acting on bad beliefs in addition to preventing leaders from acting on bad motivations. F. A. Hayek, for example, points out that "the sources of many of the most harmful agents in this world are often not evil men but highminded idealists."[23] Contrary to what we might expect, then, a leader's belief that pursuit of his goals or vision is ultimately for the good of others can lead him to behave unethically by inflating the normative force of his own commitments and ideals. Given the possibility of this kind of error, he is at least as likely as others to think that he is justified in deviating from generally applicable requirements.

It should come as no surprise that superior motivational resources are not sufficient for ethical leadership.[24] To a great extent, what leaders are motivated to do depends on what they believe is valuable, and these beliefs can sometimes be incorrect. Admittedly, Kirkpatrick and Locke do suggest that leaders are not only better motivated but also have greater cognitive ability than do followers. This is the second major distinction between leaders and followers. A question remains, though, as to whether recognition of these cognitive resources inhibits or promotes the making of exceptions. For instance, if a leader infers from the fact that he knows more than followers that he therefore knows enough to act exclusively on this knowledge, then he may be inclined to bypass processes of consent and consensus in an effort to avoid what he perceives to be misguided opposition. One noteworthy argument in support of these processes is that because "[p]owerful people make horrendous mistakes," leaders should "submit their proposals to public scrutiny, where dangerous errors can be exposed before wreaking their damage."[25] Since

---

[21] See David McClelland, "N achievement and Entrepreneurship: A Longitudinal Study," *Journal of Personality and Social Psychology* 1 (1965): 389–392.

[22] Kirkpatrick and Locke, "Do Traits Matter?" p. 53.

[23] F. A. Hayek, *Law, Legislation and Liberty: A New Statement of the Liberal Principles of Justice and Political Economy*, Vol. 1 (Chicago: University of Chicago Press, 1973), p. 70.

[24] See Chapters 2 and 5 of this book.

[25] Jamie Mayerfeld, *Suffering and Moral Responsibility* (New York: Oxford University Press, 1999), p. 204.

relatively greater cognitive ability hardly implies infallibility, this argument applies not only to the powerful but also to the intelligent.

Another reason against relying greatly on the superior cognitive ability of leaders is the risk that they will exaggerate its ethical importance, just as they might be inclined to overestimate the normative implications of a socialized power motive. Kirkpatrick and Locke, for example, construe a leader's knowledge quite narrowly, understanding it in terms of "strong analytical ability, good judgement, and the capacity to think strategically and multidimensionally."[26] As such, the particular cognitive resources to which leaders have access are hardly sufficient for accurate conceptions of value. In fact, Susan Wolf distinguishes between this kind of cognitive ability and the ability "normatively to recognize and appreciate the world for what it is."[27] On this distinction, one can have the cognitive ability "to be controlled . . . by perceptions and sound reasoning that produce an accurate conception of the world" and, nevertheless, lack the normative ability to have "one's *values* be controlled by processes that afford an accurate conception of the world."[28] Here, even if we ultimately reject Wolf's robust conception of normative competence, we must recognize that technical expertise and knowledge of the business are unlikely to get leaders very far on moral fronts.

Kirkpatrick and Locke focus on virtue to draw the third major distinction between leaders and followers. Here, they point to the traits of integrity and honesty, where "[i]ntegrity is the correspondence between word and deed and honesty refers to being truthful or non-deceitful."[29] To the credit of trait approaches to leadership, a leader's integrity and honesty can serve as substantial moral resources. First, a leader's integrity suggests that he will not make an exception of himself when it comes to behavior dictated by the values he accepts. The fact that he too must live by these values creates something of a test of his commitment to them. The moral downside, of course, is that a leader may be perfectly willing to live by an inaccurate conception of value. This is especially troublesome when a leader's conception of value is inegalitarian in nature and, consequently, demands that others bear most of the costs of his ascribing to it. The possibility of misdirected integrity

[26] Kirkpatrick and Locke, "Do Traits Matter?" p. 55.
[27] Susan Wolf, "Sanity and the Metaphysics of Responsibility," in Ferdinand Schoeman, ed., *Responsibility, Character, and the Emotions: New Essays in Moral Psychology* (Cambridge: Cambridge University Press, 1987), p. 56.
[28] Wolf, "Sanity and the Metaphysics of Responsibility," p. 55.
[29] Kirkpatrick and Locke, "Do Traits Matter?" p. 53.

can be seen as part of the motivation for the claim that leaders should also have the virtue of honesty. Under the right conditions, a leader's honesty about the values that underlie his behavior can expose these values to much-needed criticism and, as a result, redirect his integrity so that he ultimately acts on better values.

Unfortunately, if follower integrity and honesty are unwelcome or unheeded, then the integrity and honesty of leaders offer significantly less moral protection. A leader's integrity and honesty serve as checks on an inaccurate conception of value only if conditions make this conception assailable, specifically by exposing it to real critique from followers who can act on their values and say what they think. When these conditions do not exist, we may be in a position to appeal to a leader's integrity and honesty to predict what he will do, but it is unlikely that we will be able to trust him to do the right thing. This is close to a distinction Robert Solomon draws: "Trust, as opposed to prediction or confidence, presupposes a relationship. And relationships by their nature involve much more than a calculation of probabilities and outcomes. They involve values and emotions, responsibilities and the possibility of not only disappointment but betrayal."[30] In many ways, then, focusing on leader integrity and honesty can cause us to overlook the equally important place of follower integrity and honesty in the leadership process. Admirable though these traits may be in whomever they are found, understanding them as being unequally distributed among leaders and followers may preclude the very kind of relationship that serves as a safeguard against the fallibility of leaders.

Recently, the claim that traits such as integrity and honesty are predictive of human behavior has come under serious criticism from philosophers, especially those who draw on experimental evidence in social psychology to evaluate the foundational assumptions of virtue ethics.[31] This is the view that character, not action itself, is the main object of moral evaluation. On ethical theories of this sort, agents should be more

[30] Robert C. Solomon, "Ethical Leadership, Emotions, and Trust: Beyond 'Charisma,'" in Joanne B. Ciulla, ed., *Ethics, the Heart of Leadership* (Westport, CT: Praeger, 1998), p. 99.

[31] See, for example, Owen Flanagan, *Varieties of Moral Personality: Ethics and Psychological Realism* (Cambridge, MA: Harvard University Press, 1991), ch. 14; John M. Doris, "Persons, Situations, and Virtue Ethics," *Noûs* 32 (1998): 504–530; Gilbert Harman, "Moral Philosophy Meets Social Psychology: Virtue Ethics and the Fundamental Attribution Error," *Proceedings of the Aristotelian Society* 99 (1999): 315–331.

concerned with developing habits or dispositions to act virtuously than with adhering to general rules, principles, and requirements.[32] Its most compelling critics charge that the moral psychology of virtue ethics ignores strong evidence in favor of the view that behavior is determined by features of the situation, not by character traits. Here, the critiques frequently point to Darley and Batson's study of helping behavior, which was mentioned in the introduction to this chapter. Darley and Batson found that personality variables such as religiosity were not significant predictors for whether seminarians on their way to give talks – some on the parable of the Good Samaritan itself – would offer assistance to a "victim" in need. What they instead found to be significantly predictive was a single situational variable: the degree to which seminarians were in a hurry.[33]

Whatever the ultimate force of these criticisms of trait theory, they do remind us that a leader's belief that he is more virtuous than followers can sometimes be morally misleading. Even if Robert Solomon is correct that the philosophical critics of virtue ethics "are just looking at the wrong disposition" and that they should instead consider dispositions such as promptness, the problem remains that people are not very good at predicting behavior based on the beliefs they hold about their traits.[34] At the very least, experiments in social psychology teach us that many among the "virtuous" do not have the particular traits they think they have.[35] Given "how little there has been in their lives to challenge

---

[32] Alasdair MacIntyre, *After Virtue: A Study in Moral Theory*, 2nd edition (Notre Dame, IN: University of Notre Dame Press, 1981), p. 112.

[33] Darley and Batson, "'From Jerusalem to Jericho.'"

[34] Robert C. Solomon, "Victims of Circumstances? A Defense of Virtue Ethics in Business," *Business Ethics Quarterly* 13 (2003): 53. With respect to Stanley Milgram's experiments, *Obedience to Authority; An Experimental View* (New York: Harper and Row, 1974), to which these critics also appeal, Solomon says that the relevant virtue is obedience to authority. Responding to Solomon, Gilbert Harman objects that "[s]ince Solomon thinks that all the experimental subjects had these traits," he cannot appeal to promptness and obedience to explain behavioral differences within the experiment ("No Character or Personality," *Business Ethics Quarterly* 13 [2003]: 91). But Solomon's actual claim is that "*virtually* all of the subjects had been brought up ... [to do] what they were told by those in authority," which does look relevant to an explanation of why *virtually* all of the subjects obeyed the experimenter to some extent or other (p. 53, emphasis added).

[35] Commenting on one study by Milgram, *Obedience to Authority*, Flanagan notes that "thirty-nine Yale psychiatrists, thirty-one college students, and forty middle-class adults [predicted] their own maximum level of compliance. Everyone was sure he or she would break off very early. When asked to predict how far a diverse group of Americans would go, the psychiatrists predicted, on average, that fewer than

their high opinion of themselves," it is hardly shocking that they have something to learn about just how virtuous they really are.[36] But this means that the behavior of such leaders is ultimately traceable to fundamentally cognitive considerations. Specifically, they hold the mistaken moral belief that they have admirable traits on which they can rely in times of crisis.

One problematic implication of virtue theory, then, is that a leader can infer from the belief that he is virtuous that he therefore has less need for the constraints of generally applicable moral requirements. Such inferences are clearly consistent with much of virtue ethics, since this ethical theory unapologetically subordinates adherence to rules and principles to a concern for character.[37] For example, in one defense of a character view of morality, Bernard Mayo argues that "the subordination of exemplars to principles...fails to do justice to a large area of moral experience."[38] The "'black-or-white' nature of moral verdicts based on rules" conflicts with the fact that qualities of character come in degrees and, as a consequence, does not allow us to "set [heroes and saints] apart from the rest of humanity."[39] But what such arguments miss is that "many times our confidence in character is precisely what puts us at risk in morally dangerous situations."[40] This may have been true for the priest and the Levite in the parable of the Good Samaritan, and there is no reason to think that it is not also true for other leaders as well.

---

50 percent would still be obedient at the tenth level (150 volts), fewer than four in a hundred would reach the twentieth level, and fewer than one in a thousand would administer the maximum shock. It is remarkable that psychiatrists, who are trained to perceive subtle force fields in the social environment, and who are also well aware of dark, seamy, and destructive urges, could be so far off the mark here" (*Varieties of Moral Personality*, p. 295).

[36] Solomon, "Victims of Circumstances?" p. 57. As Solomon points out, the subjects that did not quit "were indeed confused" (p. 55).

[37] Solomon is probably an outlier here: "I would take Harman's and Doris's arguments as a good reason to insist on sound ethical policies and rigorous ethical enforcement in corporations and in the business community more generally, thus maximizing the likelihood that people will conform to the right kinds of corporate expectations" ("Victims of Circumstances?" p. 46). Solomon continues, "[S]uch design is important and essential and almost totally ignored by too many virtue ethicists today" (p. 58).

[38] Bernard Mayo, *Ethics and the Moral Life* (London: Macmillan and Company, 1958), pp. 214–215.

[39] Mayo, *Ethics and the Moral Life*, p. 215.

[40] Doris, "Persons, Situations, and Virtue Ethics," p. 516.

A more recent religious example – the Catholic Church's failed efforts to respond to child sexual abuse by priests – exemplifies the moral fallout of this risk. News accounts suggest that church leaders, such as Boston's former archbishop Bernard Law, repeatedly moved abusers to new parishes and protected them from criminal prosecution. One explanation of these failures is that church officials simply had too much confidence in the character of priests. Equally troublesome, however, is the fact that the crisis seems to have done little to undermine their confidence in their own abilities to draw on character to resolve these problems internally.[41] In this respect at least, Law and other church leaders show nothing short of self-confidence, the final trait that Kirkpatrick and Locke ascribe to leaders. As this case makes plain, what constitutes self-confidence from the perspective of those on the inside can be indistinguishable from overconfidence to those of us on the outside. Empirical evidence establishes that overconfidence is no stranger to military and business leadership, and it should also be flagged as a potentially problematic characteristic of religious leaders.[42]

Regardless of leadership context, leaders who are self-confident in the fact that they have superior motivation, knowledge, and virtue are vulnerable to the mistaken belief that they are justified in making exceptions of themselves. As Messick and Bazerman make the point, "The major peril is that [they] will come to see [themselves] as people for whom the normal rules, norms, and obligations do not apply."[43] If leaders believe

---

[41] Cardinal Law was widely known for his humanitarian work in the civil rights movement and his advocacy of the rights of immigrants. See, for example, Gill Donovan, "Ambition, defense of institutional church drove cardinal's career," *National Catholic Reporter* (December 27, 2002).

[42] David M. Messick and Max H. Bazerman, "Ethical Leadership and the Psychology of Decision Making," *Sloan Management Review* 37, 2 (1996): 19.

[43] Messick and Bazerman, "Ethical Leadership," p. 20. According to *Newsweek* reporters Evan Thomas and Andrew Murr, former Enron CEO Kenneth Lay "believed that the ordinary rules of business somehow did not apply to him or his company" ("The Gambler Who Blew It All: The bland smile concealed an epic arrogance. The fall of a preacher's kid who thought he had it all figured out," *Newsweek* [February 4, 2002]). Barbara Ehrenreich criticizes Wal-Mart for not holding "itself to the same standard of rectitude it expects from its low-paid employees." She suggests that this problem should not be attributed to "a rogue store manager or 'bad apple' but management as a whole" ("Two-Tiered Morality," *New York Times* [June 30, 2002]). Sports figures are no less subject to this phenomenon: "There are double standards for a Bobby Knight and the rest of the faculty. This is all explained away by Texas Tech's improved basketball record since the great man arrived, after his exile from Indiana, which took a decade too long to figure out Knight was more trouble than he was worth" (George Vecsey, "At Salad Bar with

that they really are different from followers, then they can appeal to this belief to justify deviations from generally applicable moral requirements. To the extent that trait approaches to leadership accentuate the differences between leaders and followers that give rise to this kind of self-confidence, they represent an understanding of leadership that can promote ethical failure. To be sure, it would not follow from this ethical analysis that we should reject the main thesis of these approaches – the claim that effective leaders really are different from followers. However, it would follow from the truth of this thesis that these ethical challenges arc part of the very nature of effective leadership.

IV. SITUATIONAL APPROACHES TO LEADERSHIP

Keen observers of leadership have long questioned the importance of traits for leadership. In *The Prince*, Machiavelli rejects the view that a ruler must have the traits associated with virtue, and is "so bold as to say that having and always cultivating them is harmful."[44] Machiavelli recommends instead that the leader "must be prepared to vary his conduct as the winds of fortune and changing circumstances constrain him and . . . not deviate from right conduct if possible, but be capable of entering upon the path of wrongdoing when this becomes necessary."[45] On Machiavelli's view, that is, leadership behavior should be guided by the necessity of the situation, not by the dispositional properties of princes. Although more recent social scientific critiques of trait theories of leadership do not focus on what are typically taken to be the virtues, they do hold that qualities conducive to a leader's effectiveness in one situation can be an impediment to his effectiveness in another situation.

Knight, Praise Only the Cherry Tomatoes," *New York Times* [February 8, 2004]). Finally, commenting on elite units such as the Los Angeles Police Department's Rampart Division, Brian Michael Jenkins claims that their members "easily come to regard themselves as the especially privileged combatants . . . They come to believe that rules are for the regulars, but 'we know what we have to do.' This is not always self-serving justification. Pleased with the results, the top brass may choose not to inquire too closely just how it is being accomplished. The operators interpret this as a wink of approval" ("Perspective on Policing; Elite Units Troublesome, but Useful; We Need Them for Tough Assignments, but They Require Skillful Management, Strong Leadership," *Los Angeles Times* [March 27, 2000]).

[44] Niccolò Machiavelli, *The Prince*, eds. Quentin Skinner and Russell Price (Cambridge: Cambridge University Press, 1988), p. 62.

[45] Machiavelli, *The Prince*, p. 62.

For example, in an early and influential critique, Ralph Stogdill claims that "[t]he persistence of individual patterns of human behavior in the face of constant situational change appears to be a primary obstacle encountered not only in the practice of leadership, but in the selection and placement of leaders."[46]

Contemporary *situational approaches to leadership* dispense with traits discourse altogether. According to these approaches, effective leadership is a matter of fitting particular styles of leadership with features of situations. At the most basic level, leadership styles can be differentiated in terms of whether a leader's behavior is oriented to the task at hand or to his relationships with followers. This standard distinction runs through traditional behavioral understandings of leadership, and it is variously referred to as initiating structure or consideration,[47] job-centered supervision or employee-centered supervision,[48] and concern for production or concern for people,[49] respectively. Relying on the assumption that styles of leadership are less rigid than character traits, most of these approaches hold that leaders can adjust their styles to suit the demands of the situations they face. A notable exception, however, is Fiedler's Contingency Theory.[50] This theory denies that leaders have very much behavioral flexibility when it comes to task-motivated or relationship-motivated behavior and suggests that the most we can do is match particular leaders to situations.[51]

---

[46] Ralph Melvin Stogdill, "Personal Factors Associated with Leadership: A Survey of the Literature," *Journal of Psychology* 25 (1948): 65.

[47] Edwin A. Fleishman, "The Description of Supervisory Behavior," *Journal of Applied Psychology* 37 (1953): 1–6.

[48] Rensis Likert, *New Patterns of Management* (New York: McGraw-Hill, 1961).

[49] Robert Rogers Blake and Jane Srygley Mouton, "The Managerial Dilemma," in their *The Managerial Grid: Key Orientations for Achieving Production Through People* (Houston: Gulf Publishing Company, 1964), pp. 5–17.

[50] Fred Edward Fiedler, *A Theory of Leadership Effectiveness* (New York: McGraw-Hill, 1967).

[51] Machiavelli claims that "[s]omeone who is used to proceeding in a particular way will never change . . . , so it is inevitable that when the times change and become unsuitable for his particular style, he will be ruined" (Niccolò Machiavelli, *Discourses on the First Ten Books of Titius Livius*, in Michael L. Morgan, ed., *Classics of Moral and Political Theory*, 3rd edition [Indianapolis: Hackett Publishing Company, 2001], pp. 486–487). Leaders are unable to change their styles, he thinks, because they are largely constrained by their own natures and inclined to adhere strictly to styles that were successful in the past. It is for this reason that Machiavelli prefers republics to monarchies, the former being made up of people with a variety of characters.

Hersey and Blanchard's model of Situational Leadership serves as a popular example of a situational approach that assumes individual leaders can alter their styles for effective leadership.[52] First, these authors understand task-oriented behavior and relationship-oriented behavior as falling along separate axes, so that a leader's orientation to task need not interfere with his orientation to relationship. Second, the situations to which leaders respond are construed narrowly to focus on levels of follower maturity or readiness, specifically on their "ability and willingness...to perform a particular task."[53] Putting these two components of the model together, leaders should adopt a high-task/low-relationship style when followers are at the lowest levels of ability and willingness, and they should use a low-task/low-relationship style when followers are at the highest levels of ability and willingness. A high-task/high-relationship style is appropriate when followers have moderate ability and high willingness, whereas a low-task/high-relationship style is called for when followers have high ability and variable willingness.

How do situational approaches to leadership support a leader's view that he is justified in making an exception of himself? After all, the variability in behavior they recommend need not be understood to imply a universal situational ethic, just contingency with respect to the leadership styles that should be adopted.[54] None of these approaches, that is, goes nearly so far as to take up the Machiavellian suggestion that whether a leader should deviate from generally applicable moral requirements is determined solely by the situation. Nevertheless, situational approaches to leadership do ascribe to a markedly instrumental view of the value of showing concern for followers. First, the appropriateness of relationship-oriented behavior is contingent on the connection between this component of leadership style and overall effectiveness.[55] Second, when effectiveness does call for relationship-oriented behavior, concern for followers is limited to the extent necessary for

[52] Paul Hersey and Kenneth H. Blanchard, "Life Cycle Theory of Leadership," *Training and Development Journal* 23, 5 (1969): 26–34.

[53] Paul Hersey and Kenneth H. Blanchard, "Situational Leadership," in J. Thomas Wren, ed., *The Leader's Companion: Insights on Leadership Through the Ages* (New York: Free Press, 1995), pp. 207–208.

[54] James O'Toole, I think, incorrectly makes this assumption. See his *Leading Change: The Argument for Values-Based Leadership* (New York: Ballantine Books, 1996).

[55] See Joanne B. Ciulla, "Leadership Ethics: Mapping the Territory," in Joanne B. Ciulla, ed., *Ethics, the Heart of Leadership* (Westport, CT: Praeger, 1998), pp. 3–25.

task performance. Given these instrumentalist commitments, situational leaders will have reason to believe that they are justified in making exceptions of themselves both when effectiveness competes with the moral requirement that they show concern for followers and when the relationship-motivated behavior necessary for effectiveness is well short of what genuine moral concern would require.[56]

A second ethical critique of situational approaches to leadership draws upon a well-established phenomenon in social psychology called *actor-observer divergence*. Actors are inclined to attribute their behavior to features of the situation, whereas observers attribute this same behavior to features of the actors themselves. Jones and Nisbett introduce the phenomenon with the following example:

In their autobiographies, former political leaders often report a different perspective on their past acts from that commonly held by the public. Acts perceived by the public to have been wise, planful, courageous, and imaginative on the one hand, or unwise, haphazard, cowardly, or pedestrian on the other, are often seen in quite a different light by the autobiographer. He is likely to emphasize the situational constraints at the time of the action – the role limitations, the conflicting pressures brought to bear, the alternative paths of action that were never open or that were momentarily closed – and to perceive his actions as having been inevitable.[57]

This example underscores the disparate understandings that leaders and followers can have of leadership behavior, and the underlying social psychological phenomenon to which these authors appeal goes some way toward making sense of the historical preoccupation that the study of leadership has had with trait theory. Our inclination is to look for dispositional, not situational, explanations for the behavior of leaders. Given the relative generality of this phenomenon, there is also reason to think that leader understandings of follower behavior would be similarly subject to actor-observer divergence. In fact, Martin Chemers notes several studies that use attribution theory to make sense of supervisor perceptions of follower performance.[58]

---

[56] Here, my discussion owes much to comments from Tom Wren.

[57] Edward E. Jones and Richard E. Nisbett, "The Actor and the Observer: Divergent Perceptions of the Causes of Behavior," in Edward E. Jones, David E. Kanouse, Harold H. Kelley, Richard E. Nisbett, Stuart Valins, and Bernard Weiner, eds., *Attribution: Perceiving the Causes of Behavior* (Morristown, NJ: General Learning Press, 1972), pp. 79–80.

[58] Martin M. Chemers, "Contemporary Leadership Theory," in J. Thomas Wren, ed., *The Leader's Companion: Insights on Leadership Through the Ages* (New York: Free

Leaders can be related to action as actors engaging in the behavior itself or as observers of the behavior of other actors. One kind of behavior with which they can be associated in either of these two ways is a deviation from a generally applicable moral requirement. Actor-observer divergence implies that the attributions that leaders make as actors, attributions regarding their own deviations, will differ from the attributions they make with respect to the deviations of followers. This is just what we would conclude about this phenomenon for human behavior more generally. Leaders are subject to the same biases in attribution to which the rest of us are susceptible. But there are additional reasons to suspect that actor-observer divergence might be more pronounced for leaders. The argument for this claim draws attention to what Jones and Nisbett call "powerful cognitive forces" in their explanation of the phenomenon.[59] According to this explanation, "Our responses to immediately impinging stimuli are ... biased in two ways: they are too salient and they are too 'real.'"[60] These two biases, as we shall see, are relevant for understanding why situational leaders might be especially inclined to think that they are justified in making exceptions of themselves.

In their examination of these cognitive forces, Jones and Nisbett appeal directly to differences in information processing. First, observers find the action itself salient because "[w]hile the environment is stable and contextual from the observer's point of view, action is figural and dynamic."[61] In contrast, as a result of physiological barriers to taking this kind of perspective on his own action, the actor "is less likely to focus his attention on his behavior than on the environmental cues that evoke and shape it."[62] This explanation gets empirical support from research on the attribution effects of manipulating perceptual orientation. By means of videotape recordings and other devices, "visual

---

Press, 1995), p. 93, lists Stephen G. Green and Terence R. Mitchell, "Attributional Processes of Leaders in Leader-Member Interactions," *Organizational Behavior and Human Performance* 23 (1979): 429–458; Terence R. Mitchell and Robert E. Wood, "Supervisors' Responses to Subordinate Poor Performance: A Test of an Attributional Model," *Organizational Behavior and Human Performance* 25 (1980): 123–138; Terence R. Mitchell and Laura S. Kalb, "Effects of Outcome Knowledge and Outcome Valence in Supervisors' Evaluations," *Journal of Applied Psychology* 66 (1981): 604–612.

[59] Jones and Nisbett, "The Actor and the Observer," p. 80.
[60] Jones and Nisbett, "The Actor and the Observer," p. 86.
[61] Jones and Nisbett, "The Actor and the Observer," p. 85.
[62] Jones and Nisbett, "The Actor and the Observer," p. 85.

gaze" can be redirected to decrease actor-observer divergence.[63] However, if perceptual orientation can be manipulated to undermine actor-observer divergence, it might also be manipulated to exacerbate the phenomenon. In other words, we might assume that focal characteristics that contribute to actor-observer divergence can be made more salient for some actors and, accordingly, have increased effects on their behavior.

When cognitive challenges having to do with this first difference in information processing are coupled with situational approaches to leadership, leaders may be more apt than others to see their own behavior as a justified response to cues that – from their perspective – are features of the situation and less apt than others to see the behavior of followers as being similarly caused. My reasoning is that situational approaches aim to increase the salience of the very features that drive this phenomenon. These approaches often recommend that leaders take special consideration of follower characteristics when deciding what leadership styles they should adopt as actors. On the assumption that these characteristics really have increased salience for effective leaders, it is plausible to infer that the perceptual orientation that these leaders take will make them particularly susceptible to actor-observer divergence. Leaders who adopt these approaches may be peculiar in their tendencies to understand their own behavior as well as the behavior of followers as being determined by characteristics of the followers themselves, thus more readily lending their behavior as leaders to situational justifications. In other words, situational leaders may be inclined to reserve judgments of justification for their own exceptions because – as actors – they see the characteristics in question as features of the situation, whereas – as observers – they see these characteristics simply as features of other actors.

Few situational approaches hold that appropriate leadership style is determined exclusively by follower characteristics. House and Mitchell's path-goal theory, for instance, recommends a broadened view of what features of situations are relevant to the choices leaders make

---

[63] Shelley Duval and Robert A. Wicklund, *A Theory of Objective Self Awareness* (New York: Academic Press, 1972); Michael D. Storms, "Videotape and the Attribution Process: Reversing Actors' and Observers' Points of View," *Journal of Personality and Social Psychology* 27 (1973): 165–175; Shelley E. Taylor and Susan T. Fiske, "Point of View and Perceptions of Causality," *Journal of Personality and Social Psychology* 32 (1975): 439–445.

among these styles.[64] According to these authors, "The two contingency variables are (a) personal characteristics of the subordinates and (b) the environmental pressures and demands with which subordinates must cope in order to accomplish the work goals and to satisfy their needs."[65] By utilizing leadership styles that incorporate incentives or eradicate disincentives to taking the path to a goal, effective leaders respond to subordinate characteristics and environmental conditions in ways that increase follower expectancies of satisfaction. As a result, productivity is also increased. For example, when subordinates are authoritarian or the task is ambiguous, directive leadership may be effective because followers find it personally satisfying or because this style of leadership decreases ambiguity, thereby removing an obstacle to goal achievement.

By attending to both environmental conditions and subordinate characteristics, perhaps situational leaders can mitigate the potential effects of actor-observer divergence. Understanding follower behavior as being partly a function of environmental conditions having to do with task – in addition, that is, to subordinate characteristics such as ability and motivation – might check the tendency of these leaders to rely too heavily on the features of followers in the causal attributions they make about follower performance. Still, this broadened view of what features of the situation are relevant to leadership style does nothing to increase the salience of the actor characteristics of leaders themselves. In fact, focusing the attention of situational leaders on environmental conditions, as opposed to their own actor characteristics, may make them more prone to the second cognitive pressure that Jones and Nisbett claim can issue in actor-observer divergence – namely, the inclination to privilege our own subjective evaluations of reality. As they make the argument, "The effect of . . . differential attribution tendencies is amplified by bias from another source, the tendency to regard one's reactions to entities as based on accurate perceptions of them. Rather than humbly regarding our impressions of the world as interpretations of it, we see them as understandings or correct apprehensions of it."[66]

Drawing out the ethical implications of actor-observer divergence, we can articulate this evaluative bias in terms of the nature of belief

---

[64] Robert J. House and Terence R. Mitchell, "Path-Goal Theory of Leadership," *Journal of Contemporary Business* 3, 4 (1974): 81–97.

[65] House and Mitchell, "Path-Goal Theory," p. 85.

[66] Jones and Nisbett, "The Actor and the Observer," pp. 85–86.

itself. To hold a belief, an actor must accept its truth. Based on this commitment to truth, the actor would not readily distinguish between his belief, say, that a situation has certain features, and the facts as to whether the situation does indeed have these features. However, there is no parallel conceptual conflict for observers. Since an observer can distinguish between an actor's subjective beliefs and what he – the observer – takes to be the objective facts, the observer will be more likely to attribute the actor's behavior to characteristics of the actor – for example, to the actor's subjective beliefs – than he would be to make a similar attribution in his own case. The cognitive overconfidence to which this evaluative bias gives rise is critical to understanding ethical failures in leadership because it helps explain why leaders would believe that their own assessments of situations are sufficient to justify the exceptions they make of themselves. Most important for our purposes, cognitive pressures on leaders to privilege the reality of their evaluations make it easier for them to overestimate the objective value of the task at hand and, as a consequence, to believe that situational constraints justify them in deviating from generally applicable moral requirements.

There is some evidence to suggest that the behavior of individuals who make exceptions of themselves can be the result of mistaken beliefs about the *importance* of what they are doing. In a follow-up experiment to Darley and Batson's study of helping behavior,[67] Batson et al. found that beliefs about the importance of the tasks to which subjects were assigned turned out to be significant predictors as to whether these subjects would stop to help a "victim" in need.[68] If we assume that the subjects accepted a generally applicable moral requirement prescribing helping behavior, we might conclude that they also believed that the objective value of their tasks outweighed the normative force of the relevant requirement. Interestingly, a later study by Radant et al. failed to confirm any significance for *objective* task importance.[69] But it is worth noting that even the authors of this study posit that their results may have been due to the fact that they did not look at subjective measures indicated by variables such as "speed of transition" and "the subject's perception

---

[67] Darley and Batson, "'From Jerusalem to Jericho.'"

[68] C. Daniel Batson, Pamela J. Cochran, Marshall F. Biederman, James L. Blosser, Maurice J. Ryan, and Bruce Vogt, "Failure to Help When in a Hurry: Callousness or Conflict?" *Personality and Social Psychology Bulletin* 4 (1978): 97–101.

[69] Nancy Radant, Richard Blackford, Tamara Porch, Paul Shahbaz, and Richard E. Butman, "From Jerusalem to Jericho Revisited: A Study in Helping Behavior," *Journal of Psychology and Christianity* 4 (1985): 48–55.

of . . . importance."[70] It is just this kind of *subjective* assessment of the situation that is apt to influence ethical reasoning by generating mistaken justifications.

The phenomenon of actor-observer divergence thus creates a serious ethical challenge for leaders who adopt situational approaches to leadership. The perspective that these leaders must take to meet the recommendation that they develop special insights into task and subordinate characteristics is worrisomely close to the second cognitive pressure that issues in differential attributions – namely, the inclination to privilege subjective interpretations of reality. Accordingly, situational leadership can exacerbate ordinary evaluative biases, thereby putting leaders at an increased risk of treating their own situational justifications more favorably than they treat the situational justifications of followers. The resulting exceptions that these leaders make of themselves might be attributed either to the fact that they take their own justifications too seriously or to the fact they do not take the justifications of followers seriously enough. In other words, we can expect that situational leaders will be mistaken about the permissibility of their own deviations from generally applicable moral requirements as well as about the impermissibility of similar deviations that followers seek to justify. In either case, the justificatory framework for exception making by leaders is supported by the basic assumptions that situational approaches bring with them.

V. TRANSACTIONAL APPROACHES TO LEADERSHIP

The idea that there can be fundamentally disparate requirements on leaders and followers is commonplace in historical thinking about leadership. There is no greater defense of this idea than the main line of argument found in the political writings of Thomas Hobbes. Published at the end of the English civil war, Hobbes's *Leviathan* makes the classic case for absolute sovereignty, holding that the goods of political stability necessitate that subjects give up their rights to govern themselves: "This is the generation of that great Leviathan . . . For by this authority, given him by every particular man in the commonwealth, he hath the use of so much power and strength conferred on him, that by terror thereof, he is enabled to conform the wills of them all to

---

[70] Radant et al., "From Jerusalem to Jericho Revisited," p. 53.

peace at home, and mutual aid against their enemies abroad."[71] It is by their consent, that is, that subjects authorize the absolute rule of the sovereign in exchange for the peace and security that such leadership promises. As a result, although subjects are bound by the requirements of justice, whatever the sovereign does "can be no injury to any of his subjects."[72]

The differential requirements of justice to which Hobbes ascribes can thus be understood by appeal to the nature of the agreement itself. On his version of social contract theory, "Because the right of bearing the person of them all, is given to him they make sovereign, by covenant . . . of one to another, and not of him to any of them; there can happen no breach of covenant on the part of the sovereign."[73] In fact, making the sovereign subject to the contract would defeat its primary purpose: the resolution of conflicts that characterize the state of nature.[74] To resolve these conflicts, the sovereign must have "the whole power of prescribing the rules, whereby every man may know, what goods he may enjoy and what actions he may do, without being molested by any of his fellow subjects."[75] Nevertheless, there remains a sense in which even absolute sovereignty is ultimately conditional for Hobbes. Subjects are bound by the rules authorized by the sovereign only "as long, and no longer, than the power lasteth, by which he is able to protect them. For the right men have by nature to protect themselves, when none else can protect them, can by no covenant be relinquished."[76] So, despite the fact that the sovereign is not himself bound by the contract, the normative force of his rule is very much dependent upon the provision of the peace and security that motivates the original exchange.

In the field of leadership studies, the importance of exchange in the generation of requirements on leaders and followers finds its most straightforward expression in *transactional approaches to leadership*. Transactional approaches start with the assumption that leaders are more than repositories of traits and followers are more than components of the situation to which leaders respond. On these approaches, leaders and followers are better understood as parties to relationships of exchange. As

[71] Adapted from Thomas Hobbes, *Leviathan*, ed. Richard Tuck (Cambridge: Cambridge University Press, 1991), p. 120.
[72] Hobbes, *Leviathan*, p. 124.
[73] Hobbes, *Leviathan*, p. 122.
[74] Hobbes, *Leviathan*, p. 123.
[75] Hobbes, *Leviathan*, p. 125.
[76] Hobbes, *Leviathan*, p. 153.

James MacGregor Burns characterizes transactional leadership, "The exchange could be economic or political or psychological in nature: a swap of goods or one good for money; a trading of votes between candidate and citizen or between legislators; hospitality to another person in exchange for willingness to listen to one's troubles."[77] The exact nature of the relationships between leaders and followers is therefore determined by what they bring to the exchange. Since they are often in positions to make contributions differing in kind and amount, outcomes of these exchanges – defined in terms of privileges and responsibilities – can vary dramatically between them.[78]

One such variation in outcome is the degree to which leaders and followers can deviate from normal behavioral constraints. Given inequalities in input, that is, the relationship between leaders and followers need not be one of equals bound by the same demands. E. P. Hollander, an early advocate of transactional approaches to leadership, identifies the currency of these transactions as "idiosyncrasy credits."[79] Marking the status of individuals within the group, idiosyncrasy credits track the attainment and maintenance of leadership influence. According to Hollander, status can be understood in terms of

the differentiated view of one individual held by others . . . Briefly, then, a differentiated perception, with effects upon interpersonal expectancies, conditions a particular behavioral approach to the object person. Since the expectancies applicable to the behavior of this person are in some way special, he is perceived, reacted to, and expected to behave uniquely . . . The genesis of this perceptual differentiation comes about from social interaction . . . Within a group framework, two main dimensions appear to be central to this process: the behavior of the object person in accordance with interpersonal expectancies, and his contribution to group goals . . . [A]n individual achieves status by fulfilling common expectancies and demonstrating task competence . . . As he continues to amass credits he may eventually reach a threshold which permits deviation and innovation, insofar as this is perceived by the others to be in the group's interests.[80]

---

77 James MacGregor Burns, *Leadership* (New York: Harper and Row Publishers, 1978), p. 19.
78 Contemporary "contractualist" theorists, such as John Rawls, argue for fair bargaining conditions to control for inequalities in outcome. See his *A Theory of Justice* (Cambridge, MA: Belknap Press of Harvard University Press, 1971).
79 E. P. Hollander, *Leaders, Groups, and Influence* (New York: Oxford University Press, 1964), pp. 26–29.
80 Hollander, *Leaders, Groups, and Influence*, pp. 157–159. Rousseau traced civil society itself to the perception of difference: "[People] accustomed themselves to

In other words, in exchange for past conformity and task competence, leaders emerge from groups with idiosyncrasy credits, leaving them relatively free to deviate from behavioral requirements.[81] They are then in a position to use this freedom to achieve group goals.[82]

The results of Hollander's experimental research on problem-solving groups support the importance of the idiosyncrasy model for our understanding of why leaders might think they are justified in making exceptions of themselves. In one study, early conformity by a confederate who was especially adept at "solving" problems for the group led to ready acceptance of his deviations from normal behavioral constraints.[83] Typical deviations included the following: "[H]e would break in with his choice immediately after an earlier respondent had spoken and before the next in sequence could do so; when there were periods of silence during a trial he would observe aloud that maybe majority rule did not work so well; and he would show a lack of enthusiasm for the choice offered by various others on the matter . . ."[84] This kind of non-conformity, especially when it occurred late in the trial, "went unhindered" and "yielded a rubber stamping of his choice."[85] For these cases, the confederate was allowed to violate requirements previously chosen to regulate the behavior of participants, for example, "by speaking out of prescribed turn" and "by questioning the utility of majority rule," even though it was the participants themselves who had decided upon these requirements in pre-trial discussions.[86]

Do these instances of non-conformity on the part of emerging leaders constitute potential ethical failures? Put another way, to what extent can

---

assemble before their huts round a large tree; singing and dancing, the true offspring of love and leisure, became the amusement, or rather the occupation, of men and women thus assembled together with nothing else to do. Each one began to consider the rest, and to wish to be considered in turn; and thus a value came to be attached to public esteem. Whoever sang or danced best, whoever was the handsomest, the strongest, the most dexterous, or the most eloquent, came to be of most consideration; and this was the first step towards inequality . . . " (Jean-Jacques Rousseau, *A Discourse on the Origin of Inequality*, in his *The Social Contract and Discourses*, trans. G. D. H. Cole [London: J. M. Dent Ltd., 1973] p. 90).

[81] Hollander, *Leaders, Groups, and Influence*, p. 159.

[82] Indeed, leaders are expected to do so and suffer losses of credits when they act otherwise. See Hollander, *Leaders, Groups, and Influence*, p. 158.

[83] Hollander, *Leaders, Groups, and Influence*, ch. 17.

[84] Hollander, *Leaders, Groups, and Influence*, p. 199.

[85] Hollander, *Leaders, Groups, and Influence*, p. 203.

[86] Hollander, *Leaders, Groups, and Influence*, p. 199.

behaviors such as interrupting group members and sabotaging demo-cratic processes be understood as deviations from generally applicable moral requirements? The strongest case for the claim that the confed-erates in Hollander's study deviated from requirements with genuine moral content appeals to the fact that participants in the study explicitly agreed that they would conform their behavior to these requirements. This line of argument locates the potential ethical lapses of the confed-erate in his failure to do what he expressly said he would do. To be sure, he never really intended to conform his behavior to the requirements that he speak in turn and respect majority rule. Nevertheless, we can assume that what participants took to be *"public affirmation* of member intent"[87] was sufficient, initially at least, for the legitimate expectation that the confederate would discharge the ethical obligations that con-sent implies. The important point, then, is that the pre-trial decisions generated what group members might reasonably view as generally applicable moral requirements yet group members allowed deviations from these requirements.

To say that a leader's deviations are potential ethical failures does not imply that he lacks justification for the exceptions he makes of himself. It is rather to say that there are at least prima facie reasons against these deviations, reasons that might be defeated by other considerations. In keeping with the moral foundations of transactional leadership, one such consideration is that followers themselves can consent to devia-tions from generally applicable moral requirements, thereby releasing leaders from what would be characterized as defeasible ethical obli-gations. On the idiosyncrasy model, for example, follower consent is considered to be necessary for the attainment of status and therefore of-fers itself as an obvious means of justification for the exceptions leaders make of themselves. In Hollander's words, leaders derive their status "from followers who may accord or withdraw it, in an essentially free interchange within a group context. Group consent is therefore a central feature of the leader-follower relationships."[88] But if followers consent to deviations from generally applicable requirements, how can there be any room for moral complaint? For, according to the widely accepted doctrine *volenti non fit injuria,* there can be no wrong to which one has freely consented.

---

[87] Hollander, *Leaders, Groups, and Influence,* p. 199.
[88] Hollander, *Leaders, Groups, and Influence,* p. 16.

In what sense do followers consent to the exceptions that leaders make of themselves? This question is especially germane when these exceptions are not themselves subject to the *"public affirmation of member intent"* to which Hollander refers in his analysis of pre-trial discussions of procedures.[89] With respect to the confederate's deviations in the problem-solving study, for instance, at no time did the participants explicitly agree that he was no longer bound by these requirements. Here, perhaps the advocate of transactional approaches to leadership has in mind something such as the Lockean distinction between express consent and tacit consent.[90] The justification for the confederate's deviations from generally applicable requirements might appeal to the fact that participants consented to these deviations simply by offering no objections to them.[91] Indeed, there is some evidence to support this line of argument. The behavior of participants toward early conformists differed dramatically from that shown to early non-conformists, with the latter receiving "such comments of censure as 'That's not the way we agreed to do it, five.'"[92] Thus, from the fact that participants withheld consent to some deviations by voicing objections to them, we might therefore conclude that their silence constituted giving consent to other confederates who deviated from these requirements.

It is questionable, though, whether advocates of transactional leadership can draw this inference outside of laboratory contexts. Unlike the participants in Hollander's experiment, ordinary followers can face major obstacles to meaningful dissent, not least because of power differentials between leaders and followers. The two kinds of power most likely to undermine the conditions for consent are what French and Raven identify as legitimate power and coercive power.[93] The former refers to the formal authority of leaders within an organization, and the latter to their ability to sanction or punish followers. To use John Simmons's

---

[89] Hollander, *Leaders, Groups, and Influence*, p. 199.

[90] John Locke, *Two Treatises of Government*, ed. Peter Laslett (Cambridge: Cambridge University Press, 1988), ch. 8.

[91] Tiffany Keller and Fred Dansereau, "Leadership and Empowerment: A Social Exchange Perspective," *Human Relations* 48 (1995): 128, for example, suggest that "unlike economic exchange, social exchange is not an explicit, contractually based arrangement."

[92] Hollander, *Leaders, Groups, and Influence*, p. 203.

[93] John R. P. French, Jr., and Bertram Raven, "The Bases of Social Power," in Dorwin Cartwright, ed., *Studies in Social Power* (Ann Arbor, MI: Institute for Social Research, 1959), pp. 150–167.

language, employees may be willing to tolerate unethical behavior from a manager because inequalities in legitimate and coercive power imply that followers do not know that their "consent is appropriate" in the situation or, although they have this knowledge, dissent would be "extremely detrimental to the potential consenter."[94] When follower acceptance of the exceptions that leaders make of themselves is well short of consent, we should have reservations about the morality of the relationships between leaders and followers. This, despite the fact that these relationships are the outcome of a series of exchanges between them.

There is all the more reason to question the normative force of such acceptance when deviations from generally applicable requirements extend beyond the behavior of leaders to include the behavior of particular followers as well. In Hollander's problem-solving study, for example, the confederate's deviations tended to be "taken up by some others" when these deviations were successful.[95] One promising way of understanding this kind of behavior looks to a contemporary transactional approach to leadership called Leader-Member Exchange Theory (LMX). According to the earliest incarnation of this theory, individual followers engage in satisfying performance to negotiate with leaders for behavioral latitude.[96] As a result of the negotiations, some followers become "'special' assistants" to leaders and obtain the privileges that such associations carry.[97] To whatever extent permissions to deviate from generally applicable moral requirements are included within these privileges, justification for exception making cannot be grounded in the consent of the group. Since the relationships at issue are understood solely in terms of leader-follower dyads on LMX, the question of consent from other followers does not even arise.

---

[94] A. John Simmons, "Tacit Consent and Political Obligation," *Philosophy and Public Affairs* 5 (1976): 279–280.

[95] Hollander, *Leaders, Groups, and Influence*, p. 203.

[96] George Graen and James F. Cashman, "A Role-Making Model of Leadership in Formal Organizations: A Developmental Approach," in James G. Hunt and Lars L. Larson, eds., *Leadership Frontiers* (Kent, OH: The Comparative Administration Research Institute, 1975): 143–165.

[97] George Graen, "Role-Making Processes Within Complex Organizations," in Marvin D. Dunnette, ed., *Handbook of Industrial and Organizational Psychology* (Chicago: Rand McNally College Publishing, 1976), p. 1241. Susan Walton, ex-wife of basketball great Bill Walton, claims that UCLA coach John Wooden "let Bill smoke pot but not the other players" (Pat Jordan, "Bill Walton's Inside Game," *New York Times Magazine* [October 28, 2001]).

There is a parallel problem in thinking that follower consent, in cases in which it is sufficiently robust, releases leaders not only from group norms but also from moral principles that are widely accepted within the larger society. This problem for the ethics of transactional leadership is rooted in the fact that there is hardly any sense in which we might say that outsiders are willing to forego the protections they get from generally applicable moral requirements. Since the exceptions that leaders make of themselves can sometimes wrong individuals outside of their groups, a consent-based justification of exception making requires that these exceptions be limited to the group context itself or else that leaders get consent from third parties. Accordingly, transactional leadership must isolate deviations from generally applicable moral requirements so that they do not spill over into other parts of social, political, and professional life.

The question arises as to whether meeting this requirement is psychologically feasible. Without denying the possibility of substantial moral compartmentalization, we can say – at the very least – that there are bound to be cognitive costs associated with making such distinctions. When these costs are steep, there is the risk that leaders will reduce them by making exceptions of themselves outside of group contexts – for example, as family members or as citizens. If virtue theory gets nothing else right, it is that immoral behavior is to some extent habituated. Even if we assume that deviations from generally applicable moral requirements can be limited to behavior within targeted groups, a second question asks how leaders might contain the effects of their deviations. To alter John Donne's adage, no group is an island. So, putting aside the issue of whether it is psychologically feasible for leaders to make relevant distinctions between normative domains of work and home or the private and the public, advocates of transactional leadership can still expect considerable difficulty in guaranteeing that potentially harmful consequences of the exceptions that followers find acceptable are borne only by consenting followers and by leaders themselves.

An appeal to ethical issues having to do with the nature of consent thus explains why leaders who adopt transactional approaches to leadership might think that they are justified in deviating from generally applicable moral requirements. On such approaches, it is ultimately followers who set limits on the extent to which leaders can make exceptions of themselves, and followers are often willing – in varying degrees – to accept these exceptions. As we have seen, Hollander embraces this basis of norms, arguing that their force ultimately depends "upon how the others in that situation feel about each other."[98] But what we should notice is that we can admit the truth of the descriptive claim that whether leaders conform their behavior to generally applicable moral requirements is a function of what they are allowed to do, without making the additional concession that the actual normative force of these requirements is determined by follower acceptance. This is certainly not to deny that followers sometimes go so far as to expect deviations from generally applicable moral requirements in the belief these exceptions are necessary for attaining the benefits of goal achievement. Rather it is to point out that transactional leadership makes leaders vulnerable to overestimations of the normative force of follower acceptance, both with respect to the treatment of followers themselves and with respect to the treatment of third parties. Not unlike the priest and the Levite in the parable of the Good Samaritan, these leaders can be mistaken as to whether their special relationships with followers entail freedom from the behavioral constraints of generally applicable moral requirements.

Why do leaders mistakenly believe that they are justified in deviating from generally applicable moral requirements? My contention is that an explanation of the exceptions leaders make of themselves must appeal to more than the fact that justification is not always transparent to actors. While leaders certainly face the same impediments that the rest of us face when it comes to determining the conditions under which exceptions are justified, they are also part of a social process that brings with it fairly standard assumptions about the special characteristics of leaders, the special situations in which leadership is exercised, and the special relationship between leaders and followers. These assumptions are variously highlighted by three very general ways of thinking about leadership: trait approaches, situational approaches, and transactional approaches. Each approach to leadership emphasizes particular grounds on which leaders can readily draw in their efforts to justify deviations from generally applicable moral requirements. In so doing, trait approaches, situational approaches, and transactional approaches embody understandings of leadership that can promote ethical failure.

---

[98] Hollander, *Leaders, Groups, and Influence*, p. 152.

Chapter 4

Justifying Leadership

I. INTRODUCTION

When are leaders justified in making exceptions of themselves? Under what conditions, that is, is it permissible for them to deviate from moral requirements that apply to the rest of us? Initially at least, it might seem that leaders can never be justified in making such exceptions. First, to deviate from what morality requires is to do what is morally wrong. In other words, it is to fail to engage in behavior supported not only by prima facie moral reasons but also by conclusive moral reasons against the deviation. Second, justification implies that the actor does no wrong by engaging in the behavior in question. That is to say, if a leader's behavior is justified, then it is *a* morally right thing to do in the circumstances, perhaps among other perfectly permissible alternatives. It may also be *the* right thing to do, in which case his behavior is required in addition to being permissible. It would seem, then, that the claim that a leader's behavior is justified minimally requires that he do no wrong when he engages in it. But if justified behavior is permissible in just this sense, and deviations from the requirements of morality are always morally wrong, then leaders are never justified in making exceptions of themselves. Plainly stated, it cannot be right for them to do what is wrong.

We must therefore assume from the outset that the claim that leaders can be justified in making exceptions of themselves does not mean that leaders do no wrong when they fail to do what morality really requires of them. This assumption leaves us with two options for thinking about how leaders might be justified in deviating from moral requirements. Either their deviations are not morally wrong after all, or there is some weaker sense in which it is meaningful to say that leaders are justified in doing what is morally wrong, one that leaves them with something short of full moral justification. On the first option, which we might call the *reconciliation view*, the exceptions that leaders make of themselves can be fully justified because morality, properly understood, does not prohibit this kind of leadership behavior. On the second option, which we might call the *realist view*, these exceptions need not be reconciled with the demands of morality, possibly because they cannot be reconciled with these demands. According to advocates of this view, good, or indeed great, leadership often requires that leaders do some moral wrong. In these cases, justification for the behavior of leaders is incomplete at best.

It is sometimes difficult to tell the reconciliation view and the realist view apart, mainly because realism rarely eschews all justificatory appeals to morality. Even on ostensibly amoralist varieties of realism, substantial moral considerations often lurk in the background. For example, when Dean Acheson, who advocated quick military action in the Cuban missile crisis, claims that "[m]oral talk did not bear on the problem," we can interpret him not as rejecting morality altogether but rather as privileging some moral considerations over others.[1] After all, he defends the perspective he took in these circumstances by appeal to his role as "a public servant."[2] Given the nature of the expectations associated with this kind of leadership, it would be odd to think that Acheson's justification is devoid of moral content. For purposes of distinguishing the reconciliation view from the realist view, then, the most important question is whether in meeting these expectations, the leader has nonetheless done some moral wrong. The advocate of reconciliation claims that he is fully justified, whereas the realist concedes that his justification is, at most, limited.

II. THE NATURE OF JUSTIFICATION

One way to justify the exceptions that leaders make of themselves is to appeal to the distinction between deviations from generally applicable moral requirements and behavior that is actually morally wrong. On this distinction, generally applicable moral requirements are prescriptions or proscriptions that usually or almost always bind the behavior of actors but can be overridden by other more weighty moral considerations. For

[1] Quoted in Stephen A. Garrett, "Political Leadership and the Problem of 'Dirty Hands,'" *Ethics and International Affairs* 8 (1994): 164.
[2] Garrett, "Political Leadership and the Problem of 'Dirty Hands,'" p. 164.

example, those who promote reconciliation between exception making by leaders and the genuine demands of morality point to the variable authority of moral requirements to argue that, in some circumstances, these requirements fail to apply to the behavior of leaders or they apply with insignificant normative force – in either case – because of the good that can be achieved or the evil that can be avoided by deviating from them. This line of argument thus holds that when leaders make exceptions of themselves for the sake of appropriately higher causes, the ends of leadership have sufficient moral weight to override generally applicable moral requirements.[3] As a consequence, the exceptions in question can be seen as fully justified.

The difficulty for any defense of exception making, of course, is in specifying the conditions under which deviations from generally applicable moral requirements might be justified. All plausible moral theories agree, for example, that deception and manipulation are generally wrong. Even exponents of ethical egoism – the view that morality directs us always to act in our self-interest – can appreciate the fact that people generally have moral reasons to avoid these behaviors, especially when it comes to those individuals with whom we most often interact.[4] Where moral theories disagree is on the issue of when, if ever, it is permissible to deviate from the commonplace prohibitions on deception or manipulation and from other generally applicable moral requirements of their kind. Disagreement is just what we should expect, however, given that moral theories are essentially competing accounts of justification. Since these theories are distinguished from each other on the basis of the reasons that make behavior permissible, required, or prohibited, they will also differ when it comes to the justification of exceptions.

To be sure, this does not mean that a moral theory can allow exceptions that constitute a departure from what that theory says about morality. If it were to allow exceptions of this kind, then the exceptions would serve as counterexamples to the theory itself. What a moral theory can do, though, is offer reasons to which leaders might appeal to show that their behavior can be justified despite the fact that it deviates from generally applicable moral requirements. All this is to say that what justifies an exception on a moral theory can be no different

---

[3] See, for example, James MacGregor Burns, *Leadership* (New York: Harper and Row Publishers, 1978), pp. 429–432.

[4] See, for example, Edwin Locke's argument in Bruce J. Avolio and Edwin A. Locke, "Contrasting Different Philosophies of Leader Motivation: Altruism Versus Egoism, *Leadership Quarterly* 13 (2002): 169–191.

from what justifies all behavior on that theory. To the extent that the moral theory permits deviations from generally applicable moral requirements, it will do so on grounds of what it deems to be the relevant moral reasons. Whether the exceptions that leaders make of themselves really are morally justified is thus a matter of how competing reasons from the various moral theories are incorporated within a normative theory of leadership. In essence, it is nothing short of determining what normative theory of leadership is correct.

Deontological moral theory holds that only features of an action itself are relevant to a determination of its morality. As such, these theories take the position that justification excludes consideration of consequences. For Immanuel Kant, the primary historical exponent of deontological ethics, the feature of an action on which its morality turns is its connection to reason, a connection that can be characterized in either of two ways. First, the formal structure of reason dictates that we act only in ways that it would be possible for everyone else to act and, moreover, that we would be willing to have them act. In Kant's words, *"Act as if the maxim of your action were to become through your will a universal law of nature."*[5] Second, the absolute value of our rational nature dictates that we respect the capacity of persons to use their reason, treating them *"never simply as a means, but always at the same time as an end."*[6] So, for example, Kant infamously argues from the "categorical" nature of these directives that it would be morally wrong to lie to a murderer to save the life of his victim.[7] The bad consequences that the truth might bring about justify neither an exception for the potential liar nor the disrespect that lying would show the rational agency of the murderer.

In contrast, consequentialist moral theory holds that the morality of an action is determined strictly by the results to which it gives rise. Utilitarianism, easily the most influential version of consequentialism, assesses these results in terms of overall happiness or well-being. Accordingly, on most varieties of utilitarianism, deception and manipulation can be justified when the utility produced by deviating from prohibitions against these behaviors is greater than that produced by

---

[5] Immanuel Kant, *Groundwork of the Metaphysic of Morals,* trans. H. J. Paton (New York: Harper and Row Publishers, 1964), p. 89.

[6] Kant, *Groundwork*, p. 96.

[7] See Immanuel Kant, "On a Supposed Right to Lie from Philanthropy," in his *Practical Philosophy*, trans. and ed. Mary J. Gregor (Cambridge: Cambridge University Press, 1996), pp. 605–615.

conformity to them.[8] Of course, there may be all kinds of utilitarian reasons to conform our behavior to these generally applicable moral requirements and perhaps to treat them as if they were deontological constraints on action. Not least of all is the fact that deception and manipulation by leaders can erode the trust of others, making it difficult to maximize utility in the long run. Nevertheless, considerations of happiness or well-being on the whole establish the normative force of the prohibitions on deception and manipulation and, in at least some circumstances, would seem to allow exceptions to them. Insofar as lying to save the life of another is one such case, utilitarianism offers a way of explaining the intuition that an exception in this situation must surely be justified.

It is often difficult to characterize normative theories of leadership as being committed to either deontological or consequentialist moral theory.[9] James MacGregor Burns's theory of *transforming leadership*, for instance, ascribes to what seems to be a deontological constraint on leaders – namely, that they are forbidden from "treat[ing] people as things."[10] In fact, Burns seems to think that respecting this constraint is partially definitive of leadership and, for this reason, differentiates between leaders and mere *"power wielders."*[11] But normative theories such as Burns's must also assign significant moral weight to attaining the ends of leadership. Because leadership is fundamentally a goal-oriented activity, advocates of these theories would be remiss were they not to make consequences a prominent focus in the evaluation of leadership behavior.[12] As Burns himself puts it, "[T]he test of the extent and quality of power and leadership is the degree of *actual accomplishment*

---

[8] Rule utilitarianism is the obvious exception here. This version of utilitarianism holds that rules, not acts, are the proper object of moral deliberation. We should act according to those rules that, if followed by everyone, would maximize utility.

[9] Joanne B. Ciulla, "Leadership Ethics: Mapping the Territory," in Joanne B. Ciulla, ed., *Ethics, the Heart of Leadership* (Westport, CT: Praeger, 1998), pp. 15–18.

[10] Burns, *Leadership*, p. 18.

[11] Burns, *Leadership*, p. 18. See my Introduction (present book) for a discussion of Burns's definition.

[12] Charles F. Rauch, Jr., and Orlando Behling, for example, follow Ralph Melvin Stogdill, *Handbook of Leadership: A Survey of Theory and Research* (New York: Free Press, 1974) and define leadership as "the process of influencing the activities of an organized group toward goal achievement" ("Functionalism: Basis for an Alternate Approach to the Study of Leadership," in James G. Hunt, Dian-Marie Hosking, Chester A. Schriesheim, and Rosemary Stewart, eds., *Leaders and Managers: International Perspectives on Managerial Behavior and Leadership* [New York: Pergamon Press, 1984], p. 46).

of the promised change."[13] It would seem, then, that the main challenge for normative theories of leadership is to articulate the connection between this strong consequentialist commitment and any morally binding deontological constraints.[14]

One way to ease the tensions between these competing ethical considerations is to claim that most, if not all, deontological constraints are better understood in terms of generally applicable moral requirements that can be overridden to achieve good or avoid evil. If the normative force of these requirements is ultimately determined by consequentialist considerations, then the ends of leadership do all of the justificatory work. As we shall see, this is just the strategy that normative theories of leadership are inclined to adopt. It presupposes, however, that these ends are themselves derived from the dictates of consequentialist moral theory. In other words, this strategy assumes that the ends to which leaders and followers commit themselves can be identified with consequences that morally ought to be pursued. Only on this kind of identification can the ends of leadership justify the exceptions that leaders make of themselves. So, before asking whether these ends justify deviations from generally applicable moral requirements, we must first ask whether the ends themselves can be justified on consequentialist ethics. If these ends cannot be justified, then it is hard to see how advocates of reconciliation might use them to justify anything else.

III. THE ENDS OF LEADERSHIP

People engage in the leadership process because it is instrumental to the achievement of goals established by, or in some cases for, the group, organization, or society of which they are a part. In the standard cases, sports leadership aims at victory for the team, business leadership at profitability for the firm, and political leadership at protecting state or national interests. This is not to deny that there can be goods internal to the leader-follower relationship and, moreover, that leaders and followers can come to see these goods as being more valuable than whatever external goods they seek to attain. Here, the intrinsic value of collaboration, reciprocity, and participation immediately comes to mind. Out of respect for this kind of value, sports leaders sometimes strive for teamwork, business leaders for fair labor practices, and political leaders for

---

[13] Burns, *Leadership*, p. 22.
[14] I will suggest, however, that this contrast oversimplifies the challenge.

genuine democracy. But even these internal goods are more likely to be understood as instrumental to the achievement of collective ends, simply because this particular understanding of their value fits better with the nature of the leadership process itself. Without some ends at which leaders and followers might aim, there is hardly room for leadership at all.

It is the instrumental nature of leadership that drives its consequentialist logic. As Gary Yukl puts it, "Most researchers evaluate leadership effectiveness in terms of the consequences of the leader's actions for followers and other organization stakeholders."[15] On this standard of evaluation, effective leadership gives rise to good consequences, as measured by "the extent to which the leader's organizational unit performs its task successfully and attains its goals."[16] Accordingly, what constitutes success can be as varied as both the tasks in which leaders and followers engage and the goals at which they aim. As a result of this variability, the primary beneficiaries of "the most commonly used measure of leader effectiveness"[17] can range from members of the organization itself to others within the broader society in which it operates. In all cases, however, the reputed goodness of the ends to which this standard of effectiveness aspires, as well as the beneficiaries of their attainment, is relative to the context in which leadership is exercised.

It might seem that the consequentialist logic of leadership would make for ready compatibility with consequentialist moral theory. Since effectiveness is evaluated by appeal to behavioral outcomes, leadership is in some ways well suited to a standard of moral analysis that focuses solely on consequences. However, given the variability of the ends of leadership, this important conceptual similarity actually creates potential conflicts between these ends and consequentialist moral theory. Any reasonably acceptable version of this theory would assess actions not simply in terms of whether they produce effects reflecting the goals of a group, organization, or society but rather on the basis of the actual goodness of these effects. This means that the ends of leadership will be significantly constrained by the particular ends to which consequentialist ethics is committed. Common aspirations of leader effectiveness such as "profits, profit margin, sales increase, market share,

[15] Gary Yukl, *Leadership in Organizations*, 5th edition (Upper Saddle River, NJ: Prentice Hall, 2002), p. 8.
[16] Yukl, *Leadership in Organizations*, p. 8.
[17] Yukl, *Leadership in Organizations*, p. 8.

sales relative to targeted sales, return on investment, productivity, cost per unit of output, costs in relation to budgeted expenditures, and so on"[18] will be justified, then, only insofar as consequentialist moral theory deems them valuable as a means to the achievement of something more fundamentally good such as utility maximization.

One way to defend the stronger claim that the ends of leadership are indeed grounded in consequentialist moral theory appeals to the connection between preference satisfaction and goal achievement. Goal achievement is utilitarian, so the argument goes, because it satisfies the preferences of those who have the goals, thereby contributing directly to the goods of happiness and well-being. Unfortunately, what this line of argument ignores is that consequentialist moral theory does more than tell us that goods such as happiness and well-being serve to justify behavior. It also has much to say about the conditions under which we are justified in being the primary beneficiaries of these goods. For example, utilitarianism holds that the right action is the action that maximizes *overall* happiness or well-being, not the happiness or well-being of those engaged in the leadership process. So even if we draw on purely subjective interpretations of happiness and well-being to accommodate the variability in the ends of leadership, it is doubtful that those who benefit from the attainment of these ends will be the same beneficiaries as dictated by utilitarianism.

Other authors have suspected that the relationship between the consequentialist logic of leadership and consequentialist moral theory will not be exactly harmonious. For example, Bass and Steidlmeier anticipate conflicts of value.[19] They write:

Conflicts in values are a continuing occurrence in utilitarian organizations. Which is more important? Productivity? Safety? Cost Reduction? Efficiency? Employee and manager well-being? Profitability? Survival? Growth? Some say stockholder interests are paramount. Others argue that morality requires maximizing the well-being of the employees.[20]

But the potential for value conflict is actually much deeper than their diagnosis of the problem allows. While there may be difficulties in offering a complete specification of the ends of utilitarianism and the best means of achieving them, the source of the value conflicts in such organizations

---

[18] Yukl, *Leadership in Organizations*, p. 8.
[19] Bernard M. Bass and Paul Steidlmeier, "Ethics, Character, and Authentic Transformational Leadership Behavior," *Leadership Quarterly* 10 (1999): 181–217.
[20] Bass and Steidlmeier, "Authentic Transformational Leadership Behavior," p. 208.

is not indeterminacy within the moral theory itself. Utilitarianism is more than clear enough both that it aspires to the maximization of overall happiness or well-being and that its values cannot simply be indexed to the goals of an organization and to the well-being of its members. The deeper source of value conflict is rather that leaders and followers regularly work together to achieve goals that diverge from the ends of utilitarianism and benefit them in ways that this theory proscribes.

When would the ends of leadership be justified on utilitarianism? Given technological advances that provide ready access to information on suffering throughout the world and make us capable of responding quickly to it, we can no longer accept John Stuart Mill's nineteenth-century understanding of the practical implications of utilitarianism.[21] Specifically, we must discard the outdated assumption that there are few occasions on which a person can be "a public benefactor," that "private utility, the interest or happiness of some few persons, is all he has to attend to."[22] Today, the most obvious cases in which utilitarianism would justify the ends of leadership are those in which leaders pursue ends that would make dramatic contributions to the happiness or well-being of others outside their particular group, organization, or society. Efforts to eliminate poverty, hunger, and disease would be likely candidates for satisfying this condition. But not even *servant leadership*, one of the most popular normative conceptions of leadership, requires that leaders show this kind of concern for outsiders. Instead, the test of this form of leadership focuses primarily on the led, asking whether "those served grow as persons . . . Do they, *while being served*, become healthier, wiser, freer, more autonomous, more likely themselves to become servants?"[23]

This is not to suggest that outsiders are forgotten on the theory of servant leadership. But the expectations for their treatment are importantly weaker than are the expectations for the treatment of insiders. Greenleaf asks, "[W]hat is the effect on the least privileged in society; will they benefit, *or, at least, not be further deprived*?"[24] In other words, the test of

---

[21] Peter Singer, "Famine, Affluence, and Morality," *Philosophy and Public Affairs* 1 (1972): 232.

[22] John Stuart Mill, *Utilitarianism*, ed. George Sher (Indianapolis: Hackett Publishing Company, 1979), p. 19.

[23] Robert K. Greenleaf, *Servant Leadership: A Journey into the Nature of Legitimate Power and Greatness* (New York: Paulist Press, 1977), pp. 13–14. See, however, James MacGregor Burns's epilogue to *Transforming Leadership: A New Pursuit of Happiness* (New York: Atlantic Monthly Press, 2003).

[24] Greenleaf, *Servant Leadership*, p. 14, emphasis added.

this form of leadership can be met by making the least well-off members of society no worse off, that is, by simply sustaining the status quo for these individuals. Placing such limited demands on leaders is not only counter to the Rawlsian proposal that "the social order is not to establish and secure the more attractive prospects of those better off unless doing so is to the advantage of those less fortunate" but also counter to the view that the least privileged have the most to gain in terms of utility and, as a result, could likely make better utilitarian use of whatever resources might otherwise be expended on insiders.[25] Admittedly, there will be cases in which the best way to maximize overall happiness or well-being is by attending to the needs, interests, and preferences of those involved directly in the leadership process. Leadership within disadvantaged and oppressed communities will sometimes meet this condition fairly easily, and it will also be met when focusing on the happiness or well-being of leaders and followers in the short run is instrumental to maximizing overall utility in the long run. We might nonetheless conclude that the number of cases in which the ends of leadership are truly utilitarian will be comparatively quite small.[26]

Despite our presuppositions to the contrary, deontological moral theory may better accommodate the variability in the ends of leadership. Since this theory does not assess actions on the basis of their consequences, it creates considerable moral space in which leaders and followers might pursue their ends. Of course, some means of pursuing these ends will be limited by deontological constraints on action. For example, Kant argues for a strict or narrow duty against the deceptive practice of using false promises for goal achievement. This duty is grounded in the fact that any attempt to universalize the practice generates a *contradiction in conception* for the potential actor:

I then see straight away that this maxim can never rank as a universal law of nature and be self-consistent, but must necessarily contradict itself. For the universality of a law that every one believing himself to be in need can make any promise he pleases with the intention not to keep it would make promising, and the very purpose of promising, itself impossible, since no one would believe

---

[25] John Rawls, *A Theory of Justice* (Cambridge, MA: Belknap Press of Harvard University Press, 1971), p. 75. Of course, Rawls's proposal is indexed to institutions, not to individual actors, and is developed as an alternative to utilitarianism.

[26] Similar conflicts will arise with respect to other versions of consequentialist moral theory. Since each will be committed to its own view of the good, there will be little room for the variability in the ends of leadership.

he was being promised anything, but would laugh at utterances of this kind as empty shams.[27]

So, even when there is no other means to goal achievement, the conceptual impossibility of universalizing a practice will generate a prohibition on the attainment of the ends of leadership. Nevertheless, for a great many cases, it is fair to say that the ends of leadership as well as the means for attaining them will be consistent with Kant's strict or narrow duties.

In addition to duties derived from contradictions in conception, Kant also defends the place of duties derived from *contradictions in will*. Among these duties is the duty to help others in need. According to Kant, while it is possible to conceive of a world in which no one helps anyone else,

it is impossible to *will* that such a principle should hold everywhere as a law of nature. For a will which decided in this way would be in conflict with itself, since many a situation might arise in which the man needed love and sympathy from others, and in which, by such a law of nature sprung from his own will, he would rob himself of all hope of the help he wants for himself.[28]

In effect, willing that no one help anyone is inconsistent with willing the kind of help that we will surely need ourselves. We have a duty to help others in need, that is, not because of the good that we can do for them or even the good that we can expect in return but because it would be contradictory to will that people universally do otherwise. Whatever our ends, we eventually *need* and, therefore, *will* the help of others.[29]

Does a commitment to this kind of duty preclude accommodating the variability in the ends of leadership? After all, there will always be others for whom we might abandon our ends in an effort to help them with theirs. Such a sacrifice, however, would clearly defeat the Kantian rationale for the conclusion that we should help others in need. Without our own ends for which we might need the help of others, there is no contradiction in willing that no one help anyone. In other words, it is by virtue of these ends that we have a duty to help others in the first place. As a consequence, discharging this duty must be consistent with their pursuit. Kant guarantees this kind of consistency by placing

[27] Kant, *Groundwork*, p. 90.
[28] Kant, *Groundwork*, p. 91.
[29] The word *need* here must be read as having none of its ordinary psychological, physiological, or social components.

a restriction on the scope of the duty to help others, calling it a broad or meritorious duty to distinguish it from the strict or narrow duties. Broad or meritorious duties give actors significant freedom to decide, for example, when they will help others in need. Within the freedom allowed by duties of this kind, there is substantial moral space to pursue the ends of leadership.[30]

Versions of deontological moral theory such as Kantianism have comparatively little trouble accommodating the variability in the ends of leadership, essentially because of the value that they assign to individual autonomy. Ultimately, this variability allows people to draw on their rational nature to make autonomous choices about the ends they will pursue. But a Kantian defense of leadership is not without costs of its own. If the ends of leadership are justified not on the basis of consequentialist considerations but rather on the basis of deontological considerations, then the value of these ends cannot be used to reconcile the exceptions that leaders make of themselves with actual moral demands on leadership behavior. Since these demands would themselves be grounded in the value of autonomy, leaders who fail to conform their behavior to deontological constraints would show disrespect for the very values that justify the ends of leadership. Accordingly, it is not easy to see how the ends of leadership and the exceptions that leaders make of themselves might both be justified on a normative theory of leadership.

IV. TRANSFORMING LEADERSHIP

To be successful, the reconciliation view must restrict variability in the ends of leadership by committing leaders to purposes morally robust enough to justify the exceptions that leaders make of themselves. No normative theory of leadership has made more progress on this score than James MacGregor Burns's theory of transforming leadership. In his seminal book *Leadership*, Burns defends this theory against transactional varieties by appeal to a distinction between end-values and modal values.[31] He writes, "The chief monitors of transactional leadership are *modal values*, that is, values of means – honesty, responsibility, fairness, the honoring of commitments . . . Transformational leadership

---

[30] This interpretation of Kant's broad or meritorious duties thus contrasts sharply with that of Susan Wolf, "Moral Saints," *Journal of Philosophy* 79 (1982): 419–439.
[31] Burns, *Leadership*, p. 43.

is more concerned with *end-values*, such as liberty, justice, and equality."[32] Exactly twenty years after the publication of this work, Burns's restatement of the values of leadership adds what he calls *ethical values*. These values include "'old-fashioned character tests' such as sobriety, chastity, abstention, kindness, altruism, and other 'Ten Commandments' rules of personal conduct," values most closely associated with "'status-quo' leaders."[33] Reflecting on this categorization, he muses: "Wouldn't it be lovely, in this fragmented world, if these three sets of values, and hence all these forms of leadership, could exist in happy harmony? Alas, it cannot be."[34]

To articulate the "basic dilemma" of leadership, Burns approvingly quotes Herbert Kelman on the moral costs and benefits of manipulation: "On the one hand, for those of us who hold the enhancement of man's freedom of choice to be a fundamental value, any manipulations of the behavior of others constitutes a violation of their essential humanity . . . On the other hand, effective behavior change inevitably involves some degree of manipulation and control, and at least an implicit imposition of the change agent's values on the client or the person he is influencing."[35] Greenleaf similarly writes, "Part of our dilemma is that all leadership is, to some extent, manipulative."[36] The leadership dilemma, then, can be understood in terms of the conflict between the deontological value of agency to which Kelman and others refer and the kind of leadership behavior that is sometimes necessary for good consequentialist reasons. For advocates of the reconciliation view, solving this dilemma is a matter of finding the proper ordering of our values, one on which threats to autonomy are compatible with actual moral demands on leadership behavior.

---

[32] Burns, *Leadership*, p. 426. This quote is ambiguous between the claim that transformational leadership is more concerned with end-values than it is concerned with modal values and the claim that transformational leadership, by comparison with transactional leadership, is more concerned with end-values. I have opted for the former reading for several reasons, not least because Burns makes it clear that transactional leadership is not at all concerned with end-values, which would make it superfluous to say that transformational leadership, by comparison with transactional leadership, is more concerned with these values.

[33] Burns, "Foreword," in Joanne B. Ciulla, ed., *Ethics, the Heart of Leadership* (Westport, CT: Praeger, 1998a), p. x.

[34] Burns, "Foreword," p. x.

[35] Burns, "Foreword," p. x. Burns's reference is to Herbert C. Kelman, "Manipulation of Human Behavior: An Ethical Dilemma for the Social Scientist," *Journal of Social Issues* 21, 2 (1965): 31–46.

[36] Greenleaf, *Servant Leadership*, p. 42.

In keeping with his respect for the dilemma, Burns's normative theory of leadership embraces values quite similar to those found on deontological moral theory. First, transforming leadership "occurs when one or more persons *engage* with others in such a way that leaders and followers raise one another to higher levels of motivation and morality."[37] As a defining feature of this mutual transformation, those engaged in the leadership process realize genuine moral agency by curbing subjective wants so that they might meet objective needs, needs characterized in terms of "higher and higher searches for individual and social fulfillment."[38] Here, Burns's skepticism about the place of desires and preferences within a normative theory of leadership is akin to Kant's concerns about a moral theory "based on feelings, impulses, and inclinations."[39] Although their views contrast rather sharply with one another on the issue of whether morality can be grounded in "*characteristics of human nature*,"[40] both hold that merely subjective influences are insufficient for the genuine moral agency with which they are most concerned.

A second feature of transforming leadership that makes for ready comparison with deontological moral theory is implicit in Burns's claim that this form of leadership "converts followers into leaders."[41] Not only does transforming leadership contribute to the moral agency of followers by encouraging them to act on their highest needs and values, but it also uses motivational and moral transformation to get them to see the broader importance of these transformative effects and, upon this recognition, to become transforming leaders themselves. Within deontological moral theory, a similar feature drives the second version of the Kantian argument for a broad or meritorious duty to help others in need. After exposing the contradiction in will that grounds this duty, Kant appeals to the value of "*humanity as an end in itself*," arguing that "the ends of a subject who is an end in himself must, if this conception is to have its *full* effect in me, be also, as far as possible, *my* ends."[42] The commonality shared by the two theories, then, is that both are committed to the view that realizing one's own moral agency generates a parallel responsibility to contribute to the moral agency of others.

---

[37] Burns, *Leadership*, p. 20.
[38] Burns, *Leadership*, p. 72.
[39] Kant, *Groundwork*, p. 102.
[40] Kant, *Groundwork*, p. 92.
[41] Burns, *Leadership*, p. 4.
[42] Kant, *Groundwork*, p. 98.

These similarities aside, transforming leadership is much more closely aligned with consequentialist moral theory than with deonto-logical moral theory. Most telling is the fact that Burns subordinates concerns for the means utilized by leaders to concerns about particu-lar ends that might be achieved. In other words, when not all values can be satisfied, some are rightly sacrificed to others. Subordination of the means cannot be taken to suggest that leaders should be indiffer-ent to the modal values listed earlier. For example, Burns tells us that leaders are judged morally against these values "by the extent to which they advanced or thwarted fundamental standards of good conduct in humankind."[43] Still, this consequentialist commitment to the modal val-ues diverges significantly from adherence to deontological constraints on the means to which leaders might appeal. To expose this divergence, we need only notice that leaders can advance, rather than thwart, stan-dards of good conduct without strictly adhering to the modal values themselves. In fact, as Burns shows by appeal to Franklin Roosevelt's manipulation of Joseph Kennedy in the 1940 presidential campaign, be-ing in a position to foster these standards within society may require that individual leaders sometimes ignore the modal values when it comes to their own leadership behavior.[44]

What makes Burns's commitment to the modal values consequen-tialist is that he gives them a purely conditional role within the theory of transforming leadership. Although he recognizes that these values can have intrinsic worth, suggesting that "[m]odes [of conduct] some-times are goals in themselves,"[45] this is a far cry from making them unconditional constraints on action. In lieu of an appeal to the uncon-ditional normative force of the modal values, transforming leaders are instead encouraged to conform their behavior to these values on the grounds that "insufficient attention to means can corrupt the ends."[46] Interestingly enough, Joanne Ciulla singles out this caution as a po-tential obstacle to any consequentialist characterization of transforming

---

[43] Burns, *Leadership*, p. 426.
[44] Burns, *Leadership*, pp. 32–33. Burns also notes Roosevelt's manipulation of other "political rivals" such as John L. Lewis and Huey Long (p. 114).
[45] Burns, *Leadership*, p. 75.
[46] Burns, *Leadership*, p. 426. For instance, in one of Michael Walzer's examples, a politician believes that "if he makes [a deal with a dishonest ward boss] he may not be able later on to achieve those ends that make the campaign worthwhile" ("Political Action: The Problem of Dirty Hands," *Philosophy and Public Affairs* 2 [1973]: 166).

leadership, a characterization that she herself seems inclined to accept.[47] But if Burns's warning is meant to imply that leaders should attend to the modal values lest they distort the end-values, then his argument will hardly be any less consequentialist for it. Whether the end-values are defined as "standards" to be advanced rather than thwarted or as "collective goals,"[48] what constitutes insufficient attention to the modal values will ultimately be determined by what is necessary to attain these ends.

On this interpretation of the Burnsian value framework, the normative force of the modal values is conditional on their connection to the end-values. By and large, transforming leaders should attend to the modal values because failure to do so can frustrate "the fundamental standards of good conduct in humankind," making it difficult to achieve collective goals.[49] Plainly, however, circumventing what are effectively generally applicable moral requirements can sometimes be a reasonable strategy for actualizing end-values. To use Burns's example, "Roosevelt's court-packing plan, with its use of dubious means to attain high ends, is a case in point."[50] It is precisely this conditionality that makes the advocate of transforming leadership well placed to reconcile such exceptions with the actual demands that morality makes on leadership behavior. For, as we have seen, the prospects of reconciliation would be slim indeed if these demands were best captured by deontological constraints. By detaching the modal values from deontological moral theory, Burns allows that leaders might be justified in deviating from generally applicable moral requirements.

Unlike standard versions of consequentialism, Burns's theory of transforming leadership does not call for maximization of overall happiness or well-being. This is not to say that happiness and well-being do not matter for Burns; on the contrary, leaders are "judged in the balance sheet of history by their impact on the well-being of the persons whose lives they touched."[51] It is rather to say that Burns advances neither the happiness nor well-being of the whole nor even the happiness or well-being of those within a leader's group, organization, or society as the chief end of transforming leadership. In fact, in his most recent work,

[47] Ciulla, "Mapping the Territory," p. 16.
[48] Burns, *Leadership*, p. 74.
[49] Burns, *Leadership*, p. 426.
[50] Burns, *Leadership*, p. 43. Burns later says that this might have been a "political" mistake (p. 115). As far as I can tell, he does not think that it was a moral mistake.
[51] Burns, *Leadership*, p. 426.

Burns appeals to the family of Enlightenment values catalogued in the Declaration of Independence: life, liberty, and *the pursuit of* happiness. He writes,

The trinity draws its stirring, event-making power from the interdependence of these values. Life – order, security, "safety" in eighteenth century terms – without liberty can diminish the potentials of human lives, even to the extent of being life-denying. Liberty without order can turn to license, even anarchy and violence. The fullest meaning of these values becomes manifest in their mutuality, each secured – fulfilled – through the power of the other.[52]

So too, then, the value of happiness – or, more accurately put, *its pursuit* – can be understood in terms of its relation to the value of life and liberty.

Burns's commitment to life, liberty, and the pursuit of happiness is consistent with his earlier statement that he "would grant priority to *liberty*" over any other end-value.[53] This assumes, of course, that we understand the first element of the trinity as a precondition for liberty and the third element as something such as a "guarantee to all persons *the conditions* for pursuing happiness."[54] Yet giving first priority to liberty does raise a substantive question about the exact sense in which this value commitment is consequentialist. After all, rights theorists are similarly committed to the value of individual liberty, typically understood as grounding unconditional prohibitions on leadership behavior. Accordingly, some understandings of the prioritization of liberty would make it difficult for Burns to show how leaders might be justified in deviating from generally applicable moral requirements such as Kantian prohibitions on manipulating others. An alternative, of course, would be to understand the value of liberty in Millian fashion as "one of the principal ingredients of human happiness, and quite the chief ingredient of individual and social progress."[55] But, again, the relative inattention to happiness and well-being in Burns's work does not support a utilitarian reading: "The ultimate attainment of happiness is a cherished dream, but as a goal of transforming leadership we must view it more as a process, a pursuit."[56]

---

[52] Burns, *Transforming Leadership*, p. 227.

[53] Burns, *Leadership*, p. 432.

[54] Burns, *Transforming Leadership*, p. 228, emphasis added.

[55] John Stuart Mill, *On Liberty*, ed. Elizabeth Rapaport (Indianapolis: Hackett Publishing Company, 1978), p. 54.

[56] Burns, *Transforming Leadership*, p. 239.

Burns ultimately addresses these issues by treating liberty itself as a "social good," not an individual good.[57] As such, the liberty of particular individuals can be traded off when so doing is necessary to achieve the specific collective goal to which he thinks we should aspire – namely, "equal liberty" in society.[58] This particular treatment thus distinguishes Burns's commitment to the end-value of liberty, for example, from Kantian views of autonomous agency as an end itself. For Kant, respect for individual agency cannot be traded away for any good, social or otherwise. Burns's consequentialism also explains how Roosevelt, whose willingness "to persuade one person by argument, another by charm, another by a display of self-confidence, another by flattery, another by an encyclopedic knowledge"[59] was anything but Kantian, can nevertheless be said to have come to the White House with "a generalized belief in liberty and equality."[60] In service of these social goods, the president sometimes had to make an exception of himself "by retiring behind the protection of rules, customs, and conventions when they served his needs and evading them when they did not – and always by persuading, flattering, juggling, improvising, reshuffling, harmonizing, conciliating, manipulating."[61]

How does Burns's theory fare at reconciling the exceptions that leaders make of themselves with actual moral demands on leadership behavior? If these demands are determined solely by the end-values, then leaders who deviate from generally applicable moral requirements need only appeal to the value of the ends themselves to justify their behavior. Beyond the prioritization of liberty as a social good, though, Burns's view of the ends of transforming leadership is less than resolute.

Dare we speculate about these end-values and ultimate purposes? Only to a degree. Probably the worldwide debate over principle and purpose will focus even more directly, over the decades ahead, on the mutually competing and supporting values, the paradoxical trade-offs, of *liberty* and *equality* . . . How these values will be defined; how they will relate to one another in hierarchies of principles or priorities of purposes; how 'subvalues' – liberty as privacy, for example, or equality as opportunity – will support or contradict related subvalues;

---

[57] Burns, *Leadership*, p. 432.
[58] Burns, *Leadership*, p. 432. For a discussion of the value of liberty, see Will Kymlicka, *Contemporary Political Philosophy: An Introduction* (Oxford: Clarendon Press, 1990), ch. 4.
[59] Burns, *Leadership*, p. 375.
[60] Burns, *Leadership*, p. 393.
[61] Burns, *Leadership*, p. 393.

how idiosyncratic talent and freedom of innovation will be protected under the doctrine of liberty of expression – these and many other questions can only be roughly answered . . . Leaders who act under conditions of conflict within hierarchies of needs and values, however, must act under the necessity of choosing between certain *kinds* of liberties, equalities, and other end-values."[62]

In effect, this normative theory of leadership leaves the practical task of reconciliation to transforming leaders themselves. It is by means of the leadership process that they *"exploit conflict and tension within persons' value structures"* in order to come to terms with what morality really requires.[63]

In the midst of value conflict, what is to serve as a moral constraint on the behavior of transforming leaders? Is the fact that a leader sees it as necessary to actualize a particular conception of what he takes to be the weightiest end-value enough to justify an exception? Allowing leaders this much freedom to make exceptions of themselves should strike us as a recipe for unjustified deviations from generally applicable moral requirements. Of course, Burns does say that these requirements, when properly construed, have significant normative force for leaders: "*At the highest level* modal values are rights defined on the basis of a conscience that expresses the broadest, most comprehensive, and universal principles; hence they merge with the end-values of justice, equity, and human rights."[64] But if a proper construal of the modal values is derived from the end-values themselves, then leaders cannot appeal to these higher-level modes of conduct to constrain their pursuit of Burnsian end-values. It will do little good, that is, simply to identify the binding modal values with what generates the conflict in the first place – namely, particular conceptions of the content of end-values and their relative weightings. Leaders need modal values unconnected to these controversial ends.

Given the uncertainties within Burns's value framework, transforming leaders might be better served by relying on generally applicable moral requirements that capture lower-level modal values such as "honesty, responsibility, fairness, the honoring of commitments."[65] Even on the view that these requirements can be trumped by end-values of liberty and equality, leaders are justified in making exceptions of

[62] Burns, *Leadership*, pp. 431–432.
[63] Burns, *Leadership*, p. 42.
[64] Burns, *Leadership*, p. 430.
[65] Burns, *Leadership*, p. 426.

themselves only when so doing is called for by the right interpretation of these end-values. By hypothesis, however, questions about their content and weightings "can only be roughly answered."[66] This assumption therefore creates a strong epistemic argument for the presumption that leaders should adhere to generally applicable moral requirements. If nothing else, these requirements are necessary to constrain the behavior of transforming leaders who ascribe to incorrect interpretations of the end-values. So, simply because leaders "must act under the necessity of choosing between certain *kinds* of liberties, equalities, and other end-values,"[67] it does not follow that they must also subordinate the modal values to the choices they make. Only these values stand between transforming leaders and the unjustified pursuit of their ends.

V. THE PROBLEM OF DIRTY HANDS

Like Burns, Michael Walzer understands the exceptions that leaders make of themselves in terms of a dilemma between moral requirements of an absolutist variety and consequentialist considerations that work to the advantage of the greater good.[68] Yet Walzer gives us little reason to be sanguine about the possibility of any kind of reconciliation. To expose the force of the dilemma, he raises what he calls "the problem of 'dirty hands,'" arguing that the nature of the moral reality in which leaders act does not always allow for complete justification of their behavior.[69] Given permanent ethical disunity or a lack of "coherence and harmony of the moral universe," achieving our greater good sometimes leaves leaders with no choice but to do wrong.[70] According to Walzer, however, the realist view "does not mean that it isn't possible to do the right thing while governing. It means that a particular act of government (in a political party or in the state) may be exactly the right thing to do in utilitarian terms and yet leave the man who does it guilty of a moral wrong."[71]

Unlike utilitarian strategies for solving the problem of dirty hands, then, "[t]he notion of dirty hands derives from an effort to refuse

---

[66] Burns, *Leadership*, p. 432.
[67] Burns, *Leadership*, p. 432.
[68] Walzer, "The Problem of Dirty Hands," pp. 160–180.
[69] Walzer, "The Problem of Dirty Hands," p. 161.
[70] Walzer, "The Problem of Dirty Hands," p. 161.
[71] Walzer, "The Problem of Dirty Hands," p. 161.

'absolutism' without denying the reality of the moral dilemma."[72] It is questionable, though, whether even the consequentialist nature of leadership can be captured in utilitarian language. The dirty hands argument sets the realities of leadership against more general commitments to moral idealism, not just against absolutism. In fact, some of the most obvious realities in political contexts will be pressures to deviate from the impartial demands that utilitarianism might be said to make of political leaders. For instance, since political leaders typically represent the interests of constituents, they can hardly afford to be indifferent in their identification of the primary beneficiaries of goods such as happiness and well-being. When these leaders work "for *our* greater good" and their efforts "redound to the benefit . . . of all of *us* together,"[73] there is no mistaking the focus of their perspective. To quote Walzer once again, "In most cases of dirty hands moral rules are broken for reasons of state."[74] Such reasons very often belie a concern for the good of all, which would seem to include the good of political outsiders as well as political insiders.

What stands in need of justification in dirty hands cases, therefore, are not straightforward utilitarian deviations from generally applicable moral requirements. In fact, were the exceptions that leaders make of themselves really for the *good of all*, not just for *our good*, there would be greater reason to think that these leaders are fully justified in their behavior, that their hands are not dirty after all. We might even go so far as to say that it is the fact that leaders have recourse only to the justificatory force of *our good* that leaves them with dirty hands in the first place. By embracing partiality, that is, dirty hands analyses effectively abandon straightforward strategies of reconciliation. Accordingly, on this understanding of the exceptions that leaders make of themselves, it is not surprising that their deviations from generally applicable moral requirements cannot be reconciled with actual moral demands on leadership behavior. What moral theory would allow such exceptions simply on the grounds that they work to the benefit of followers?

Initially at least, the leadership dilemma raised by dirty hands cases seems to be less the result of straightforward conflicts within morality itself, say, between utilitarian and deontological commitments, than the result of conflicts generated by the manifestly partial nature of

---

[72] Walzer, "The Problem of Dirty Hands," p. 162.
[73] Walzer, "The Problem of Dirty Hands," pp. 162–163, emphases added.
[74] Walzer, "The Problem of Dirty Hands," p. 179.

leadership. Conflicts of this kind are hardly unrelated to morality. Indeed, many moral theories take as one of their primary purposes the articulation of a response to the demands of group rationality by specifying the limits of justified partialism, in much the same way that they provide standards for limiting behavior sanctioned by individual rationality.[75] As we have seen, the foundational commitments of utilitarianism make this particular moral theory an unlikely source of justification in dirty hands cases characterized by considerable partiality. In other words, it is predictable that utilitarian moral theory will prove insufficient for a full justification of the exceptions that leaders make of themselves in such cases. For if it is a mistake to appeal to utilitarianism in an attempt to justify the partiality of leadership, then it is surely too much to ask that this theory show that leaders do no wrong whatsoever when they engage in dirty hands behavior.

By focusing on utilitarian justificatory strategies, dirty hands analyses of exception making ignore alternative normative responses to partiality. In so doing, they underestimate the possibility that moral theory might generate complete justifications of the exceptions that leaders make of themselves. This is certainly not to suggest that all dirty hands cases ultimately lend themselves to this kind of reconciliation. In addition to making room for cases in which the behavior of leaders can be shown to be fully unjustified, I want to allow that there might also be cases in which the best that leaders can do gives them no choice but to do some wrong, genuinely leaving them with only limited justification in the end. Rather, my main contention is that the presence of viable possibilities for complete justification should inform our understanding of the moral psychology behind dirty hands behavior. Given these possibilities, an explanation of the moral fallout of exception making by leaders may be best served by an appeal to the epistemic realities of leadership, not its metaphysical realities.

Identifying possibilities for full justification requires a rough categorization of dirty hands cases.[76] One way to categorize these cases

[75] Bruce J. Avolio alludes to group rationality in Avolio and Locke, "Different Philosophies of Leader Motivation," pp 175–178. For a defense of group rationality, see Andrew Oldenquist, "Group Egoism," in Markate Daly, ed., *Communitarianism: A New Public Ethics* (Belmont, CA: Wadsworth Publishing, 1994), pp. 255–267.
[76] My thinking about the categories has benefited greatly from Kenneth I. Winston's related typology in his "Necessity and Choice in Political Ethics: Varieties of Dirty Hands," in Daniel E. Wueste, ed., *Professional Ethics and Social Responsibility* (Lanham, MD: Rowman and Littlefield, 1994), pp. 37–66. See also Bernard

distinguishes leadership behavior on the basis of the parties potentially wronged by it. In some cases, leaders potentially wrong *other leaders* by engaging in behavior that deviates from generally applicable moral requirements. For example, we might expect this kind of behavior from leaders when it is necessary to undermine the efforts of those individuals with whom they compete for resources such as political power, financial support, or public opinion. There are also dirty hands cases in which *followers* themselves are potentially wronged. In these instances, collective ends demand that individual members be treated in ways prohibited by generally applicable moral requirements. Still other cases return us to the issue of potential wrongs done by leaders to genuine *outsiders*. Given standard assumptions about the nature of morality, the partiality required by this kind of dirty hands behavior makes it perhaps the most difficult to justify. However, as I shall argue in Section VI of this chapter, there is a standard line of justification for the potential wrongs in this category of cases, just as there are in the others.

Consider, first, cases in which other leaders are potentially wronged by leadership behavior that deviates from generally applicable moral requirements. Political realists from Machiavelli to Max Weber argue that such behavior is not so exceptional after all. On this view, one of the first lessons the political leader must learn is that "a ruler who does not do what is generally done, but persists in doing what ought to be done, will undermine his power rather than maintain it."[77] For politics is home to "many unscrupulous men"[78] or, more cynically put, "the world is governed by demons."[79] Despite the seeming amoralism implicit in such characterizations of political life, this version of realism has also been used to support the conclusion that political leaders who deviate from generally applicable moral requirements do no wrong, and therefore that they are fully justified in their behavior.[80] Under conditions of

Williams, "Politics and Moral Character," in his *Moral Luck: Philosophical Papers 1973–1980* (Cambridge: Cambridge University Press, 1981), pp. 54–70. According to Williams, "There are victims outside politics, and there are victims inside it who get worse than they could reasonably expect" (p. 61).

[77] Niccolò Machiavelli, *The Prince*, eds. Quentin Skinner and Russell Price (Cambridge: Cambridge University Press, 1988), p. 54.

[78] Machiavelli, *The Prince*, p. 54.

[79] Max Weber, "Politics as a Vocation," in H. H. Gerth and C. Wright Mills, eds., *From Max Weber: Essays in Sociology* (New York: Oxford University Press, 1946), p. 123.

[80] For example, see C. A. J. Coady, "Politics and the Problem of Dirty Hands," in Peter Singer, ed., *A Companion to Ethics* (Oxford: Blackwell Publishers, 1993), pp. 373–383. Coady writes, "The insight behind the accusation [that it is folly

extreme conflict and competition, where success requires adherence to behavior patterns not dissimilar to those found in a Hobbesian state of nature, leaders might be said to function beyond the scope of much of common morality, with the result that they are essentially unbound by its dictates. As Kenneth Winston makes the point, "[A] public official's obligations in a given situation depend crucially on what other people in the situation are doing. If others are acting badly, the ordinary rules of morality are no longer dispositive of what the official ought to do."[81]

It is worth noting that this justification for dirty hands behavior need not posit egoism as its starting point. In fact, egoistic assumptions might leave us wondering why some political leaders have to learn what Machiavelli seems to suggest they must – namely, how not to be good. The more general justificatory point being advanced is not based on "a limit in human motivation (the influence of self-interest)"[82] but rather on the premise that it is no significant exception to act against impartial moral constraints where partiality is the rule, regardless of whether it is the partiality of individual or group projects that supports the behavior. Understanding dirty hands behavior as aiming at a good beyond leaders themselves therefore strengthens the plausibility of the case for full justification in political contexts.[83] For one thing, non-egoistic motivational assumptions are relevant to the justification of leadership behavior that potentially wrongs followers themselves. This second category of dirty hands cases includes "[t]he public official [who] cannot always wait [for deliberation and consensus]. And since others may not agree, indeed may not even understand what is being proposed, prudent officials find it necessary sometimes to resort to manipulation, deception, even coercion – for the public good."[84] Justification of dirty hands behavior

---

to behave virtuously in such a situation] is that there is some fundamental point to morality which is undermined by the widespread non-co-operation of others" (p. 381). A parallel argument can be made in business contexts.

[81] Winston, "Necessity and Choice in Political Ethics," p. 39.

[82] Winston, "Necessity and Choice in Political Ethics," p. 39.

[83] Garrett points out that "[t]hose who are prone to write a blank check for political leaders often suggest that even if statesmen do evil, they are not acting in their own interests, after all, but in our own. Absent a selfish motive, therefore, we ought to go easy on them" ("Political Leadership and the Problem of 'Dirty Hands,'" p. 161).

[84] Winston, "Necessity and Choice in Political Ethics," p. 38. Winston calls this kind of contingency "empirical" to distinguish it from the "normative" contingency that characterizes the first category of cases (pp. 38–39). But there are important elements of normative contingency in this second set of cases as well, even though it is not the normative contingency that comes to bear on justification of dirty hands behavior toward other leaders.

toward followers thus turns on the truth of the assertion that it is ultimately *for the followers* that the leader acts as he does.

There are two main understandings of what it means to act *for followers*. On a purely interest-based reading, justification turns simply on the fact that it is *for their own good* that they are manipulated, deceived, and coerced in the circumstances at hand. Central to the argument for deviating from generally applicable moral requirements in these conditions is the claim that followers are the primary recipients of the benefits of the deviations. When the benefits to followers are great, or the costs of adhering to generally applicable moral requirements are very high, we might think that there is full justification for dirty hands behavior that potentially wrongs followers. However, there is also a consent-based understanding of what it means to act *for followers*. As Walzer says of the leader who gets his hands dirty, "He doesn't merely cater to our interests; he acts on our behalf, even in our name."[85] This line of argument allows us to say that the leader can represent or embody the beliefs and values of followers, not just their interests, when he deviates from generally applicable moral requirements.

The consent-based understanding thus takes the leader who potentially wrongs followers to be acting not only for their own good, but also in a way that is ultimately grounded in follower agency.[86] Within the social contract tradition, for example, leaders arguably act on the authority they are granted by followers themselves. Exposing the normative connection between follower agency and leadership behavior, Thomas Hobbes argues that "every particular man is author of all the sovereign doth; and consequently he that complaineth of injury from his sovereign, complaineth of that whereof he himself is author; and therefore ought not to accuse any man but himself; no nor himself of injury; because to do injury to one's self is impossible."[87] Even John Locke, who shows far greater care than Hobbes when it comes to the transfer of authority that would be needed to justify potential wrongs to followers, nevertheless defends the place of significant leader discretion or *prerogative*, suggesting that the people should "[permit] their rulers, to do several things of their own free choice, where the law was silent,

---

[85] Walzer, "The Problem of Dirty Hands," p. 162.

[86] Of course, these two often go together. It is because he acts for our own good that we consent. See David Schmidtz, *The Limits of Government: An Essay on the Public Goods Argument* (Boulder, CO: Westview Press, 1991), ch. 1.

[87] Adapted from Thomas Hobbes, *Leviathan*, ed. Richard Tuck (Cambridge: Cambridge University Press, 1991), p. 124.

and sometimes too against the direct letter of the law, for the public good."[88]

Is the consent-based argument similarly plausible as a justification for leadership behavior that potentially wrongs other leaders or outsiders?[89] It would be difficult to say of the first category of dirty hands cases that the leader who does a potential wrong to other leaders does it *for them*, on either meaning of this expression, but it does make sense to say that these particular recipients of dirty hands behavior knew what they were getting into when they chose political careers. While we certainly do not want to infer from this that leaders therefore deserve whatever bad treatment comes their way, we can conclude that the politician's case for moral complaint about the dirty hands behavior of other leaders is significantly weaker than the case for moral complaint by outsiders who are potentially wronged by these leaders. Perhaps this is because an appeal to consent is clearly out of place in this third category of dirty hands cases. There is no sense at all in which outsiders consent to potential wrongs connected to the exceptions that leaders make of themselves.[90] The absence of any consensual relationship or, for that matter, any connection to their interests, is just what makes them genuine outsiders. What would be helpful to an analysis of dirty hands behavior, then, is a plausible justificatory strategy for the third category of cases.

VI. JUSTIFYING PARTIALITY

One such strategy posits morally fundamental distinctions between members of one's own group, organization, or society – on the one hand – and individuals who lack such membership – on the other. Standard absolutist and consequentialist moral theories prohibit dirty hands behavior characterized by significant partiality simply because they cannot recognize the normative force of these distinctions.[91] But communitarian critics of liberal moral theory, of which Kantianism and utilitarianism are paradigm examples, charge that liberalism's

[88] Adapted from John Locke, *Two Treatises of Government*, ed. Peter Laslett (Cambridge: Cambridge University Press, 1988), p. 377.
[89] See Section V of Chapter 3.
[90] This is not to deny that such behavior might be justified on interest-based grounds, as part of a system that promotes general well-being.
[91] See A. John Simmons, "Too Much Patriotism?" Keynote Address, 2002 Meeting of the Virginia Philosophical Association.

commitment to impartiality is ultimately grounded in a mistaken view of moral identity and, as a result, generates a problematic account of the nature of our obligations to others.[92] Michael Sandel, for example, holds that "our roles are partly constitutive of the persons we are – as citizens of a country, or members of a movement, or partisans of a cause ... [T]he story of my life is always embedded in the story of those communities from which I derive my identity – whether family or city, tribe or nation, party or cause."[93] Drawing on the importance of these narratives, communitarian moral theory locates the source of our obligations in the "moral particularity" of the communities of which we are members.[94] As Alasdair MacIntyre puts it, "Detached from my community, I will be apt to lose my hold upon all genuine standards of judgment. Loyalty to that community, to the hierarchy of particular kinship, particular local community and particular natural community, is on this view a prerequisite for morality."[95]

By privileging loyalty to particular communities, communitarian moral theory offers an alternative account of morality's scope. In contrast to liberalism's adherence to impartiality, this moral theory allows for the types of variability in scope necessary for plausible justifications of dirty hands behavior. First, communitarian moral theory makes room for substantial role differentiation within the group, organization, or society. As a result of this differentiation, moral requirements can vary in their application to individual members. On the assumption that "what is good for me has to be the good for one who inhabits these roles,"[96] individuals in particular roles need not be seen as bound by all the same requirements that apply to individuals within other roles. For our purposes, the relevance of this line of argument is that leaders and followers are also typically understood to be distinguished from one another primarily by role differentiation. Communitarian moral theorists are therefore in a position to make sense of behavior in the second category of dirty hands cases by pointing to restrictions on the scope of moral requirements that apply more generally to followers. The claim

---

[92] See Alasdair MacIntyre, *After Virtue: A Study in Moral Theory*, 2nd edition (Notre Dame, IN: University of Notre Dame Press, 1981); and Michael J. Sandel, *Liberalism and the Limits of Justice* (Cambridge: Cambridge University Press, 1982).

[93] Michael J. Sandel, "Morality and the Liberal Ideal," *New Republic* 190 (May 7, 1984).

[94] Sandel, "Morality and the Liberal Ideal."

[95] Alasdair MacIntyre, "Is Patriotism a Virtue?" in Markate Daly, ed., *Communitarianism: A New Public Ethics* (Belmont, CA: Wadsworth Publishing, 1994), p. 312.

[96] MacIntyre, *After Virtue*, p. 220.

that a leader's deviations from these requirements potentially wrong followers incorrectly assumes "that the standpoint of the moral agent constituted by allegiance to these rules is one and the same for all moral agents."[97]

The second type of variability in morality's scope sanctioned by communitarian moral theory can be understood in terms of its denial of another claim central to liberalism – namely, that moral requirements that apply within one community offer equal protection to members of other communities. For example, MacIntyre endorses patriotism, which "requires that I strive to further the interests of my community and you strive to further those of yours."[98] In effect, the patriotic loyalty that he seems to have in mind precludes my seeing the moral requirements by which I am bound as protecting the interests of outsiders and their leaders in the same way that these requirements protect members of my own community. Patriotism can also be a morally appropriate response, MacIntyre thinks, to the fact that communities are differentiated by "rival and competing sets of beliefs about the best way for human beings to live."[99] Whether these conflicts between communities are ultimately rooted in the clash of interests or in contradictory beliefs and values, the communitarian position holds that "my allegiance to the community and what it requires of me – even to the point of requiring me to die to sustain its life – could not meaningfully be contrasted with or counterposed to what morality required of me."[100] Strictly interpreted, this view of the source of our obligations implies that we cannot make conceptual sense of the complaints of genuine outsiders in the third category of dirty hands cases.

Does this strategy for defending partiality show that the exceptions leaders make of themselves are fully justified after all? Put another way, is most dirty hands behavior ultimately reconcilable with the demands of the correct moral theory? Like other attempts to explain away the gravity of deviations from generally applicable moral requirements, the communitarian argument lends itself to the charge that it does not fully appreciate the problem of dirty hands. Most telling is the fact that it prompts us to ask why leaders still feel as though they have done at least some moral wrong when they make exceptions of themselves, even if

---

97 MacIntyre, "Is Patriotism a Virtue?" p. 310.
98 MacIntyre, "Is Patriotism a Virtue?" p. 309.
99 MacIntyre, "Is Patriotism a Virtue?" p. 310.
100 MacIntyre, "Is Patriotism a Virtue?" p. 312.

exception making is necessary for the good of the group. In this respect, communitarian attempts at reconciliation ignore what Bernard Williams calls "the moral remainder" or "the uncancelled moral disagreeableness" that often accompanies dirty hands behavior.[101] On Williams's argument, an acceptable analysis of dirty hands behavior must offer an explanation of the residual feelings to which it gives rise, in addition – that is – to an account of its moral status.

According to such advocates of dirty hands analyses, "the moral remainder" is best explained by metaphysical realities of leadership that determine the moral status of dirty hands behavior. Simply put, leaders feel regret and guilt as a result of the fact that these realities sometimes preclude full justification of their actions. But this explanation assumes that leaders have epistemological access to the metaphysical realities of leadership. When leaders experience such feelings, they would have to know that their behavior is neither fully justified nor fully unjustified. In other words, the analysis assumes not only that there are genuine dirty hands cases but also that leaders recognize when they are in them. As we have seen, however, there are distinct reasons for leaders to think that they might be fully justified in deviating from generally applicable moral requirements in each of the three categories of dirty hands cases. Without the assumption that leaders can identify genuine dirty hands cases, the psychological phenomena in question can be understood as a response to epistemic challenges inherent in all justificatory strategies.

The fact that there are alternative normative responses to partiality does not imply, then, that any of these reasons is sufficient for full justification of the exceptions that leaders make of themselves. What follows from these justificatory possibilities is that we cannot expect leaders in dirty hands cases to be in a position of epistemic certainty when it comes to a judgment of the extent to which their behavior is justified. So, even if such leaders believe that they have full justification, perhaps even based on one of these possibilities, there will also be competing reasons to think that they might well be wrong. Focusing on the capacity of leaders to recognize the risk that they are mistaken about what morality requires of them thus generates an alternative explanation of the feelings associated with dirty hands behavior. Rather than inferring that these feelings are necessarily the result of wrongdoing, we can see them as more mundane psychological responses to the epistemic realities of leadership. On this understanding of the problem of dirty hands, regret

---

[101] Williams, "Politics and Moral Character," p. 61.

and guilt can accompany a leader's dirty hands behavior because he cannot be certain that his behavior is fully justified.

Brian Rosebury makes the parallel point in the context of a discussion of moral luck, arguing that an agent's feelings "tell him that he may have been [wrong] in some respect not yet clear to him."[102] Indeed, we often expect this kind of response of the leader who must act in a difficult situation, and "we would think less of him (morally) if he had complete confidence in his reason and senses under such circumstances."[103] Moreover, this expectation stands even when we think that the leader is fully justified in his behavior. Just as it is for other moral agents, the emotional aspects of ethical reflection should impinge upon leaders well after a decision or action, especially when they are less than certain as to what the right decision or action would have been. Accordingly, we need not take the leader's residual feelings as "the only evidence he can offer us, both that he is not too good for politics and that he is good enough."[104] For the fact that he has them does not prove that he has done anything wrong; at most, it proves that he does not know that what he has done is right.

The counterclaim to this account is that leaders who engage in dirty hands behavior do not worry over whether they have done wrong; to the contrary, they are certain of it. Williams says of the cases that he has in mind that "the sense that a discreditable thing has been done is not the product of uncertainty, nor again of a recognition that one has made the wrong choice."[105] But being certain that one lacks full justification would not preclude uncertainty as to whether one has even limited justification for getting one's hands dirty. So an epistemic alternative to dirty hands analyses need not infer from a leader's certainty about his wrongdoing that he will be able to recognize those cases in which he has made "the wrong choice" and, accordingly, is fully unjustified in his behavior. This false dichotomy recalls the primary weakness of dirty hands analyses – namely, that there is little reason to expect that leaders will know when they are truly in circumstances in which they must do wrong in order to do right. Taking the epistemic realities of leadership seriously, leaders can admit this very real possibility while at the same

[102] Brian Rosebury, "Moral Responsibility and 'Moral Luck,'" *Philosophical Review* 104 (1995): 515. See also Terry L. Price, "Faultless Mistake of Fact: Justification or Excuse," *Criminal Justice Ethics* 12 (1993): 22–24.

[103] Rosebury, "Moral Responsibility and 'Moral Luck,'" p. 515.

[104] Walzer, "The Problem of Dirty Hands," pp. 167–168.

[105] Williams, "Politics and Moral Character," pp. 59–60.

time thinking – mistakenly perhaps – that they have done the best that they can do.

An appeal to uncertainty at this level further contributes to an explanation of the feelings associated with dirty hands behavior. A leader's knowing that he has done the best that he can do – as dirty hands analyses would have it – is only slightly more compatible with feelings of regret and guilt than is his knowing that he is fully justified. For if we assume that the leader knows that he has done the best he can do, then we might also ask in such cases why he experiences regret and guilt, where these feelings are understood in terms of Strawsonian self-reactive attitudes,[106] as opposed to something such as objective disappointment in the fact that "no overarching viewpoint exists from which the duties generated by . . . separate spheres can be compared and weighed against one another."[107] A leader's uncertainty with respect to whether he has even limited justification makes straightforward sense of these feelings. In fact, even realist accounts of dirty hands behavior resort to this kind of explanatory appeal. For example, Walzer concedes that part of the reality for political leaders is that "[t]hey override the rules without ever being certain that they have found the best way to the results they hope to achieve,"[108] and Winston's characterization of realism moves unsystematically between the metaphysical commitment that "moral justification is not unitary" and the epistemological point that the presence of tragic choices "reveals a limit in human rationality."[109]

What are the implications of the view that leaders have only limited epistemic access to the justificatory force of moral reasons that guide their behavior? The problem of dirty hands generates a second epistemic argument for the claim that leaders should adhere to generally applicable moral requirements. If leaders cannot recognize genuine dirty hands cases, then they can hardly appeal to the fact that they are indeed in them for limited justification of the exceptions they make of themselves. It does not help, of course, that advocates of dirty hands analyses have very little to say about the frequency of cases in which leaders must do some wrong in order to do right, compared with cases in which deviations from generally applicable moral requirements would

---

[106] Peter Strawson, "Freedom and Resentment," in John Martin Fischer and Mark Ravizza, eds., *Perspectives on Moral Responsibility* (Ithaca: Cornell University Press, 1993), pp. 45–66.
[107] Winston, "Necessity and Choice in Political Ethics," p. 42.
[108] Walzer, "The Problem of Dirty Hands," pp. 179–180.
[109] Winston, "Necessity and Choice in Political Ethics," p. 39.

be fully justified or fully unjustified. The most ever offered on this score is that "many men have faced [the dilemma of dirty hands], or *think they have*"[110] and that it is "part of the business: not too often part of the business, one hopes, but part of the business all the same."[111] Determining a normative response to leaders who suspect they are in dirty hands cases may thus be more important than determining whether there really is a dilemma of dirty hands and, moreover, whether it is part of the business of leadership after all.

[110] Walzer, "The Problem of Dirty Hands," p. 161, emphasis added.
[111] Williams, "Politics and Moral Character," p. 60.

Chapter 5

The Ethics of Authentic Transformational Leadership

I. INTRODUCTION

In Act 1, Scene 3 of Shakespeare's *Hamlet*, Polonius councils Laertes: "This above all, to thine own self be true ... "[1] Polonius's endorsement of authenticity is certainly no stranger to the leadership literature. Warren Bennis and Burt Nanus, for example, tell us that "[l]eaders acquire and wear their visions like clothes. Accordingly, they seem to enroll themselves (and then others) in the belief of their ideals as attainable, and their behavior exemplifies the ideas in action."[2] Similarly, Gilbert Fairholm claims that "[t]he leader's task is to integrate behavior with values,"[3] and Ronald Heifetz encourages "[a]daptive work ... to diminish the gap between the values people stand for and the reality they face."[4] John Gardner, in his book *On Leadership*, articulates the ethic behind the Shakespearean dictum this way: "One of the tasks of leadership – at all levels – is to revitalize those shared beliefs and values, and to draw on them as sources of motivation for the exertions required of the group."[5]

Reprinted with revisions from Terry L. Price, "The Ethics of Authentic Transformational Leadership," *Leadership Quarterly* 14 (2003): 67–81, Copyright © 2003 Elsevier. Reprinted with permission from Elsevier.

[1] William Shakespeare, *The Complete Works of William Shakespeare* (Cambridge: Cambridge University Press, 1987), p. 837 [78].

[2] Warren G. Bennis and Burt Nanus, *Leaders: The Strategies for Taking Charge* (New York: Harper and Row Publishers, 1985), p. 46.

[3] Gilbert W. Fairholm, *Perspectives on Leadership: From the Science of Management to Its Spiritual Heart* (Westport, CT: Quorum Books, 1998), p. 57.

[4] Ronald A. Heifetz, *Leadership Without Easy Answers* (Cambridge, MA: Belknap Press of Harvard University Press, 1994), p. 22.

[5] John W. Gardner, *On Leadership* (New York: Free Press, 1990), p. 191.

On each of these views, leadership puts behavior in line with values so that we might be true to ourselves.

Even the most influential moral treatise in the field, James MacGregor Burns's *Leadership*, can be read as an argument about the kinds of selves to which leaders should be true. "That people can be *lifted* into their better selves," Burns tells us, "is the secret of transforming leadership . . ."[6] In fact, it is the possibility of this kind of transformation that gives leadership its moral purpose. On Burns's normative account of leadership, "The leader's fundamental act is to induce people to be aware or conscious of what they feel – to feel their true needs so strongly, to define their values so meaningfully, that they can be moved to purposeful action."[7] In its characterization of the self to which we should be true, transforming leadership thus contrasts sharply with *transactional leadership*. Whereas transforming leadership raises leaders and followers to "higher levels of motivation and morality,"[8] transactional leadership takes the selves to which we should be true simply as given. The transactional leader "recognizes the other [party to the exchange] as a *person*. Their purposes are related, at least to the extent that the purposes stand within the bargaining process and can be advanced by maintaining that process. But beyond this the relationship does not go."[9] In other words, transactional leadership adopts a markedly uncritical view of the selves engaged in these exchanges, appealing to leaders and followers simply as they are, whatever their desires and preferences might be and regardless of their perhaps questionable normative force.

This means that transformational leadership will fare better than transactional leadership on what Burns calls "the ultimate test of moral leadership": Leadership must have the "capacity to transcend the claims of the multiplicity of everyday wants and needs and expectations."[10] In this chapter, however, I challenge an assumption underlying this test – namely, that we need worry about the ethics of transformational leadership only when desires and preferences compete with morality. As with all theories that lean heavily on volitional understandings of ethical failure, the theory of transformational leadership underestimates the complexity of the moral psychology of leaders. First, this theory

---

[6] James MacGregor Burns, *Leadership* (New York: Harper and Row Publishers, 1978), p. 462.
[7] Burns, *Leadership*, p. 44.
[8] Burns, *Leadership*, p. 20.
[9] Burns, *Leadership*, pp. 19–20.
[10] Burns, *Leadership*, p. 46.

misses the fact that the threats to ethical leadership cannot be reduced to egoism. Second, it ignores one of the primary cognitive challenges that leadership brings with it: Leadership can induce and maintain a leader's belief that he is somehow excepted from moral requirements that apply more generally to the rest of us. Here, for example, I have in mind prohibitions on manipulating rational agents, on using oppressive means to secure legitimate ends, and on harming innocents. Even transformational leaders can come to believe that they are justified in violating these prohibitions. Such leaders fail to do what they should do, not because of self-interest, but because they think that generally applicable moral requirements are overridden by the other-regarding values to which they are committed. The conclusion that this chapter draws, therefore, is that transformational leadership can be morally troublesome regardless of whether the leaders who exercise it are true to their better selves.

II. TRUTH TO SELF

The ethical critique of transactional leadership turns on the claim that we often have desires and preferences with which we would not want to identify ourselves for the purposes of moral evaluation. It is not my self, or – better – the self to which I want to be true, that desires to pummel the discourteous driver on my way home from work or to skip my workout for a cold beer when I get there. If my self were to be identified with any of my desires in these cases, one would think that the identification should fix upon my desires to show patience and compassion toward strangers and a firm commitment to my exercise regimen. With good reason, then, we should expect leaders to do more than respect just what we say we want. In fact, we justifiably hold them blameworthy when they pander to our baser motivations – for example, when they appeal to our greed, our jingoism, or our cowardice. Moral leadership implies a responsibility to look beyond the uninformed preferences and desires of followers. The difficulty, though, is in finding a way to distinguish between those desires with which identification is appropriate and those desires from which we might be normatively inclined to distance ourselves.[11]

---

[11] This paragraph draws on Douglas A. Hicks and Terry L. Price, "An Ethical Challenge for Leaders and Scholars: What Do People Really Need?" in the *Selected Proceedings of the Leaders/Scholars Association* (College Park, MD: James MacGregor Burns Academy of Leadership, 1999), pp. 53–61.

Philosophers sometimes mark off our better selves by distinguishing between first-order and second-order desires.[12] First-order desires are desires to engage in particular forms of action – for instance, to eat certain foods, to take part in certain activities, and to have certain material goods. But these are not the only kind of desires that we have. As Harry Frankfurt explains, "Besides wanting and choosing and being moved *to do* this or that, [we] may also want to have (or not to have) certain desires and motives."[13] On this distinction, second-order desires have not actions, but other desires, as their content. Frankfurt's way of identifying our better selves accounts for the fact that we can have desires to do violence to rude strangers or to act contrary to the demands of healthy living, while at the same time desiring that we not have desires to do these things. In this way, the selves to which we should be true can be associated with our second-order desires and disassociated from those first-order desires that do not lend themselves to higher-level endorsement. Truth to self requires that our first-order desires and, more importantly, the actions based on those desires, accord with the results of a higher-level evaluation of the motives potentially issuing in action.[14] Put another way, we are true to ourselves when our effective desires, the desires that actually result in action, are in line with our second-order desires.

We might ask, however, what is it that privileges our higher-order desires? What gives them the normative force necessary for a characterization of the self to which we should be true? After all, they are still merely desires. Second-order desires need to be set off normatively not only from the first-order desires below them but also from higher-order desires above them. On this point, Gary Watson writes that "[i]t is unhelpful to answer that one makes a 'decisive commitment,' where this just means that an interminable ascent to higher orders is not going to be permitted. This *is* arbitrary."[15] In Frankfurt's more recent work, his response to this objection has been to argue that an interminable ascent to ever higher-order desires is unnecessary. We sometimes decide to cut off deliberation at a level of particular higher-order desires because (1) we think that we are correct to do so, or (2) we think that the benefits

---

[12] Harry G. Frankfurt, "Freedom of the Will and the Concept of a Person," *Journal of Philosophy* 68 (1971): 5–20.

[13] Frankfurt, "Freedom of the Will," p. 7.

[14] Frankfurt calls these higher-order desires "second-order volitions" ("Freedom of the Will," p. 10).

[15] Gary Watson, "Free Agency," *Journal of Philosophy* 72 (1975): 218.

of making the correction would not outweigh the costs of further deliberation. But Watson holds that a non-arbitrary distinction must draw on a distinct *source* of motivation. Here, Watson appeals to the notion of an agent's *values*: "those principles and ends which he – in a cool and non-self-deceptive moment – articulates as definitive of the good, fulfilling, and defensible life."[16] It is our "valuational system," Watson thinks, that must ultimately drive a normative assessment of our desires.[17] On this view, our normatively relevant selves, the selves to which we should be true, are identified with our valuational systems.

Frankfurt likens the process of desire assessment to an agent's mathematical calculation: "[A] sequence of calculations might end because . . . he is unequivocally confident that this result is correct, and therefore believes that there is no use for further inquiry. Or perhaps he believes that even though there is some likelihood that the result is not correct, the cost to him of further inquiry – in time or in effort or in lost opportunities – is greater than the value to him of reducing the likelihood of error."[18] It seems, however, that Frankfurt's comparison simply concedes the main point of Watson's argument for the place of an agent's values in desire assessment. How can we decide, in a non-circular fashion, that we have happened upon the correct higher-order desires, unless we appeal to something outside of the set of our higher-order desires, for example, to our values? Similarly, a determination of whether to bear the costs of further deliberation requires that assumptions be made about the value of continuing the process. These assumptions cannot be made on the basis of the higher-order desires, since it is their very legitimacy that is in question. In other words, both of Frankfurt's methods for privileging particular higher-order desires make an implicit appeal to an agent's values. If this is right, Frankfurt's response supports the value-based account, not his own desire-based account.

The values-based account of the self offers a way to ground the distinctively moral agenda of transforming leadership. By identifying our better selves not with desires and preferences but with values that lead to the satisfaction of real need, transforming leaders work from the perspective of these values to get us to act on our better selves. Or, as Bernard

[16] Watson, "Free Agency," p. 215.
[17] Watson, "Free Agency," p. 215.
[18] Harry G. Frankfurt, "Identification and Wholeheartedness," in Ferdinand Schoeman, ed., *Responsibility, Character, and the Emotions: New Essays in Moral Psychology* (Cambridge: Cambridge University Press, 1987), p. 36.

Bass puts it, they achieve the requisite transformation "[b]y raising our level of awareness, our level of consciousness about the importance and value of designated outcomes, and ways of reaching them."[19] Advocates of transformational leadership must assume, then, that leaders have knowledge of the value levels to which followers should be raised.[20] Unlike followers, transformational leaders know the importance and value of designated outcomes, and they use this knowledge to transform followers into their better selves. When untransformed followers fail to act in accord with what really is valuable, their behavior can thus be attributed to ignorance about what values ought to be pursued. In Burns's language, followers sometimes act on what they want because they do not know what it is they need. Getting followers to be true to themselves, according to Bass, "requires a leader with vision, self-confidence, and inner strength to argue successfully for what he sees is right or good, not for what is popular or is acceptable according to the established wisdom of the time."[21]

An analysis of the ethics of transformational leadership will therefore be closely connected to the question of why leaders behave immorally. As we have seen in earlier chapters, the standard view in applied ethics and moral theory holds that ethical failure should be attributed to problems of will, not to problems of belief and knowledge: Even though we have epistemic access to the requirements of morality, we are moved by self-interest to do something other than what we know we morally ought to do.[22] Indeed, it is easy to see why advocates of transformational leadership would be committed to this account of ethical failure. By hypothesis, transformational leadership *"operates at need and value levels higher than those of the potential follower."*[23] As such, its leaders "are distinguished by their quality of *not* necessarily responding to the wants of 'followers,' but to wants transformed into needs. Leaders respond to subjective wants and later to more objective needs *as leaders define those*

[19] Bernard M. Bass, *Leadership and Performance Beyond Expectations* (New York: Free Press, 1985), p. 20.

[20] Joseph C. Rost, *Leadership for the Twenty-First Century* (New York: Praeger, 1991), pp. 123–128.

[21] Bass, *Leadership and Performance*, p. 17.

[22] In the leadership literature, see Michael R. Carey, "Transformational Leadership and the Fundamental Option for Self-Transcendence," *Leadership Quarterly* 3 (1992): 217–236; and Michael Keeley, "The Trouble with Transformational Leadership: Toward a Federalist Ethic for Organizations," in Joanne B. Ciulla, ed., *Ethics, the Heart of Leadership* (Westport, CT: Praeger, 1998), pp. 111–144.

[23] Burns, *Leadership*, p. 42.

wants and needs."[24] So, advocates of this form of leadership are inclined to infer that when transformational leaders fail ethically, it is not because these leaders are mistaken about what morality requires of them. Rather, it must be because they selfishly choose to act in ways they know they should not. The validity of this inference, as well as an analysis of the ethics of transformational leadership, rests on the acceptability of the volitional account of ethical failures in leadership.

III. AUTHENTIC TRANSFORMATIONAL LEADERSHIP

Bernard Bass and Paul Steidlmeier distinguish between *authentic* transformational leadership and *inauthentic* or *pseudo*-transformational leadership. Following Burns, they suggest that transformational leadership must be grounded in "a moral foundation of legitimate values."[25] To articulate the notion of legitimacy, Bass and Steidlmeier claim that authentic transformational leadership is characterized by behavior that is "true to self and others."[26] This characterization signals that authenticity is indexed to values that reflect more than just the interests of leaders. As Bass and Steidlmeier make the argument, "[T]he exclusive pursuit of self-interest is found wanting by most ethicists. Authentic transformational leadership provides a more reasonable and realistic concept of self – a self that is connected to friends, family, and community whose welfare may be more important to oneself than one's own."[27] Accordingly, this form of leadership can be understood as representing "an *ideal moral type*"[28] against which the behavior of leaders can be judged at the level of character, the values they pursue, and the processes in which they engage with followers.[29]

---

[24] Burns, *Leadership*, p. 69, emphasis added.

[25] Bernard M. Bass and Paul Steidlmeier, "Ethics, Character, and Authentic Transformational Leadership Behavior," *Leadership Quarterly* 10 (1999): 184. See Burns, *Leadership*.

[26] Bass and Steidlmeier, "Authentic Transformational Leadership Behavior," p. 191.

[27] Bass and Steidlmeier, "Authentic Transformational Leadership Behavior," pp. 185–186.

[28] Bass and Steidlmeier, "Authentic Transformational Leadership Behavior," p. 191.

[29] Bass and Steidlmeier, "Authentic Transformational Leadership Behavior," p. 182. Historically, this view of authenticity is probably better attributed to thinkers such as Rousseau and Marx than to thinkers such as Heidegger and Sartre. Bass and Steidlmeier reference Sartre's notion of "bad faith" to articulate the kind of behavioral consistency they have in mind. But Sartre's commitment to autonomous choice hardly supports their strongly communal ethic. See Bass and

The fact that authentic transformational leadership looks to "commitments beyond the self"[30] does not mean that there is agreement between the values of leaders and followers. Being true to self and others, that is, is not meant to imply that the actions of leaders will conform to the values that followers actually hold. Followers may fail to recognize the values advocated by authentic transformational leaders as reflecting their interests, and there is no guarantee that followers will eventually come to this recognition. After all, it is the goal of this form of leadership to transform people so that they might accurately identify their real interests as members of a group, organization, or society, and come to accept the values that would serve to advance these interests. A commitment to authenticity, then, does not directly address inequalities in power that might allow transformational leaders to impose their values on others, especially on those with minority interests.[31] Rather, what such a commitment does ensure is that a leader will pursue "a cause that transcends . . . her individual egoistic needs, a cause that benefits the larger community."[32]

Bass and Steidlmeier recognize that because the components of transformational leadership are themselves morally neutral, the theory must constrain the ways in which transformational leaders can be legitimately motivated. In this respect, their argument for authentic transformational leadership concedes Michael Carey's point that when "the gifts of charisma, inspiration, consideration and intellectual strength are abused for the self-interest of the leader, the effect on followers ceases to be liberating and moral, and becomes instead oppressive and ideological."[33] Here, Bass and Steidlmeier draw upon the work of Howell and Avolio, claiming that "only socialized leaders concerned for the common good can be truly transformational."[34] Authentic transformational leadership therefore guards against abuses of self-interest by requiring that leaders

Steidlmeier, "Authentic Transformational Leadership Behavior," p. 184; and Jean-Paul Sartre, *Being and Nothingness: An Essay on Phenomenological Ontology*, trans. Hazel E. Barnes (New York: Philosophical Library, 1956).

[30] Gardner, *On Leadership*, p. 190.

[31] Keeley, "The Trouble with Transformational Leadership."

[32] Jean Lipman-Blumen, *Connective Leadership: Managing in a Changing World* (Oxford: Oxford University Press, 1996), p. 245.

[33] Carey, "Transformational Leadership," p. 232.

[34] Bass and Steidlmeier, "Authentic Transformational Leadership Behavior," p. 186. See Jane M. Howell and Bruce J. Avolio, "The Ethics of Charismatic Leadership: Submission or Liberation?" *Academy of Management Executive* 6, 2 (1992): 43–54.

Behavior

		Congruent	Incongruent
Values	Altruistic	Authentic Transformational Leadership (1)	Incontinent Pseudo-Transformational Leadership (2)
	Egoistic	Base Pseudo-Transformational Leadership (3)	Opportunistic Pseudo-Transformational Leadership (4)

FIGURE 5.1. A two-dimensional framework for authentic and pseudo-transformational leadership. Reprinted from: Price, Terry L., "The Ethics of Authentic Transformational Leadership," *Leadership Quarterly* 14 (2003): 67–81. Copyright © 2003 Elsevier. Reprinted with permission of Elsevier.

act on socialized, as opposed to personalized, power motives.[35] As Bass and Steidlmeier put it, "The authentic are inwardly and outwardly concerned about the good that can be achieved for the group, organization, or society for which they feel responsible."[36] In other words, only when the values from which leaders act are altruistic in content can we assume that their leadership is morally legitimate. The relationship between the values and behavior of authentic transformational leadership is illustrated in quadrant 1 of Figure 5.1.

[35] Jane M. Howell, "Two Faces of Charisma: Socialized and Personalized Leadership in Organizations," in Jay A. Conger, Rabindra N. Kanungo, and Associates, eds., *Charismatic Leadership: The Elusive Factor in Organizational Effectiveness* (San Francisco: Jossey-Bass Publishers, 1988), pp. 213–236.

[36] Bass and Steidlmeier, "Authentic Transformational Leadership Behavior," p. 188.

Transformational leadership is inauthentic when leaders lack a commitment to altruistic values or behave in ways that are out of line with these values. As we might expect from Bass and Steidlmeier's understanding of authenticity, the inauthenticity that characterizes pseudo-transformational leadership is ultimately grounded in failures of volition. Although pseudo-transformational leaders know what they ought to do given the other-regarding values they sometimes claim to accept, such leaders act against these values for the sake of self-interest. Bass and Steidlmeier suggest, for example, that pseudo-transformational leaders are "predisposed toward self-serving biases."[37] Most obviously, this motivational predisposition undercuts a leader's authenticity in either of two ways: It can lead him to be untrue both to self and to others or, alternatively, to be true to self but untrue to others. Aristotle would call these pseudo-transformational leaders "incontinent" and "base," respectively, and he makes the relevant distinction this way: "In fact the incontinent person is like a city that votes for all the right decrees and has good laws, but does not apply them . . . The base person, by contrast, is like a city that applies its laws, but applies bad ones."[38]

Corresponding to Aristotle's distinction, we can derive two versions of pseudo-transformational leadership. On the first version, pseudo-transformational leaders have at least some commitment to altruistic values but, nevertheless, act against them to satisfy self-interest. Accordingly, we can call them *incontinent pseudo-transformational leaders* and depict the relationship between their values and their behavior in quadrant 2 of Figure 5.1. Although incontinent pseudo-transformational leaders can be motivated by values that reflect the interests of others, these values are sometimes insufficient for motivation when there is a strong temptation to act egoistically. Perhaps Bass and Steidlmeier would appeal to this version of pseudo-transformational leadership to make sense of how leaders who "see themselves as honest and supportive of their organization's mission" can nevertheless act in ways that are "inconsistent and unreliable."[39] At least some of Bill Clinton's presidency might be understood by appeal to this way of thinking about pseudo-transformational leadership. It appreciates the fact that temptations to deviate from altruistic values can be very strong for leaders,

---

[37] Bass and Steidlmeier, "Authentic Transformational Leadership Behavior," p. 190.
[38] Aristotle, *Nicomachean Ethics*, trans. Terence Irwin (Indianapolis: Hackett Publishing Company, 1985), p. 197 [1152a20–1152a24].
[39] Bass and Steidlmeier, "Authentic Transformational Leadership Behavior," p. 187.

especially when the by-products of success undermine normal incentives to behave morally.[40]

On the second version of pseudo-transformational leadership, leaders are committed to egoistic values, and their actions reflect these values. Such leaders can be referred to as *base pseudo-transformational leaders*, and the relationship between their values and their behavior is represented in quadrant 3 of Figure 5.1. There is a sense in which the base pseudo-transformational leader is true to self, but the problem is that he is true to "an inner self that is false to the organization's purposes."[41] To the extent that egoistic values were behind the utilization of questionable partnerships at Enron, company executives might be characterized in terms of this version of pseudo-transformational leadership. On this motivational assumption, the allegation that Enron executives inflated profits to get rich at the expense of stockholders and employees is unsurprising given the values to which they were committed. It is for this reason that we might be inclined to attribute their behavior to baseness, not incontinence. Unlike leaders on the first version of pseudo-transformational leadership, that is, these leaders hold what are ultimately the wrong values.

A third version of pseudo-transformational leadership falls outside of the Aristotelian framework. On this version, leaders sometimes act in ways that advance the interests of others. However, when they so act, their concern for these interests is merely instrumental. In other words, pseudo-transformational leaders of this sort are motivated to act in accord with what seem to be altruistic values because of a contingent connection between this kind of behavior and their own egoistic values. As such, we can label them *opportunistic pseudo-transformational leaders* and portray the relationship between their values and behavior in quadrant 4 of Figure 5.1. This way of thinking about pseudo-transformational leadership is consistent with a plausible interpretation of the behavior of religious charlatans such as Jim Bakker, and it is implicit in Bass and Steidlmeier's claim that pseudo-transformational leaders choose to do what is wrong when doing what is right "conflict[s] with their own narcissistic interests."[42] Ultimately, the real commitment of these leaders is to egoistic values. It turns out, though, that self-interest is often

---

[40] Dean C. Ludwig and Clinton O. Longenecker, "The Bathsheba Syndrome: The Ethical Failure of Successful Leaders," *Journal of Business Ethics* 12 (1993): 265–273.
[41] Bass and Steidlmeier, "Authentic Transformational Leadership Behavior," p. 187.
[42] Bass and Steidlmeier, "Authentic Transformational Leadership Behavior," p. 189.

well served by behavior that has the appearance of having altruistic origins.[43]

All three versions of pseudo-transformational leadership assume the volitional account of ethical failures in leadership.[44] Ethically failed leaders recognize that their conduct is not grounded in altruistic values, but they engage in this conduct nonetheless in the belief that it is in their self-interest to do so. When incontinent pseudo-transformational leaders allow their desires and preferences to override their commitments, these leaders may be weak willed, but they are not mistaken about what they morally ought to do. Base pseudo-transformational leaders similarly put self-interest ahead of what they know to be altruistic values. In the case of these leaders, however, they do so because they subordinate altruistic values to the values of egoism. Opportunistic pseudo-transformational leaders who "mislead, deceive, and prevaricate"[45] must also be aware of the disparity between the values to which they espouse commitment and what really motivates their actions. Otherwise, they would be unable to take advantage of this disparity to satisfy their self-interest. On all three versions of pseudo-transformational leadership, then, ethical failure can be attributed to problems of will, not to problems of belief and knowledge. Opportunistic leaders care about "justice, equality, and human rights"[46] only when it is in their self-interest to do so; base leaders do not care about these values at all; and incontinent leaders simply care too little.

IV. THE ETHICS OF AUTHENTICITY

Can transformational leaders fail ethically even when they are unwilling to deviate from the requirements of morality for the sake of self-interest? My critique of authenticity turns on the claim that the threats to morality cannot be reduced to egoism. Opposition to this claim is rooted perhaps in a standard assumption in many of the social sciences that human behavior, whether in its moral or immoral varieties, can be adequately explained by an appeal to self-interest. However, drawing on recent

---

[43] There is thus a sense in which the behavior of opportunistic pseudo-transformational leaders really is congruent with their egoistic values. My point, however, is that on the surface, this behavior, unlike the behavior of base pseudo-transformational leaders, looks congruent with altruistic values.

[44] But see Chapter 2 for an alternative account of self-interested leadership behavior.

[45] Bass and Steidlmeier, "Authentic Transformational Leadership Behavior," p. 188.

[46] Bass and Steidlmeier, "Authentic Transformational Leadership Behavior," p. 192.

social scientific research,[47] Miller and Ratner conclude that individual self-interest often has less explanatory power than do personal values and a concern for collective outcomes.[48] Put another way, people sometimes act on altruistic values for the good of their group, organization, or society. In fact, as we have seen, this is just what authentic transformational leadership must assume.[49] For the purposes of my analysis here, though, the question this assumption raises is whether altruistic values and a concern for collective outcomes can themselves compete with morality.

Jean Hampton introduces what can be taken to be alternative threats to morality in the following passage:

> Normally, one opposes morality for the sake of self-interest, which may or may not be rationally tutored. This is why the question, 'Why are we immoral?' is so naturally answered by saying, 'Because we're selfish.' A legal norm might also come to oppose the moral authority, and the agent might be tempted to serve that norm, rather than the more important moral norm. Whatever the source of temptation, the agent gives into it when he installs that source over morality as her reason-giving authority.[50]

The most obvious way of reading this passage is to say that agents are tempted to serve norms that compete with morality because so doing promotes their self-interest. For example, a citizen obeys an unjust law to avoid punishment or, in keeping with office norms, a worker lies for a sexually predatory boss to avoid being fired.

It is worth noting that this understanding of the threats to morality makes their normative force purely derivative. People conform their behavior to competing norms because of a contingent connection between these norms and desire-satisfaction. In other words, these threats to morality have no independent normative force. Their force is derived from the fact that violating them would harm self-interest. But there is

---

[47] David O. Sears and Carolyn L. Funk, "Self-Interest in Americans' Political Opinions," in Jane J. Mansbridge, ed., *Beyond Self-Interest* (Chicago: University of Chicago Press: 1990), pp. 147–170; and Robyn M. Dawes, Alphons J. van de Kragt, and John M. Orbell, "Not Me or Thee but We: The Importance of Group Identity in Eliciting Cooperation in Dilemma Situations: Experimental Manipulations," *Acta Psychologica* 68 (1988): 83–97.

[48] Dale T. Miller and Rebecca K. Ratner, "The Power of the Myth of Self-Interest," in Leo Montada and Melvin J. Lerner, eds., *Current Societal Concerns about Justice* (New York: Plenum Press, 1996), p. 25.

[49] Bass and Steidlmeier, "Authentic Transformational Leadership Behavior," p. 188.

[50] Jean Hampton, "*Mens Rea*," *Social Philosophy and Policy* 7, 2 (1990): 16–17. Hampton's view is addressed at length in Chapter 2.

little reason to assume that people conform their behavior to norms that compete with morality simply on the basis of a link between these norms and desire-satisfaction. Indeed, we might expect that at least some individuals and groups will abide by competing norms even when so doing conflicts with the rational pursuit of self-interest. An extreme example is the behavior of the September 11 hijackers. The most straightforward explanation of such behavior is that people can believe that alternative norms, which in this particular case were quasi-religious norms, have authority over the norms of rationality and, as a consequence, require the sacrifice of self-interest.

More critical to the purposes of this chapter, people can mistakenly believe that these alternative norms have authority over generally applicable moral requirements. In some cases, we might want to attribute the cause of this kind of ignorance to features of the situation itself. Commenting on the Milgram experiments, John Doris suggests that "perhaps experimental pressures prevented some of his subjects from recognizing their situation as one where the moral demands for compassion towards the victims should override their obligation to help the experimenter."[51] Other cases suggest that subjects can believe that the importance of the good served by an alternative norm justifies an exception from a generally applicable moral requirement. As noted in Chapter 3, a follow-up to Darley and Batson's famous study "From Jerusalem to Jericho" found that a subject's perception of the importance of his task was significant with respect to whether he would help an individual in need.[52]

If moral authority can run up against alternative norms in just this fashion, then so too can generally applicable moral requirements come into conflict with "the good that can be achieved for the group, organization, or society for which [leaders] feel responsible."[53] Harry Truman almost certainly had the good of others in mind when he deviated from the moral prohibition on killing civilians and authorized the dropping of the atomic bomb on Hiroshima and Nagasaki. He later wrote in his

---

[51] John M. Doris, "Persons, Situations, and Virtue Ethics," *Noûs* 32 (1998): 511. For the original Milgram experiments, see Stanley Milgram, *Obedience to Authority; An Experimental View* (New York: Harper and Row, 1974).

[52] C. Daniel Batson, Pamela J. Cochran, Marshall F. Biederman, James L. Blosser, Maurice J. Ryan, and Bruce Vogt, "Failure to Help When in a Hurry: Callousness or Conflict?" *Personality and Social Psychology Bulletin* 4 (1978): 97–101. For the original study, see John M. Darley and C. Daniel Batson, "'From Jerusalem to Jericho': A Study of Situational and Dispositional Variables in Helping Behavior," *Journal of Personality and Social Psychology* 27 (1973): 100–108.

[53] Bass and Steidlmeier, "Authentic Transformational Leadership Behavior," p. 188.

memoirs that he "never had any doubt that it *should* be used," which gives us reason to think that he was sincere in the conviction that he was justified in making an exception of himself.[54] We might assume that Abraham Lincoln and Franklin Roosevelt were similarly motivated in their wartime efforts to circumvent Congress and public opinion.[55] Even if we grant that Lincoln, Roosevelt, and Truman were ultimately justified in their decisions, it can hardly be denied that all three faced significant tensions between generally applicable moral requirements and the other-regarding values to which they were committed.

On the assumption that authentic transformational leaders are not tempted to deviate from the requirements of morality because of self-interest alone, the search for potential sources of immorality thus fixes on the beliefs that these leaders hold about the normative force of their altruistic values. Specifically, it focuses on the belief that these values sometimes trump generally applicable moral requirements. When authentic transformational leaders fail ethically, they mistakenly believe that their behavior is justified in the end because the importance of "the good that can be achieved for the group, organization, or society for which they feel responsible"[56] outweighs the moral costs of deviating from these requirements. This consideration grounds the central ethical concern about authentic transformational leadership: Authenticity entails commitment to a type of good that too easily overrides the authority of morality. Even if authentic transformational leaders are unwilling to privilege their own desires and preferences, they might be perfectly willing to supplant generally applicable moral requirements in service of their other-regarding values.

Ethical success calls for more than authenticity since even authentic transformational leaders can be mistaken about what morality requires with respect to the pursuit of values that reflect the interests of others. Unlike pseudo-transformational leaders, that is, they can recognize not only the relevant moral requirement but also the authority of this requirement as it relates to their own desires and preferences and nonetheless be mistaken about its normative force in a given set of circumstances. Ethical failures in leadership thus result when authentic

---

[54] Jonathan Glover, *Humanity: A Moral History of the Twentieth Century* (New Haven: Yale University Press, 2000), p. 104, emphasis added.
[55] Bass and Steidlmeier, "Authentic Transformational Leadership Behavior," pp. 192, 198.
[56] Bass and Steidlmeier, "Authentic Transformational Leadership Behavior," p. 188.

transformational leaders overestimate the importance of their other-regarding values and, on the basis of this kind of error, make moral exceptions of themselves. In some cases (for example, Truman's decision to allow the deaths of hundreds of thousands of innocent people), respecting the relevant moral requirement would have protected non-group members from the leader's decisions. In other cases (for example, Mao Zedong's use of repression, torture, and execution to "raise the standards of health and literacy" and "to revive the revolutionary spirit of ordinary people"[57]), respecting the relevant moral requirement would have served to protect followers themselves.

When authentic transformational leaders are mistaken as to whether generally applicable moral requirements apply to them, they may appeal to their altruistic values in an attempt to distinguish themselves ethically from pseudo-transformational leaders. After all, their authenticity implies that they really do have a "strong attachment to their organization and its people."[58] Because of the justificatory force of this attachment, they can see their behavior as morally permissible, and perhaps even required. To the extent that followers share a leader's values and sanction the high level of commitment required by the ethics of authenticity, we can expect that they too will readily accept the justifications that he uses to make an exception of himself. In these cases, value congruence between leaders and followers exacerbates the moral risk of authentic transformational leadership. So it is indeed true that transformational leaders can "wear the black hats of villains or the white hats of heroes."[59] The problem, however, is that leaders and followers sometimes fail to see the color of their own hats.

V. THE JUSTIFICATORY FORCE OF LEADERSHIP

Why are authentic transformational leaders susceptible to cognitive errors that result in ethical failure? The answer to this question appeals to the general claim that leadership is bound up with the notion of justification and that this link structures the moral psychology of leaders. As we have seen, leadership brings with it special normative expectations about the importance of pursuing collective goals. These expectations play a justificatory role in the way that we think about leaders and in

---

[57] Glover, *Humanity*, p. 284.
[58] Bass and Steidlmeier, "Authentic Transformational Leadership Behavior," p. 187.
[59] Bass and Steidlmeier, "Authentic Transformational Leadership Behavior," p. 187.

the way that they think about themselves. For example, the most obvious way to assess leaders is by checking for consistency between their behavior and the collective goals to which their positions of leadership commit them. One relevant line of justification for their actions, then, is indexed to these goals. It is the tight connection between leadership and this line of justification that makes the ethics of authenticity so attractive to leadership studies in the first place. Authenticity puts leadership behavior in line with goals that represent the interests of the group, organization, or society.

Joanne Ciulla was the first to note that our definitions of leadership have always been rich in normative connotations. She argues that scholars who advance particular conceptions of leadership have been "sloppy about the language they use to describe and prescribe."[60] Descriptive claims are appropriate to an articulation of "technically good or effective" leadership, but prescriptive claims must be reserved for "morally good" leadership.[61] The temptation, of course, is to try to push the two together.

Are leaders more effective when they are nice to people, or are leaders more effective when they use certain techniques for structuring and ordering tasks? One would hope that the answer is both, but that answer is not conclusive in the studies that have taken place over the last three decades. The interesting question is What if this sort of research shows that you don't have to be kind and considerate to other people to run a country or a profitable organization? Would scholars and practitioners draw an *ought* from the *is* of this research?[62]

Here, Ciulla is concerned with the *ought* of morality, and she is correct to criticize leadership scholars who draw conclusions about what one morally ought to do from non-moral premises about effectiveness. But it is not quite right to say that non-moral premises about effectiveness are merely descriptive. Although attributions of "technically good" or effective leadership are not fundamentally moral claims, they are nonetheless normative claims. These claims attach to leaders who, in a very important way, do what they *ought* to do: realize collective goals they have set out to achieve with followers. So Ciulla's contention that "definitions of leadership have normative implications"[63] is even more to the point

---

[60] Joanne B. Ciulla, "Leadership Ethics: Mapping the Territory," in Joanne B. Ciulla, ed., *Ethics, the Heart of Leadership* (Westport, CT: Praeger, 1998), p. 13.
[61] Ciulla, "Mapping the Territory," p. 13.
[62] Ciulla, "Mapping the Territory," p. 14.
[63] Ciulla, "Mapping the Territory," p. 13.

than she seems to realize. In addition to its moral norms, leadership gives rise to norms of effectiveness, and these norms play a critical role in our understanding of ethical failures in leadership.

Expectations that leaders pursue goals that privilege group interests prove to be part and parcel of the moral psychology of leadership. As followers, we commonly expect leaders to put our needs first, and most leaders expect no less of themselves. Unfortunately, this connection between leadership and effectiveness also has its moral downside. As Ciulla puts it, "[T]he traits that make corporate America admire Jack Welch are the ones that contribute most to moral amnesia, such as intense focus on reaching the next quarter's corporate goals."[64] In other words, a leader's commitment to achieving collective goals can promote ethical failures in leadership in the same way that an individual's belief about the importance of his personal commitments can be an impetus to immoral behavior. This commitment explains why strongly impartial ethical theories such as utilitarianism threaten to undermine the ordinary exercise of leadership.[65] The ordinary exercise of leadership gives special attention to these interests, sometimes to the exclusion of serious concern for the interests of outsiders. Some leaders take these particularistic expectations on their behavior to have extraordinary normative force. For instance, in an effort to protect American officials and military personnel, the administration of George W. Bush argued for considerable exceptions to the newly ratified International Criminal Court. Other leaders conform their behavior to these expectations by simply redefining group membership. Under this description we can place the CEO who defends the claim that he is "morally justified by underscoring that the downsizing was necessary for the organization's survival and for the benefit of the remaining employees and other stakeholders."[66] Not all leaders readily engage in this kind of redefinition, but most would be hardly recognizable if they put the interests of outsiders on a par with the interests of the group.

The potential for conflict between this normative feature of leadership and the demands of morality means that an appeal to a leader's self-interest is not sufficient to fill out an account of ethical failures in leadership. Our understanding of such failures must also attend to the

---

[64] Joanne B. Ciulla, "Imagination, Fantasy, Wishful Thinking and Truth," *Business Ethics Quarterly*, special issue (1998): 102.
[65] See Chapter 4 (present book).
[66] Bass and Steidlmeier, "Authentic Transformational Leadership Behavior," p. 204.

conflict between norms of effectiveness and moral norms as this conflict is played out in leadership behavior. Only by attending to normative expectations that leaders privilege group interests can we make sense of the exceptions that we allow them and that they allow themselves. These expectations on their behavior are well articulated in Michael Walzer's argument that a political leader's "decision to run [is] a commitment (to all of us who think the election important) to try to win, that is, to do within rational limits whatever is necessary to win."[67] But the type of justification that Walzer has in mind is by no means limited to politics. Leaders across sectors use norms of effectiveness to justify exceptions to generally applicable moral requirements so that they can pursue collective goals, goals that ultimately represent *our* interests. To claim that a leader's behavior is justified in this particular sense is to imply that what he did was permissible according to, or more strongly required by, values that reflect the interests of the group. The justification appeals directly to these values in order to argue that the circumstances in which the leader deviated from a moral requirement are relevantly different from the circumstances in which this requirement typically applies.[68]

The force of the justification will depend on, among other things, just how exceptional we think a leader's circumstances really are. It may also depend on the truth of the claim that only he has what it takes to get the job done – that is, that he himself is exceptional. However, this claim will not be difficult to establish for many leaders since it is the fact that they are set apart from followers by virtue of their superior experience, motivation, and skills that puts them in positions of leadership in the first place. In the end, the exceptions we make for leaders on these grounds may be an integral part of the relationship between leaders and followers. As discussed in Chapter 4, E. P. Hollander's seminal work on social exchange holds that an emergent leader "achieves status [in the form of idiosyncrasy credits] by fulfilling common expectancies and demonstrating task competencies" and that "[a]s he continues to

[67] Michael Walzer, "Political Action: The Problem of Dirty Hands," *Philosophy and Public Affairs* 2 (1973): 165.
[68] For example, Richard B. Burrow, former head of the National D-Day Memorial Foundation, who allegedly "used a $3.3 million bank loan to obtain $4.2 million in state matching funds, while simultaneously using the state matching funds as collateral to obtain the bank loan," was nevertheless "hailed [by veterans] as the man responsible for the construction of the memorial that honors those who died in the June 6, 1944, Allied invasion of Normandy during World War II" (Rex Bowman, "Not-guilty plea given in D-Day fraud trial," *Richmond Times-Dispatch* [January 31, 2004]).

amass these credits he may eventually reach a threshold which permits deviation and innovation, insofar as this is perceived by others to be in the group's interests."[69] Given the perceived permissibility of these exceptions, it should come as little surprise to us that leaders sometimes make exceptions for themselves when it comes to generally applicable moral requirements. This kind of normative fluidity can support a leader's belief that he is removed from the scope of morality. Although he recognizes the general force of moral requirements as they are applied to others, he may fail to see that these requirements also apply to him.

The problem for such leaders, then, is not so much that they need something akin to moral imagination to "project alternative ways to frame experience and thus broaden, evaluate, and even change [their] moral point of view."[70] After all, leaders may be perfectly willing to use the appropriate ethical perspective to apply moral requirements to followers as well as to other leaders. So, for these cases at least, it will not be cognitively sufficient for ethical leadership "to get at a distance from a particular point of view or the point of view of one's colleagues, one's constituents, and/or the institutional or regulatory framework in which one is operating."[71] Sometimes, distance is the last thing that leaders need. Even one who "can disengage himself from the context of specific decisions, from his particular 'movie'"[72] and find the right "script" or mental model to frame a moral challenge can still be susceptible to cognitive errors that result in ethical failure. Such individuals may simply fail to put themselves in the lens of the camera.[73]

Whatever the normative expectations on leaders, they must recognize that the justificatory force of leadership often runs out when it comes up against generally applicable moral requirements. If the pursuit of goals that represent the interests of the group means that leaders need to deny legitimate moral demands that might be made by outsiders or by individual followers themselves, then – noble though their goals may

---

[69] E. P. Hollander, *Leaders, Groups, and Influence* (New York: Oxford University Press, 1964), p. 159.

[70] Patricia H. Werhane, *Moral Imagination and Management Decision-Making* (Oxford: Oxford University Press, 1999), p. 90.

[71] Patricia H. Werhane, "Moral Imagination and the Search for Ethical Decision-Making in Management," *Business Ethics Quarterly*, special issue (1998): 88.

[72] Werhane, *Moral Imagination and Management Decision-Making*, pp. 61–62.

[73] Robert A. Wicklund and Shelley Duval, "Opinion Change and Performance Facilitation as a Result of Objective Self-Awareness," *Journal of Experimental Social Psychology* 7 (1971): 319–342.

be – leaders should defer to these requirements. Generally applicable moral requirements are essential when it comes to protecting the interests of outsiders because their interests often fail to get incorporated into the values of leaders. These requirements can be equally important to the followers, though, especially on theories of leadership that recommend that leaders work from the perspective of values that followers might reject. So if leaders are to avoid ethical failure, they will sometimes have to defy normative pressures to privilege group interests. Even though these pressures are associated with leadership itself, they often fail to justify exceptions for leaders when it comes to generally applicable moral requirements.

VI. JUSTIFICATION AND AUTHENTIC TRANSFORMATIONAL LEADERSHIP

To what extent does the ethics of authentic transformational leadership contribute to normative expectations that compete with morality? The justificatory force associated with this kind of leadership is especially high, and accordingly so is the moral risk. First, authentic transformational leadership claims to foster "the modal values of honesty, loyalty, and fairness, as well as the end values of justice, equality, and human rights."[74] In contrast, "pseudo-transformational leadership endorses perverse modal values such as favoritism, victimization, and special interests and end values such as racial superiority, submission, and Social Darwinism."[75] What this way of drawing the line between ethical and unethical leadership ignores is that the modal and end values translate directly into moral behavior only when they are given real content. When it comes to the modal values, for example, we would be hard pressed indeed to determine what constitutes favoritism, victimization, and special interests without a particular conception of fairness from which to work.

A similar claim can be made with respect to end values. Even Jim Jones's Peoples Temple "opposed the divisions of modern society, and the invidious distinctions of racism, and favored instead a new communal ideology in which everyone would be treated equally and share in the common good."[76] Here, the more general point is that most leaders

---

[74] Bass and Steidlmeier, "Authentic Transformational Leadership Behavior," p. 192.
[75] Bass and Steidlmeier, "Authentic Transformational Leadership Behavior," p. 192.
[76] Charles Lindholm, *Charisma* (Cambridge, MA: Basil Blackwell, 1990), p. 138.

can be said to support the values of authentic transformational leadership. They disagree widely, however, on the specific demands of fairness as well as on what constitutes justice, equality, and human rights. This is where the real challenge of leadership lies, and to dismiss the importance of this challenge is to give leaders and followers false confidence in the normative force of their own value commitments. To be sure, the perversity of a leader's means or ends might well incline us properly to identify him as a pseudo-transformational leader. But Bass and Steidlmeier's formal characterization of moral means and ends creates something of a caricature of unethical leaders, and in doing so leaves us with an overly inclusive class of ethical leaders. It allows us to exclude leaders of Hitler's ilk but not much else. Ethical analysis must do more than identify the very worst leaders among us.

Second, authentic transformational leaders are set apart normatively from followers. For instance, when authenticity is assessed at the level of character, these leaders are to be compared to "the sage and the superior person [who] live under the restraint of virtue and aim to transform society accordingly. The common, inferior or small person either does not know or does not follow the way and is not a positive moral force."[77] Perhaps this is the critical distinction behind Bass and Steidlmeier's assertion that "[a]uthentic transformational leaders may have to be manipulative at times for what they judge to be the common good."[78] Put differently, these authors acknowledge that what is required by virtuous character and altruistic values will sometimes conflict with what followers take to be the morality of processes such as consent and consensus. As we have seen, this kind of exception making can result in ethical failures in leadership. This is true regardless of whether (and sometimes *because*) leaders are committed to the ethics of authentic transformational leadership.

Third, authentic transformational leadership generates normative expectations that are compatible with what Alice Eagly and Steven Karau call "the injunctive norms of gender roles."[79] Under these norms, "social perceivers . . . expect and prefer that women exhibit *communal* characteristics," specifically, that women demonstrate "concern with the welfare of other people" and that they are "affectionate, helpful, kind,

---

[77] Bass and Steidlmeier, "Authentic Transformational Leadership Behavior," p. 195.
[78] Bass and Steidlmeier, "Authentic Transformational Leadership Behavior," p. 186.
[79] Alice H. Eagly and Steven J. Karau, "Role Congruity Theory of Prejudice Toward Female Leaders," *Psychological Review* 109 (2002): 576.

sympathetic, interpersonally sensitive, nurturant, and gentle."[80] An appeal to role congruity theory thus helps to explain why it is generally hard for women to emerge from groups as leaders.[81] To put the findings in Hollander's language, women are more likely to face impediments in their attempts to move from the stage of conformity and competence to the stage of permissible deviation and innovation. But, as Eagly, Johannesen-Schmidt, and van Engen suggest in a later article, "Transformational leadership style may be congenial to women . . . because at least some of its components are relatively communal."[82] Given the resulting overlap between the normative expectations on women and the normative expectations of authentic transformational leadership, this form of leadership would make leader emergence relatively easier for women. In so doing, however, authentic transformational leadership puts women in a position to engage in the deviant and innovative behaviors indicative of leadership, behaviors generally considered to be male. An additional moral risk of this form of leadership, then, is that exception-making behavior by women leaders is more likely to meet

[80] Eagly and Karau, "Role Congruity Theory," pp. 574, 578, emphasis added. These components contrast with *"agentic* characteristics, which are ascribed more strongly to men . . . [and] describe primarily an assertive, controlling, and confident tendency – for example, aggressive, ambitious, dominant, forceful, independent, self-sufficient, self-confident, and prone to act as a leader" (p. 574).

[81] According to Eagly and Karau, "Leaders are expected not only to be competent but also to be appropriately confident and assertive. Therefore, behaving in this manner should help an individual gain influence and become a leader. However, a number of experiments have shown that achieving influence in this manner is more difficult for women than men, particularly when they deal with men" ("Role Congruity Theory," p. 584). Consider, for example, the case of Martha Stewart, who was convicted of lying to federal investigators about her sale of ImClone shares. Commenting on the conviction, Dan M. Kahan, professor at Yale Law School, points out that accusations that "Ms. Stewart was rude to underlings was a topic at her trial in a way that it might not have been had she been a male senior executive. 'A woman who lords it over other people and who asserts her authority is going to provoke a kind of resentment that a lot of men who do the same thing won't,' he said" (Jonathan D. Glater, "Stewart's Celebrity Created Magnet for Scrutiny," *New York Times* [March 7, 2004]).

[82] Alice H. Eagly, Mary C. Johannesen-Schmidt, and Marloes L. van Engen, "Transformational, Transactional, and Laissez-Faire Leadership Styles: A Meta-Analysis Comparing Women and Men," *Psychological Bulletin* 129 (2003): 573. See also Judy B. Rosener, "Ways Women Lead," *Harvard Business Review* 68 (November–December 1990). Rosener writes that female leaders describe themselves "in ways that characterize 'transformational' leadership – getting subordinates to transform their own self-interest into the interest of the group through concern for a broader goal."

the expectations of social perceivers because of the commitment that authentic transformational leaders show for communal ends.

This is not to say, of course, that women should not be leaders or engage in paradigmatic leadership behavior. Nor is it to suggest that leaders should no longer strive for communal ends grounded in particular conceptions of justice, equality, and human rights or even that we should reject authentic transformational leadership. It is rather to say that an appeal to authenticity will not resolve whatever ethical concerns we have about this normative conception of leadership. While it would be a mistake to deny the moral acceptability of a requirement that leadership behavior line up with values that reflect the interests of others, undue focus on issues of authenticity can actually promote unethical leadership. Explicitly stated, the theory of authentic transformational leadership misses the fact that leaders sometimes behave immorally precisely because they are blinded by these values. Virtuous though these leaders may be, their distinctive understandings of the collective good and of the processes necessary to achieve it must be constrained by generally applicable moral requirements. Burns is correct, then, that "[a] test of adherence to values is the willingness to apply principles or standards to oneself as well as to others."[83] But the more critical test may be one of adherence to morality. Leaders must be willing to sacrifice their other-regarding values when generally applicable moral requirements make legitimate demands that they do so.

[83] Burns, *Leadership*, p. 75.

Chapter 6

Change and Responsibility

I. INTRODUCTION

Change is often considered to be a defining characteristic of leadership. Referring to business contexts, John Kotter points out that "in almost every case, the basic goal has been the same: to make fundamental changes in how business is conducted."[1] Goss, Pascale, and Athos also grant the universality of this characterization of business leadership: "[E]xperienced businesspeople see the problem as 'leadership' because they see the solution as 'change.' And surely, they tell themselves, any leader deserving of that name can successfully implement change."[2] Commentators in political contexts are no less likely to forge a conceptual link between change and leadership, for instance, agreeing that "[t]he leadership process must be defined, in short, as carrying through from the decision-making stages to the point of concrete changes in people's lives, attitudes, behaviors, institutions."[3] In fact, change is so central to our understanding of this process that it is hard to see how our leaders might otherwise be identified. To make this more general point, James O'Toole draws parallels between political and business leadership

---

[1] John P. Kotter, "Leading Change: Why Transformation Efforts Fail," *Harvard Business Review on Change* (Boston: Harvard Business School Publishing, 1998), p. 2.

[2] Tracy Goss, Richard Pascale, and Anthony Athos, "The Reinvention Roller Coaster: Risking the Present for a Powerful Future," *Harvard Business Review on Change* (Boston: Harvard Business School Publishing, 1998), p. 85.

[3] James MacGregor Burns, *Leadership* (New York: Harper and Row Publishers, 1978), p. 414. More recently, Burns tells us that "[o]f all the tasks on the work agenda of leadership analysis, first and foremost is an understanding of human change, because its nature is the key to the rest" (*Transforming Leadership: A New Pursuit of Happiness* [New York: Atlantic Monthly Press, 2003], p. 17). Burns asks rhetorically: "Where does leadership begin? Where change begins" (p. 140).

and suggests that in both contexts leaders respond to "followers' natural resistance to change."[4] In essence, individuals who conform closely to what others are thinking or doing, thereby subjecting their behavior to the Millian "despotism of custom," betray their status not as leaders but as followers.[5]

Advocates of the conceptual connection between leadership and change sometimes go so far as to claim that this is what distinguishes leadership from management: "Good management brings a degree of order and consistency . . . Leadership, by contrast, is about coping with change."[6] Whether in groups, organizations, or societies, that is, leaders aim to help us move in a different direction, whereas managers – and, in the political sphere, bureaucrats – work to ensure that we stay the course indicated by our current ways of doing things. Of course, we should not make too much of this distinction. The different direction in which leadership aims to take us need not be a completely new one, since leaders can very well be proponents of tradition, urging that we return to old ways of thinking or culturally established ways of doing things. Nor would it be correct to say that managers and bureaucrats cannot exercise leadership or that leaders never need to manage and demonstrate the bureaucrat's commitment to fixed rules. Still, leadership implies recognition of something over and above the status quo – specifically, the possibility of doing things in a better way. In the background of the social phenomenon of leadership is recognition of the distinction between the way things are and they way things ought to be. This makes leadership a particularly unlikely response to complete satisfaction or contentment with the current state of affairs. Without awareness that descriptive realities and prescriptive possibilities might diverge, there would be little need for leadership and little reason to think that anyone would want to be a leader.

In preceding chapters, I have left open the possibility that leaders might sometimes be justified in making exceptions of themselves. Despite this possibility, I have argued that there are substantial epistemic reasons for leaders to adhere to generally applicable moral

---

4 James O'Toole, *Leading Change: The Argument for Values-Based Leadership* (New York: Ballantine Books, 1996), p. xi.
5 See O'Toole, *Leading Change*, ch. 12; and John Stuart Mill, *On Liberty*, ed. Elizabeth Rapaport (Indianapolis: Hackett Publishing Company, 1978), ch. 3.
6 John P. Kotter, "What Leaders Really Do," in J. Thomas Wren, ed., *The Leader's Companion: Insights on Leadership Through the Ages* (New York: Free Press, 1995) p. 115.

requirements.[7] Most important among these reasons is that the justificatory force of leadership inclines leaders to misjudge the importance of the goals they seek to achieve. Because of the tendency of leaders to overvalue collective ends and the interests these ends typically reflect, generally applicable moral requirements are necessary to prevent ethical failures in leadership. But imposing strong limits on the means to which leaders can appeal to achieve their ends makes my view fairly conservative. Simply put, it privileges rules and principles over results and, some might say, the status quo over change and progress. As such, the view so far articulated is not without potential moral costs of its own, especially when what is needed within society is moral change. If genuine moral progress requires deviations from generally applicable moral requirements, yet leaders are not permitted to make the necessary deviations, then the conservatism of my view prohibits what some would see as paradigmatic cases of moral leadership. Showing that the ordinary ends of leadership are not sufficient to justify exception making, that is, does not answer the question of how leaders should respond when they believe that exception making is necessary for the morally legitimate well-being and agency interests of followers or outsiders. What is moral leadership, one might ask, if not the willingness of leaders to stand up for their convictions and work to change society for the better?

This tension between moral progress and moral conservatism raises a serious problem for assessing responsibility in leadership.[8] Assuming that leaders can be in a position of epistemic uncertainty as to whether social change justifies their exception-making behavior, how can we blame leaders when they do the wrong thing thinking they are right? Just what should we expect of leaders by way of a response to the fact that justification is not always transparent? To generate behavioral checks on exception making for leaders, this chapter works from cases of social change for which issues of justification are now clear to us. My assumption, in other words, is that we now know whether the exception-making behavior in these cases was justified or unjustified. Working from these

---

[7] See, especially, Chapters 4 and 5 (this book).
[8] Irving L. Janis points to "the tendency for the collective judgments arising out of group discussions to become polarized, sometimes shifting toward extreme conservatism and sometimes toward riskier courses of action than the individual members would otherwise be prepared to take" (*Groupthink: Psychological Studies of Policy Decisions and Fiascoes*, 2nd edition [Boston: Houghton Mifflin Company, 1982], p. 5).

cases, I claim that we can derive moral reasons for leaders to restrict the exceptions they make of themselves to the pursuit of inclusive ends, to make both the exception-making behavior and the arguments for it reasonably public, to reserve the use of violence for those cases in which there is widespread support for these means even among outsiders, and to be willing to accept the penalty for their exception-making behavior. I do not claim, however, that these conditions are either necessary or sufficient for justification. Given my assumption that leaders sometimes face insurmountable epistemic barriers to making determinations of justification, I could hardly pretend to generate a unique set of behavioral requirements to ensure that leaders always do the right thing. Rather, what I offer is a normative response to these epistemic barriers, a response that allows leaders in some circumstances to elude attributions of responsibility when their exception-making behavior is unjustified.[9]

II. MORAL CORRECTION: SYMPATHY AND INCLUSIVENESS

Perhaps there are emotive correctives to generally applicable moral requirements that would signal when leaders are justified in making exceptions of themselves. Jonathan Bennett proposes one such corrective to morality, suggesting that feelings of sympathy should sometimes lead us to renounce strict adherence to principles.[10] Bennett's argument thus offers leaders an alternative to moral conservatism in the face of genuine epistemic uncertainty. Rather than rigidly conforming to generally applicable moral requirements, one must "keep [one's] morality open to revision, exposing it to whatever valid pressures there are – including pressures from [one's] sympathies."[11] To make this argument, Bennett first appeals to a central ethical crisis in Mark Twain's novel *Huckleberry Finn*. Based on the belief that "slave-owning is just one kind of ownership," Huck's conscience tells him that he should respect the property rights of slave-owners and turn his friend Jim over to the men hunting for runaway slaves.[12] In the end, Huck helps Jim escape, thereby deviating

---

[9] This argument reflects the idea that one can do the wrong thing but nevertheless not be blameworthy for one's unjustified behavior, an idea that is central to our blaming practices.

[10] Jonathan Bennett, "The Conscience of Huckleberry Finn," *Philosophy* 49 (1974): 123–134.

[11] Bennett, "The Conscience of Huckleberry Finn," p. 133.

[12] Bennett, "The Conscience of Huckleberry Finn," p. 125.

from what he takes to be a generally applicable moral requirement. According to Bennett, Huck does so because his sympathy prevents him from acting conscientiously on his moral principles. The pressures of sympathy, that is, serve to check "the conscience of Huckleberry Finn."

Bennett draws a sharp contrast between feelings of sympathy and beliefs about morality, noting that "[t]hese *feelings* must not be confused with *moral judgments*."[13] This distinction allows him to say that Huck's decision to help Jim does not in any way turn on his belief that it was the right thing to do. But notice that even if feelings of sympathy are not moral judgments, they are very often connected to these judgments and, specifically, to beliefs about who is protected, and to what extent, by moral requirements. Jonathan Glover makes this point in the context of his discussion of the moral psychology of waging war, noting that one way to weaken feelings of sympathy in close combat is "to distance the people on the other side."[14] In effect, by coming to believe that the enemy is fundamentally different from us, we are able to neutralize feelings of sympathy. On Bennett's view, feelings of sympathy are nevertheless cleanly differentiated from currently held moral beliefs: Huck feels sympathy for Jim, while at the same time seeing Jim as outside of the scope of the morality to which he is committed. For example, to support the claim that Huck's behavior does not ultimately rest on any belief about what is owed to Jim, Bennett says of Huck that "in his morality promises to slaves probably don't count."[15]

It is somewhat striking that Bennett rejects an explanatory appeal to Huck's beliefs about what he owes Jim, especially given that Huck decides not to turn Jim over to the slave hunters only when Jim tells him that he is "de on'y white genlman dat ever kep' his promise to ole Jim."[16] In fact, Huck's sense of obligation to Jim appears to do at least as much work in this scene as does Huck's sympathy. For instance, when Jim shares his plan to return and save his wife and children, Huck shows very little sympathy for Jim, thinking instead, "Here was this nigger which I had as good as helped to run away, coming right out flat-footed and saying he would steal his children – children that belonged to a man

[13] Bennett, "The Conscience of Huckleberry Finn," p. 124.
[14] Jonathan Glover, *Humanity: A Moral History of the Twentieth Century* (New Haven: Yale University Press, 2000) p. 50.
[15] Bennett, "The Conscience of Huckleberry Finn," p. 127.
[16] Bennett, "The Conscience of Huckleberry Finn," p. 126.

I didn't even know; a man that hadn't ever done me no harm."[17] In any case, whatever sympathy Huck has for Jim would seem to be predicated on what is at the very least a suspicion that Jim is part of the moral community and, as such, merits the protection of the moral requirements that prohibit promise breaking. Without having some cognizance of Jim's moral status, it is hard to see how Huck might feel sympathy for Jim in the first place.

In the passages cited by Bennett, Huck's strongest verbal expression of feeling toward another person is actually directed at Jim's owner, Miss Watson: "What had poor Miss Watson done to [me], that [I] could see her nigger go off right under [my] eyes and never say one single word?"[18] Bennett identifies Huck's self-reproach with conscience, but it is not clear why Huck's opinion of himself is not also connected to his sympathy for Miss Watson. Huck plainly has "a *feeling* for [her] in [her] plight."[19] As such, his emotional reaction toward Miss Watson fits neatly with Bennett's characterization of sympathy. Equally plain is the connection between Huck's feeling for Miss Watson and his belief that she is very much a member of the moral community and protected by its requirements – in particular, the property rules of the community. Of course, Huck's sympathy for Miss Watson is consistent with his having feelings of sympathy for Jim as well. Sympathy for both slaveholder and slave is just what we would expect if Huck really is caught between the cognitive commitments of two moralities. Yet the fact that Huck can feel sympathy for both Miss Watson and Jim means that he cannot easily use these feelings to check his moral principles. This is because feelings of sympathy well up within him not only when he thinks about deviating from property rules but also when he thinks about breaking his promise to Jim. It is no wonder, then, that Huck ultimately gives up on morality, insisting that "[i]t don't make no difference whether you do right or wrong, a person's conscience ain't got no sense, and just goes for him *anyway*."[20]

---

[17] Bennett, "The Conscience of Huckleberry Finn," p. 125.
[18] Bennett, "The Conscience of Huckleberry Finn," p. 125.
[19] Bennett, "The Conscience of Huckleberry Finn," p. 124.
[20] Bennett, "The Conscience of Huckleberry Finn," p. 131. Michele M. Moody-Adams follows Lionel Trilling in suggesting that Huck's use of "right" and "wrong" is ironic. See Moody-Adams, *Fieldwork in Familiar Places: Morality, Culture, and Philosophy* (Cambridge, MA: Harvard University Press, 1997), p. 160; and Lionel Trilling, "Huckleberry Finn," in his *The Liberal Imagination: Essays in Literature and Society* (Harmondsworth, Middlesex, England: Penguin Books, 1970).

We might be tempted to privilege sympathy in exactly those cases in which it serves as a personal check on the public morality.[21] Although Huck felt sympathy for both slaveholder and slave, only his feelings for Jim are consistent with challenging the general public view that slavery is morally acceptable. Indeed, Huck's socialization under this public morality is surely an important part of the explanation of why he feels sympathy for Miss Watson in anticipation of her loss. A second case from Bennett's article, however, shows that sympathy can point to deficiencies in a personal morality as well. In a speech to his SS generals at Poznan, Heinrich Himmler offers praise for the manner in which the extermination of the Jews was being accomplished in Nazi Germany:

I am referring now to the extermination of the Jews. This is one of those things everyone says easily. The Jewish people are being exterminated. It is in our program, removing the Jews, exterminating them. But most of us know what it really means when a hundred corpses are lying on the ground together, when there are five hundred or a thousand lying there. To have gone through this and to have remained decent – apart from exceptions due to human weakness – this is what has made us tough. But overall we can say that we have carried out this most arduous duty out of love for our people. We have not been harmed in doing so in our inmost being, in our soul, in our character. [22]

On Bennett's interpretation, "[Himmler] is saying that only the weak take the easy way out and just squelch their sympathies, and is praising the stronger and more glorious course of retaining one's sympathies while acting in violation of them."[23] In the end, the personal morality of Nazi leaders wins out over whatever sympathy might be associated with the public morality of Germany and, as a result, succeeds in becoming the public morality itself.[24]

Does this mean that the responsibility of leaders rests in their ability to use sympathy to correct their personal moralities when sympathetic feelings are clearly aligned with the public morality? Unfortunately, sympathy lends itself to this use only in those cases in which leaders

---

[21] See, for example, Joanne B. Ciulla's introduction to Bennett's piece in Joanne B. Ciulla, ed., *The Ethics of Leadership* (Belmont, CA: Wadsworth/Thomson Learning, 2003), p. 81.

[22] *The Trial of Adolf Eichmann*, PBS Home Video (ABC News Productions and Great Projects Film Company, 1997).

[23] Bennett, "The Conscience of Huckleberry Finn," p. 128.

[24] Daniel Jonah Goldhagen gives us reason to think that this might already have been the public morality (*Hitler's Willing Executioners: Ordinary Germans and the Holocaust* [New York: Alfred A. Knopf, 1996]).

have some sense that feelings of sympathy are appropriate. For example, unless we assume that Himmler suspected that sympathy was an appropriate reaction to the Jews and their plight, how can we expect him to have used his sympathetic feelings to come to the conclusion that there is something wrong with Nazi morality? Although Bennett attributes this perspective on sympathy to Himmler, it is far from clear whether Himmler intended by his remarks that Germans should retain their sympathetic feelings toward Jews. After all, we might think that feelings of sympathy were seen by Himmler as indicative of the very human weaknesses to which he refers.[25] Himmler's real concern seems to be that participants in the Final Solution would lose the general sensibilities necessary for decent human relations after the extermination of the Jews. On this interpretation of his speech, Himmler is primarily concerned with the indirect effects of the Final Solution on fellow Germans, not about the direct effects on the Jews themselves.[26] Since Himmler's personal morality commits him to the position that Jews are not part of the moral community, to imply that he is advocating sympathy for the Jews would be to assume that these feelings can be detached from his beliefs about moral membership. A better interpretation is that Himmler might have explained whatever sympathy remained for the Jews by appeal to the public morality that Nazism aimed to transcend, in much the same way that we might appeal to socialization to explain the sympathetic feelings that Huck has for Miss Watson.

The problem with using sympathy as a moral corrective is that advocates of social change cannot know whether these feelings indicate

---

[25] David H. Jones writes, "Even though Nazi leaders were utterly convinced by their ideology that killing the Jews was completely justified, they believed that most Germans still suffered from the 'weaknesses' of 'Christian morality' (as Himmler put it), that is, moral scruples that were the 'lingering effect of two thousand years of Western morality and ethics' that would have to be overcome" (*Moral Responsibility in the Holocaust: A Study in the Ethics of Character* [Lanham, MD: Rowman and Littlefield Publishers, 1999], p. 152). The internal quotes in the preceding sentence refer to Raul Hilberg, *The Destruction of the European Jews*, Vol. 3 (New York: Holmes and Meier, 1985). See also Glover's discussion of "hardness" in *Humanity*, chs. 2, 33.

[26] This characterization of Himmler's position bears some resemblance to Kant's argument regarding the treatment of animals. Kant writes, "If he is not to stifle his human feelings, he must practise kindness towards animals, for he who is cruel to animals becomes hard also in his dealings with men" (Immanuel Kant, "Duties towards Animals and Spirits," trans. Louis Infield, *Lectures on Ethics* [New York: Harper and Row Publishers, 1963], p. 240). See also Peter Carruthers, *The Animals Issue* (Cambridge: Cambridge University Press, 1992).

correct morality or simply represent the affective residue of a public morality that should be rejected. To be sure, Himmler should have deferred to any sympathetic feelings he might have had for the Jews, and Huck was right to act on whatever feelings of sympathy he had for Jim. In neither case, though, is the presence of sympathy by itself sufficient for determining what the agent ought to do. Bennett concedes this general point in his claim that sympathy can conflict "not just with bad moralities, but also with good ones like yours and mine."[27] These feelings can get in the way of an ethics grounded in human interests, as when we defer to sympathy and subordinate an individual's future good to his present desires.[28] Sympathy for one individual can also compete with fairness for others as well as with equal respect for the individual for whom we feel sympathy, as when we are tempted to assign a higher grade to a student than what he really deserves. So, while Bennett is concerned with "sympathy in relation to bad morality," his focus cannot be traced to the fact that "such conflicts occur only when the morality is bad" or even that they are any more likely to occur for people with bad moralities.[29] On Bennett's view, the leader who questions his morality would need to know whether it is good or bad before he can know whether he should embrace his feelings of sympathy and accept the conclusion that a deviation from a generally applicable moral requirement would be justified.

A deeper problem with using sympathy as a moral corrective is that adherents of bad moralities can lack these feelings altogether. Regardless of how we interpret Himmler's remarks on the appropriateness of sympathy for the Jews, some Nazis surely experienced these feelings. Many perpetrators, however, showed little or no signs of sympathetic opposition, some delighting in the pain and suffering they meted out. Simply put, immoral behavior does not always give rise to sympathy. A third case raised by Bennett is meant to illustrate an absence of connection between bad morality and feelings of sympathy. According to Bennett, Calvinist theologian and American philosopher Jonathan Edwards felt no sympathy for the eternally damned and, as evidenced by his sermons, seemed to enjoy contemplating the torment that these individuals would eventually face. Perhaps Bennett's portrayal of Edwards is

[27] Bennett, "The Conscience of Huckleberry Finn," p. 124.
[28] Bennett gives an example of a mother whose sympathy gets in the way of medical treatment for her child ("The Conscience of Huckleberry Finn," p. 124).
[29] Bennett, "The Conscience of Huckleberry Finn," p. 124.

not completely fair, but it is hardly an odd way to think about a man who resigned as Congregationalist minister because of his opposition to the "view that unbelievers should be admitted to the Lord's Supper in the hope that it would convert them."[30] The strength of Edwards's cognitive commitment to the exclusion of the eternally damned from the moral community seems to have left him little room for feelings of sympathy towards these individuals. With respect to his advocacy of social change, lack of sympathy would mean that he had nothing at all to privilege over his personal morality.

All this is to say that sympathy can serve neither as a reliable corrective to generally applicable moral requirements nor as a reliable check on exceptions to these requirements. What Bennett's analysis really shows is that sympathetic feelings can either support or undermine inclusiveness in the moral community. On the one hand, the feelings Huck had for Jim, the feelings some Germans had for Jews, and the feelings Edwards should have had for the eternally damned are aligned with the moral protection of outsiders. On the other hand, feelings for slaveholders such as Miss Watson, as well as for others who lose their way of life when they can no longer benefit from injustice, can risk impeding social changes that would properly extend such protections.[31] Kant's concerns about identifying moral action with the behavior of the "many spirits of so sympathetic a temper"[32] are thus exacerbated by the fact that both public and personal normative commitments about the scope of morality influence the selection of which individuals are ultimately the objects of our feelings of sympathy. The relevant determining factor in the cases Bennett raises, then, is not the presence or absence of sympathy but rather the contribution exception making would make to the identification of particular outsiders as appropriate objects of sympathy. On this alternative to using sympathy as a moral corrective, exclusivity is what signals that a deviation from a generally applicable moral requirement might be justified. The corresponding behavioral check on exception making is whether the exception would support a state of affairs in which the scope of morality is extended to those not currently protected by moral requirements.

[30] Bennett, "The Conscience of Huckleberry Finn," p. 123.
[31] Self-pity can have a similar effect.
[32] Immanuel Kant, *Groundwork of the Metaphysic of Morals*, trans. H. J. Paton (New York: Harper and Row Publishers, 1964), p. 66. As Jones points out in his discussion of pity, "too often a purely emotional response . . . can be easily assuaged by some minimal gesture" (*Moral Responsibility in the Holocaust*, p. 208).

Bennett's appeal to what may be the best example of a justified war against moral exclusion helps to make this general point: "I think it was right to take part in the Second World War on the Allied side; there were many ghastly individual incidents which might have led someone to doubt the rightness of his participation in that war; and I think it would have been right for such a person to keep his sympathies in a subordinate place on those occasions, not allowing them to modify his principles in such a way as to make a pacifist of him."[33] We can accept with Bennett, I think, that deviations from generally applicable moral requirements against killing were justified to stop the Nazis. At the time of these deviations, however, sympathy alone was not sufficient for a determination of justification. Instead, an appeal to the moral status of the victims of Nazi oppression was necessary to adjudicate between sympathetic feelings for these victims, on the one hand, and sympathy for Allied troops and even for enemy soldiers, on the other. As Auschwitz survivor Elie Wiesel puts the idea behind this more reliable corrective to generally applicable moral requirements, "We must have the courage to stand by the victim always, even if it means questioning God."[34] The presence of this kind of victimization, not sympathy, indicates the need for social change, and generally applicable moral requirements, no less than God, can be questioned when they stand in the way of the changes that would extend the scope of morality's protections. By creating room for exception making, the behavioral check of moral inclusiveness allows leaders to ask these questions.[35]

III. CIVIL DISOBEDIENCE AND SOCIAL CHANGE

The idea that deviations from generally applicable moral requirements can be justified in the name of social change has its legal analogue in the practice of civil disobedience. For example, in the American civil rights movement of the 1950s and 1960s, opponents of segregation purposefully broke the law as a way to bring about the moral inclusion of black Americans. Martin Luther King, Jr., appeals directly to the exclusive nature of segregation statutes to justify this kind of disobedience: "To use the words of Martin Buber, the great Jewish philosopher, segregation

---

[33] Bennett, "The Conscience of Huckleberry Finn," p. 133.
[34] Elie Wiesel, public lecture, University of Richmond, December 1999.
[35] As we shall see, Wiesel is also correct that those who would deviate from generally applicable moral requirements "have no right to answer" these questions (public lecture, University of Richmond, December 1999).

substitutes an 'I-it' relationship for the 'I-thou' relationship, and ends up relegating persons to the status of things. So segregation is not only politically, economically and sociologically unsound, but it is morally wrong and sinful."[36] Initially at least, the universalism that characterizes all consistent opposition to segregation statutes might lead us to question whether those who used civil disobedience to protest these laws actually made exceptions of themselves. After all, the position of the protesters was that no one should be subject to the statutes, not that legal exceptions should be made just for the protestors themselves. When these participants in civil disobedience violated the law, there was a good sense in which what they were doing was nothing more than what everyone should have been allowed to do.

How, then, can we use the notion of exception making to understand the behavior of those who engage in civil disobedience? One answer to this question appeals to Joel Feinberg's distinction between *direct* civil disobedience, which "violates the very law that is the target of the protest," and *indirect* civil disobedience, which "violates some other law whose reasonableness is not in question."[37] On this distinction, the claim that participants in civil disobedience do not make exceptions of themselves holds, at most, for cases of direct civil disobedience. Moreover, Feinberg tells us,

In fact it is surprisingly difficult to protest the most likely sorts of unjust laws and policies by direct civil disobedience. White people sitting in the black sections of segregated buses in the 1950s and war protestors burning their draft cards are good examples. But more characteristically, acts of civil disobedience in recent years have been indirect, the most familiar being those that violate local trespass ordinances, for example, "sitting in" at an atomic energy site until one must be forcibly carried away by the police in order to protest, not trespass laws, but rather the policy of building atomic power plants.[38]

---

[36] Martin Luther King, Jr., "Letter from Birmingham City Jail," in James Melvin Washington, ed., *A Testament of Hope: The Essential Writings of Martin Luther King, Jr.* (San Francisco: Harper and Row Publishers, 1986), p. 293. There is also a close parallel here with Kant's argument for the second version of the categorical imperative, which I discussed in Chapter 5: "*Act in such a way that you always treat humanity, whether in your own person or in the person of any other, never simply as a means, but always at the same time as an end*" (*Groundwork*, p. 96).

[37] Joel Feinberg, "Civil Disobedience in the Modern World," in Joel Feinberg and Russ Shafer-Landau, eds., *Reason and Responsibility: Readings in Some Basic Problems of Philosophy*, 10th edition (Belmont, CA: Wadsworth Publishing, 1999), p. 669.

[38] Feinberg, "Civil Disobedience in the Modern World," p. 669.

Even in the civil rights movement, King defends indirect civil disobedience on the grounds that "[t]here are some instances when a law is
just on its face and unjust in its application."[39] For example, he holds
both that "there is nothing wrong with an ordinance which requires a
permit for a parade" and that such an ordinance should not be applied
to protests against segregation.[40] Those who engage in indirect civil
disobedience thus make exceptions of themselves when they violate ordinances of this kind. It is simply that the ends of the protesters make
the law inapplicable, thereby justifying the violation.

Direct civil disobedience also leaves room for a charge of exception
making. Again, those who violate the laws they seek to overturn believe
that no one should be subject to these laws. But we cannot attribute to
the protesters the more general belief that people are justified in disobeying a law whenever they are opposed to it. This belief would not
have allowed opponents of segregation to reject a claim of equal justification on behalf of the segregationists. King puts the problem faced
by the protesters this way: "Since we so diligently urge people to obey
the Supreme Court's decision of 1954 outlawing segregation in the public schools, it is rather strange and paradoxical to find us consciously
breaking laws."[41] To address this problem, King contrasts segregationists and opponents of segregation, arguing that the former disobey just
laws whereas the latter disobey unjust laws. So the segregationist is not
justified in engaging in civil disobedience: "But now I must affirm that it
is just as wrong [as using immoral means to attain moral ends], or even
more so, to use moral means to preserve immoral ends."[42] This appeal
to the morality of the ends, however, does not show that civil disobedience by the opponents of segregation amounts to anything less than
exception making on their part. What it ultimately suggests is that these
exceptions must be justified by appeal to moral argument. As we might
expect, immediately after proposing that we can distinguish between
just and unjust laws, King flags the exclusive nature of segregation
statutes to defend this distinction and, so too, the exceptions that the
protesters make of themselves.

Given that the point of contention in cases of civil disobedience is
always who has justice on his side, those who engage in this kind of

---

[39] King, "Letter from Birmingham City Jail," p. 294.
[40] King, "Letter from Birmingham City Jail," p. 294.
[41] King, "Letter from Birmingham City Jail," p. 293.
[42] King, "Letter from Birmingham City Jail," p. 301. Here, King is talking about the
use of non-violence by the police.

behavior must begin with the assumption that they are making exceptions of themselves by disobeying the law and that their exception-making behavior stands to be justified. This way of framing a moral analysis of civil disobedience is closely related to what John Rawls and others call the "duty of fair play."[43] The charge that civil disobedience always constitutes exception making is grounded in the claim that it has "the characteristic of unfair play and that exploitation is at least one of its inevitable moral costs even when it is justified on balance."[44] Against this view, Feinberg contends that when "it is done sincerely for a 'higher moral cause,'" represents a means of last resort, and does not seriously threaten respect for the law more generally, civil disobedience is "not 'exploitative' of anyone. To the question, What if everyone did it? the justified civil disobedient can answer that if everyone did it (where by 'it' we mean disobedience that satisfies [this] condition), the results would not be bad at all."[45] What Feinberg seems to miss, though, is that the most convincing version of the fairness objection does not point to concerns about what would happen if everyone who is actually justified in engaging in civil disobedience were to violate the law. To the extent that this objection focuses at all on the cumulative effects of civil disobedience, it raises concerns about what would happen if everyone who *believes* that his behavior meets this condition – and, consequently, that he is justified in engaging in civil disobedience – were to violate the law.

The claim that civil disobedience, by its very nature, constitutes exception making derives in large part from what Feinberg himself grants – namely, the epistemic reality that "people can be wrong in their conscientious convictions as in any other ones."[46] A case in point is that many segregationists could say that they sincerely believed that they were acting for a "higher cause," grounding their opposition to integration in what they took to be solid moral objections. We might also note that their claim that disobedience was the only means available to them has at least as much plausibility as the parallel claim made on behalf of the opponents of segregation. Finally, even the charge that disobedience by the segregationists was relatively more dangerous to democracy would not convince anyone who sees the federal judiciary as a serious threat

---

43 John Rawls, "Legal Obligation and the Duty of Fair Play," in Sidney Hook, ed., *Law and Philosophy; A Symposium* (New York: New York University Press, 1964), pp. 3–18.
44 Feinberg, "Civil Disobedience in the Modern World," p. 678.
45 Feinberg, "Civil Disobedience in the Modern World," p. 679.
46 Feinberg, "Civil Disobedience in the Modern World," p. 669.

to majority rule, especially at the state or local level. Given that the segregationist could in this way make the argument that civil disobedience
on his part would have been justified, there remains something unfair
in expecting that he obey laws with which he disagrees and at the same
time advocating that others disobey the laws with which they disagree.
This unfairness cannot be fully captured in terms of "the costs to our
democratic institutions, our public civility, and our domestic tranquil-
ity."[47] It is better attributed to the fact that opponents of segregation
engaged in a practice that they could not endorse for the segregationist.
In the end, the only relevant distinction between the two sides was one
to which the opponents of segregation could not appeal to explain away
completely the unfairness of their behavior.

The reason that opponents of segregation could not make civil disobedience available to the segregationist is that this would have been
tantamount to advocating the very behavior they sought to eradicate
from society.[48] In this respect, engaging in direct civil disobedience is
usually quite different from exercising free speech as a form of protest,
as speech that might be used to counter one's point of view is rarely itself
the object of one's protest. Understandably, then, King is adamant that
the practice of civil disobedience not be extended to those who violate
just laws: "In no sense do I advocate evading or defying the law as the
rabid segregationist would do."[49] Yet if it was really enough to point out
that the segregationists did not have justice on their side, then why does
King nevertheless hold that when the opponents of segregation break
an unjust law, they "must do it *openly, lovingly* . . . , and with a willingness to accept the penalty?"[50] Since segregation statutes are themselves
unjust, it cannot be the normative force of these particular laws that
gives rise to behavioral conditions on civil disobedience. King's answer
is that "an individual who breaks a law that conscience tells him is unjust, and willingly accepts the penalty by staying in jail to arouse the
conscience of the community over its injustice, is in reality expressing

---

[47] Feinberg, "Civil Disobedience in the Modern World," p. 678.
[48] David Lyons writes: "Experience shows that, in the face of resistance against significant, deeply entrenched, systematic injustice, those who break the law, at least
initially, are often not resisters but officials and their supporters, employing unlawful methods against resisters and failing to arrest unlawful attacks on them
or to prosecute the perpetrators" ("Moral Judgment, Historical Reality, and Civil
Disobedience," *Philosophy and Public Affairs* 27 [1998]: 46).
[49] King, "Letter from Birmingham City Jail," p. 294.
[50] King, "Letter from Birmingham City Jail," p. 294.

the very highest respect for law."[51] The implication seems to be that the individual who engages in civil disobedience would show less than full respect for the law more generally were he to fail to make his behavior public, use violent means, or be unwilling to accept the penalty. What grounds this kind of respect?

The notion of political obligation offers one way to think about the respect that participants in civil disobedience show for the law. If we accept the notion that there is an obligation to obey both just and unjust laws, then those who engage in civil disobedience always do some wrong by making exceptions of themselves. On this view, for example, "Their submitting to arrest and punishment is taken as . . . evidence of respect for legal authority and recognition of a moral obligation to obey."[52] The notion of political obligation thus allows us to see the problem of civil disobedience as parallel to the problem of dirty hands discussed in Chapter 5. Michael Walzer explicitly draws the comparison, suggesting that "[i]n both men violate a set of rules, go beyond a moral or legal limit, in order to do what they believe they should do. At the same time, they acknowledge their responsibility for the violation by accepting punishment or doing penance."[53] However, holding participants in civil disobedience responsible for these violations would seem minimally to assume that the social systems they aim to change are "'reasonably just.'"[54] Considering paradigmatic cases of civil disobedience such as principled protest against "chattel slavery, British colonial rule, and Jim Crow," David Lyons rejects this assumption and concludes that it is a mistake to think that the resisters in these cases believed that the existing social systems were reasonably just.[55] Instead, Lyons alleges, the readiness of theorists to accept this assumption "can reasonably be characterized as a derivative but socially important form of racism."[56]

If the assumption "that political resistance requires moral justification . . . is [typically] premised on a serious moral error,"[57] then we

---

[51] King, "Letter from Birmingham City Jail," p. 294.
[52] Lyons, "Moral Judgment," p. 39.
[53] Michael Walzer, "Political Action: The Problem of Dirty Hands," *Philosophy and Public Affairs* 2 (1973): 178.
[54] Lyons, "Moral Judgment," p. 33.
[55] Lyons, "Moral Judgment," p. 33.
[56] Lyons, "Moral Judgment," p. 49.
[57] Lyons, "Moral Judgment," p. 39.

need an alternative argument for the relatively burdensome conditions that King puts on civil disobedience. A competing view of the behaviors typically identified with this practice sees them as purely practical means to social change. Lyons contends that principled resisters such as Thoreau, Gandhi, and King were committed to this approach: "Their acceptance of legal sanctions signified a strategic, not a moral judgment."[58] Admittedly, the strategic interpretation of the willingness of principled resisters to accept punishment fits well with at least one interpretation of what it means to use imprisonment "to arouse the conscience of the community over its injustice."[59] But from the claim that political obligation does not generate necessary conditions on justified civil disobedience it does not follow that participants in civil disobedience have no other moral reasons to be willing to accept the penalty for their behavior. At least for King, it seems to be morally relevant that civil disobedience violates the law, unjust though the law may be. The strategic interpretation, for instance, makes it difficult to explain why King sees willingness to accept punishment as a means of showing respect. In other words, on this interpretation, we no longer have an answer to the question, respect for what? Willingness to accept punishment for disobeying an unjust law in an unjust system is certainly an odd way to show respect for the moral law, as it is precisely the gravity of the discrepancy between law and morality that grounds the justification for civil disobedience in the first place.

The purely strategic understanding of the willingness to accept punishment cannot make sense of King's respect for the law because it returns us to the view that civil disobedience does not constitute exception making after all. In the absence of political obligation, legal statutes do not apply to anyone, so violations of the law are not exceptional. As we have seen, however, King clearly expected protesters to express respect for the law, despite the fact that they were violating unjust laws. Perhaps this expectation can ultimately be traced to a morally relevant distinction among unjust societies. Some unjust societies are on the way to becoming just or at least to becoming less unjust. In these societies, as in reasonably just societies, violating the law always involves a certain amount of unfairness. The expectation that others conform their behavior to the general demands of legality, which is necessary for

---

[58] Lyons, "Moral Judgment," p. 40.
[59] King, "Letter from Birmingham City Jail," p. 294.

the establishment of justice, implies that civil disobedience constitutes exception making even when it is done in protest of the very laws that make the system unjust. On this line of argument, the critical point is that the protesters cannot simply assume that the justice of their ends is sufficient to justify the exceptions they make of themselves by violating the law. In short, the protesters do not know whether they do some wrong by making exceptions of themselves, even though they are working to overturn laws that others may come to see as unjust. Epistemic concerns about justification at the level of means therefore generate moral reasons for leaders who engage in civil disobedience to make their behavior public, to refrain from using violence, and to be willing to accept the penalty.

There is evidence to suggest that King himself took these epistemic concerns very seriously. According to John Ansbro, King was deeply influenced by the work of Edgar Brightman, who writes in his *Moral Laws*, "All of the ideals which have hitherto entered into my life should daily be confronted by the standards of the highest insight I have yet been able to attain. This necessarily will mean that I shall have to revise or even reject today some of the standards which seemed final even as recently as four or five years ago."[60] King similarly claims in the *Playboy Interviews*, "I subject myself to self-purification and to endless self-analysis; I question and soul-search constantly into myself to be as certain as I can that I am fulfilling the true meaning of my work . . . "[61] The Montgomery boycott provides a good example of King's concerns about justification at the level of means. Ansbro says of King that "he was disturbed that his proposed method of protest was being regarded as the same as the one used by the White Citizens Councils to preserve segregation. He began to consider whether the boycott method was an ethical course of action or a basically unchristian and negative approach to the solution of a problem."[62]

Properly constrained by conditions of publicity, non-violence, and willingness to accept the penalty, civil disobedience can thus be understood as an educational exercise for society. While civil rights leaders may have held that both their ends and means were ultimately justified, they did not rely exclusively on their conscientious convictions

[60] Quoted in John J. Ansbro, *Martin Luther King, Jr.: The Making of a Mind* (Maryknoll, NY: Orbis Books, 1982), p. 84.
[61] Quoted in Ansbro, *Martin Luther King, Jr.*, p. 146.
[62] Ansbro, *Martin Luther King, Jr.*, p. 136.

about justification. King sometimes uses language that is open to this interpretation of the conditions on civil disobedience:

We merely bring to the surface the hidden tension that is already alive. We bring it out in the open where it can be seen and dealt with. Like a boil that can never be cured as long as it is covered up but must be opened with all its pus-flowing ugliness to the natural medicines of air and light, injustice must likewise be exposed, with all of the tension its exposing creates, to the light of human conscience and the air of national opinion before it can be cured.[63]

On this characterization, protest in the civil rights movement relied on the judgment of people other than opponents of segregation for determinations of justification. The use of civil disobedience forced the public to confront important questions about inclusiveness in the moral community and how to achieve it, rather than assuming that it was sufficient that leaders had answered these questions for themselves.

Even in cases in which the ends of change are inclusive, then, the conditions on civil disobedience represent the possibility that exception making might not be justified. Satisfaction of these conditions shows respect for the law by submitting questions about justification to public determination. As such, conditions on civil disobedience have a dual cognitive function. Most obviously, these conditions serve to convince others of the necessity of social change or the justice of a cause – for example, to "help men to rise from the dark depths of prejudice and racism to the majestic heights of understanding and brotherhood."[64] Less obviously, but no less importantly, publicity, non-violence, and willingness to accept the penalty can be ways to test the morality of the means used by protesters. Civil disobedience carried out in these ways harnesses both aspects of the cognitive function by juxtaposing the public's view of what means are morally acceptable with the public's view of the justice of the protesters' ends. One way to answer questions about inclusiveness in the moral community and how to achieve it is to ask what costs others are willing to bear to preserve the status quo. In cases of institutional injustice like that found in Jim Crow, these costs are embodied in the punishments leaders willingly accept for their exception-making behavior. The costs of punishing leaders for their exceptions are part of the case for the injustice and, as such, force the public to consider the importance of changing the current system. Whether the public is

---

[63] King, "Letter from Birmingham City Jail," p. 295.
[64] King, "Letter from Birmingham City Jail," p. 291.

willing to tolerate the punishment of leaders is a sign of exactly how just it takes the object of protest to be. Civil disobedience characterized by publicity, non-violence, and a willingness to accept the penalty brings any contradictions into sharp relief.

IV. BEHAVIORAL CHECKS ON EXCEPTION MAKING

Section III introduced a set of behavioral checks on a particular kind of exception making by leaders. My strategy was to supplement the behavioral check of moral inclusiveness by using an example of leadership in the civil rights movement concerning which there is now substantial agreement that exception-making behavior was justified. At the time of the civil rights movement, however, people disagreed not only about the justice of its leaders' ends but also about the morality of their means. King's "Letter from Birmingham City Jail," which was written not to segregationists but to white moderates, makes it clear that objections to civil disobedience were hardly limited to people who denied the value of ending segregation. One way to understand the moral reasons to take this kind of disagreement seriously is in terms of epistemic barriers such as those faced by King in his efforts to effect social change. Given the difficulty of making determinations of justification, the behavioral checks of moral inclusiveness, publicity, non-violence, and willingness to accept the penalty serve as normative responses to the epistemic limits of leadership. Leaders who do not know whether they are justified in making exceptions of themselves can do no better than to rely on the safeguards adopted by others who clearly had justification on their side.

When leaders have done the best that can be reasonably expected of them in their determinations of justification, making the appropriate normative response to the epistemic limits of leadership renders these leaders immune to attributions of blameworthiness for unjustified exception making.[65] In other words, by adhering to the behavioral check of moral inclusiveness and satisfying the conditions on civil disobedience, leaders who are genuinely in positions of epistemic uncertainty about justification have an excuse for the exceptions they make of themselves. This set of behavioral checks on exception making reflects the idea that

---

[65] In Chapter 7, I defend the importance of the distinction between what leaders are able to do and what can be reasonably expected of them. See also Terry L. Price, "Character, Conscientiousness, and Conformity to Will," *Journal of Value Inquiry* 35 (2001): 151–163.

there are significant cognitive issues at stake in leadership and, more-over, that the judgment of leaders is not always sufficient to resolve these issues. What we can expect of leaders, then, is that they acknowledge one of the preconditions of public life in a liberal, democratic society: the capacity of people other than themselves to make determinations of justification.[66] Leaders in politics or the professions who bypass this capacity when it comes to assessments of their own exception-making behavior take matters of justification into their own hands. Their devi-ations from generally applicable moral requirements raise the question of whether an exception is justified, and they alone get to provide an answer to this question. As a consequence, such leaders expose them-selves to attributions of blameworthiness should it turn out that their exception-making behavior is unjustified.

Does this mean that the behavioral checks are necessary conditions for eluding attributions of blameworthiness for unjustified exception making? The strongest argument for an affirmative answer to this ques-tion can be made with respect to the behavioral check of moral inclu-siveness. This check responds directly to the main epistemic limit of leadership – namely, that leaders are prone to overvalue collective ends and to overestimate what kinds of behavior these ends will justify. By restricting exception-making behavior to those cases in which it would expand the scope of moral protection, the behavioral check of moral in-clusiveness moderates beliefs about the justificatory force of leadership. Leaders who ground their exceptions in the ends of moral inclusion are least likely to give too much normative weight to the interests of follow-ers within their group, organization, or society. After all, what can be more morally important than making sure that all members of the moral community are properly recognized as falling within the scope of its protections? When followers are excluded from the moral community,

---

[66] John Locke writes: "I easily grant, that *Civil Government* is the proper Remedy for the Inconveniences of the State of Nature, which must certainly be Great, where Men may be Judges in their own Case, since 'tis easily to be imagined, that he who was so unjust as to do his Brother an Injury, will scarce be so just as to condemn himself for it: But I shall desire those who make this Objection, to remember that *Absolute Monarchs* are but Men, and if Government is to be the remedy of those Evils, which necessarily follow from Mens being Judges in their own Cases, and the State of Nature is therefore not to be endured, I desire to know what kind of Government that is, and how much better it is than the State of Nature, where one Man commanding a multitude, has the Liberty to be Judge in his own Case" (*Two Treatises of Government*, ed. Peter Laslett [Cambridge: Cambridge University Press, 1988], p. 276).

it is their well-being and agency interests that are threatened either by outsiders or by other insiders working to achieve group, organizational, or societal goals. A behavioral check of moral inclusiveness therefore significantly reduces the moral risks of exception making even for leaders who privilege the interests of followers. The risks are even smaller when the end of exception making is the moral inclusion of outsiders. Leaders can hardly be accused of according too much normative weight to follower interests in cases of this kind since the focus of moral concern is the interests of outsiders, not the interests of members of a leader's group, organization, or society.

Unfortunately, the behavioral checks of publicity, non-violence, and willingness to accept penalty do not easily translate into necessary conditions for avoiding attributions of blameworthiness for unjustified exception making. Without significant refinement, the conditions on civil disobedience would rule out potentially justifiable means to which leaders might appeal. Specifically, these behavioral checks would prevent leaders from ever using secrecy, violence, and evasion to achieve their ends. Here, we must be careful not to retreat from the idea that the epistemic limits of leadership call for significant restrictions on the exceptions leaders make of themselves. But restrictions on deviations from generally applicable moral requirements should be something short of outright prohibitions on particular means. Otherwise, the behavioral checks on exception making would fail to convey the idea that exception making might be justified in some circumstances. An absolutist understanding of ethical failures in leadership would require a theory of justification that defends a universal prohibition on exception making. Rather than mounting such a defense, the cognitive account of ethical failures in leadership makes the weaker claim that leaders sometimes behave immorally because they mistakenly believe that the goals of their group, organization, or society justify deviations from generally applicable moral requirements. Stringent behavioral checks on exception making are therefore better applied at the level of ends.[67]

---

[67] The claim that the behavioral checks, even with significant refinement, are necessary conditions on eluding attributions of blameworthiness for unjustified exception making also assumes that leaders who make exceptions of themselves were, or at least should have been, aware of these checks. In Chapter 7, I go some way toward defending this assumption for the case of contemporary leaders. These leaders, I argue, have special reasons to recognize their own fallibility and, especially, their tendency to overestimate the justificatory force of leadership when it comes to the exclusion of members of the moral community.

To appreciate the fact that the publicity check must be refined, despite its demand that leaders show respect for the ability of people other than themselves to make determinations of justification, notice that its robust application would preclude deviations from the generally applicable moral requirements that most readily lend themselves to claims of justified exception making, requirements such as prohibitions on deceptive and manipulative behavior.[68] This is because deception and manipulation are effective only when it is not public knowledge that they are being used. Requiring that leaders carry out deceptive and manipulative behavior in a way that meets the letter of the publicity check on exception making would therefore render these particular exceptions practically useless in leadership. In his efforts to bring the United States into World War II, for example, Franklin Roosevelt could hardly reveal the true origins of the infamous "secret map," a map that supposedly showed Nazi aspirations to take control of the Americas.[69] In this particular case, Roosevelt's non-public exception making did not suggest a belief on his part that he lacked justification. Such a belief would imply that any potential ethical failures were volitional in nature. Rather, there were real cognitive issues at stake – specifically, over whether bypassing the rational faculties of the American people was a justified response to the Nazi threat. The problem for Roosevelt and leaders like him is that it is sometimes impossible at the time of an exception both to engage in the exception-making behavior and to entrust a determination of its justification to others.

If a normative response to the epistemic limits of leadership is to accommodate possibilities for justified exception making, then it is surely too much to ask that leaders publicize their exceptions in ways that make it impossible for them to violate prohibitions such as those on deception and manipulation. But leaders are often in a position to share even this kind of exception making and the reasons for it with individuals

---

[68] Here, I am not arguing that deception and manipulation are ever justified, just that my account cannot assume that they are never justified. For a model of effectiveness for autocratic, consultative, and group decision procedures, see Victor Harold Vroom and Philip W. Yetton, *Leadership and Decision-Making* (Pittsburgh: University of Pittsburgh Press, 1973).

[69] John F. Bratzel and Leslie B. Rout, Jr., concede that Roosevelt may not have known that the map was a forgery but suggest that "policy considerations made it unlikely that FDR was going to question too closely the authenticity of potentially useful material. Roosevelt's greatest concern was the threat that Hitler posed to the security of the United States" ("FDR and the 'Secret Map,'" *Wilson Quarterly* 9, 1 [1985]: 172).

who are not the objects of the behavior in question. These individuals may be other trusted leaders or followers within a company or political administration, as when Roosevelt told Treasury Secretary Henry Morgenthau, Jr., "I am perfectly willing to mislead and tell untruths if it will help win the war."[70] Still, publicizing deception and manipulation in this limited way, while clearly preferable to complete secrecy, will rarely be enough to avoid an attribution of blameworthiness for unjustified exception making. Even if power differentials permit internal audiences to question a leader's exception-making behavior, insiders, who often "consider loyalty to the group the highest form of morality," will not be "inclined to raise ethical issues that imply that this 'fine group of ours, with its humanitarianism and its high-minded principles, might be capable of adopting a course of action that is inhumane and immoral.'"[71]

In his seminal work on group decision making, Irving Janis identifies this shared belief in the inherent morality of the group as a symptom of what he calls *groupthink*.[72] Here, groupthink "refer[s] to a mode of thinking that people engage in when they are deeply involved in a cohesive in-group, when the members' strivings for unanimity override their motivation to realistically appraise alternative courses of action."[73] Janis details several examples to support this phenomenon, of which I will mention only two. First, commenting on the role of Truman's policy-making group in the escalation of the Korean War, political scientist Glen Paige notes "the high degree of satisfaction and sense of moral rightness shared by the decision makers."[74] According to Janis, "It was a group of men who shared the same basic values and the dominant beliefs of the power elite of American society, particularly about the necessity of containing the expansion of 'world communism' in order to protect the 'free world.'"[75] Second, even in the case of Watergate, there is evidence to suggest that "Nixon and his aides shared a belief in the inherent morality

---

[70] John Morton Blum, *From the Morgenthau Diaries: Years of War 1941–1945* (Boston: Houghton Mifflin Company, 1967), p. 197.

[71] Janis, *Groupthink*, pp. 11–12. See also my discussion of leader-member exchange (LMX) theory in Chapter 3. According to Gary Yukl, some followers get special benefits from the leader-follower relationship by being, among other things, "more committed to task objectives" and "loyal to the leader" (*Leadership in Organizations*, 5th edition [Upper Saddle River, NJ: Prentice Hall, 2002], p. 116).

[72] Janis, *Groupthink*, p. 12.

[73] Janis, *Groupthink*, p. 9.

[74] Quoted in Janis, *Groupthink*, p. 49.

[75] Janis, *Groupthink*, p. 49.

of their group . . . "[76] On this point, Charles Colson, special counsel to the president, "alluded to a basic assumption of inherent morality that never needed to be talked about or even privately thought about: 'I believed what I was doing was right. The President, I am convinced, believed he was acting in the national interest . . .'"[77]

Assumptions of this kind explain why mistaken beliefs about justification often go relatively unobserved, at least at the time of exception making. To the extent that group members share the belief that exception-making behavior is justified, they will be less inclined to discuss issues of justification among themselves. Consequently, "[t]heir only concern in each instance *appears* to have been whether they could get away with it."[78]

Based on these considerations, if leaders cannot risk publicizing their behavior beyond internal boundaries at the time of an exception, we can expect that they do so in a much more open way after the fact. In some cases, given the assumption that the exceptions they make of themselves might be justified, later participation in public argument is the most that they can do. Qualification of the publicity check on exception making is particularly appropriate for leaders when the urgency of the situation would seem to prevent them from concurrently giving reasons for their deviations from generally applicable moral requirements. This is not to say that perceived urgency is sufficient to justify the exceptions leaders make of themselves. Because determinations of urgency are connected to beliefs about justification, the claim that an exception was a response to an urgent matter does little more than pose the very questions about justification that we seek to address. In other words, mistaken beliefs that leaders hold about the justificatory force of their ends quickly give rise to mistaken beliefs about urgency, since urgency is itself a temporal characterization of importance. To require, however, that leaders not make exceptions of themselves in times of crisis comes very close to begging the question in the other direction. That some leaders believe *"there is always a crisis"*[79] does not undermine the possibility that some crises might justify exceptions that, for practical reasons, cannot be defended at the time of the exceptions. But differentiation among crises makes room for the demand that leaders will in the future give public

[76] Janis, *Groupthink*, p. 296n.
[77] Janis, *Groupthink*, p. 296n.
[78] Janis, *Groupthink*, p. 229, emphasis added. See my Chapter 2 (this book) for a discussion of an agent's belief that he can "get away with it."
[79] O'Toole, *Leading Change*, p. 105.

arguments in response to the moral risks associated with exception-making behavior in past crises. Just how public these arguments must be made is essentially a matter of who is potentially wronged by the exceptions. At the very least, leaders have a responsibility to publicize their behavior to any followers or outsiders who might have cause for complaint.

The non-violence condition must be similarly refined so that it does not prohibit leaders from making exceptions of themselves in genuine moral emergencies. Situations that come immediately to mind are those cases in which conformity to a behavioral check of non-violence allows serious harm to be imposed on followers or outsiders. For example, Thoreau defends John Brown's raid on Harpers Ferry, arguing that "I do not wish to kill nor to be killed, but I can foresee circumstances in which both these things would be by me unavoidable . . . I think that for once the Sharp's rifles and the revolvers were employed in a righteous cause."[80] The more general point is that since self-defense and defense of third parties are typically considered paradigmatic examples of justified exceptions to prohibitions against the use of violence, we would be hard pressed indeed to defend a condition on exception making with the implication that these behaviors are never justified. Arguably, deviations from these requirements are sometimes not only permissible but also required of leaders. Political leaders who are unwilling to resort to force to protect citizens from internal or external aggression expose themselves to the charge that they have not done enough to protect followers from those who treat them as though they were not members of the moral community.[81] President Dwight Eisenhower, we can assume, was justified in using the 101st Airborne Division and the Arkansas

---

[80] Henry David Thoreau, "A Plea for Captain John Brown," *Thoreau: People, Principles, and Politics*, ed. Milton Meltzer (New York: Hill and Wang, 1963), p. 187.

[81] Of course, appeals to self-defense can also be questionable. Slobodan Milosevic pleads, "I have been indicted because I defended my people legally and with legitimate means on the basis of the right to self-defense that every nation has" (Marlise Simons, "Still Defiant, Milosevic Hears the Atrocities Read Out," *New York Times* [October 30, 2001]). Defending atrocities against Armenians in World War I, Turkish consul Djelal Munif Bey claims, "All those who have been killed were of that rebellious element who were caught red-handed or while otherwise committing traitorous acts against the Turkish Government, and not women and children," adding that during wartime "discrimination is utterly impossible, and it is not alone the offender who suffers the penalty of his act, but also the innocent whom he drags with him . . . The Armenians have only themselves to blame" (Samantha Power, *"A Problem from Hell": America and the Age of Genocide* [New York: Perennial, 2003], p. 10).

National Guard to provide this kind of protection during school de-
segregation. Similarly, we might think that military efforts necessary to
defeat Osama bin Laden and those responsible for the September 11 terrorist attacks constitute a justified response to their treatment of Western
citizens, which was based – in part at least – on a view about religious
inclusion and exclusion.[82]

Defense of followers, however, is not the only argument for permitting leaders to employ violent means. The United States has been
roundly criticized for its reluctance to use violence to save threatened
third parties in places around the world such as Iraq, Bosnia, and
Rwanda.[83] In her analysis of the United States position on Iraq's use of
chemical weapons in its war against Iran, Samantha Power claims that
"[p]olicymakers responded as if the ayatollah had removed the Iranian
people (and especially Iranian soldiers) from the universe of moral and
legal obligation."[84] One way to put the sentiment behind such criticisms
is to say that United States officials have been reluctant to expose the
economic, political, or security interests of followers when so doing is
necessary for the inclusion of outsiders in the moral community. More
generally, then, the argument for permitting violence can be grounded in
the manifestly impartial assumption that political leaders have a moral
responsibility to protect the innocent, regardless of whether these individuals are insiders or outsiders. Of course, there will be good faith
disagreement about just what kind of sacrifices leaders should be willing to impose on followers to achieve moral inclusiveness, especially
when potential sacrifices include the inevitable losses of life associated
with military action. Disagreement of this kind is the result of the cognitive difficulties involved in making determinations of justification, and
it actually supports the claim that an absolute prohibition on violence

---

[82] Quoting the Koran 4:76, bin Laden writes in his "Letter to America," "Those
who believe, fight in the Cause of Allah, and those who disbelieve, fight in the
cause of Taghut (anything worshipped other than Allah, e.g., Satan). So fight you
against the friends of Satan . . . " Bin Laden's letter was published in *The Observer*
(November 24, 2002). Bin Laden goes on to give a justification for aggression
against United States civilians. As Doug Hicks has pointed out to me, we should
keep in mind that this religious language masks a political and cultural agenda.

[83] See Power, "*A Problem from Hell.*"

[84] Power, "*A Problem from Hell,*" p. 178. Power writes, "U.S. officials justified their
soft response to Iraqi chemical weapons use on several grounds. They portrayed
it as a weapon of last resort deployed only after more traditional Iraqi defenses
were flattened" (p. 179). Moreover, "[n]othing in U.S. behavior signaled [Saddam]
Hussein that he should think twice about now attempting to wipe out rural Kurds
using whatever means he chose" (p. 187).

cannot be a behavioral check on exception making. Appeals to violence are among the very exceptions for which the difficult questions of justification arise.

Deviations from generally applicable moral requirements against the use of violence are thus compatible with the pursuit of inclusive ends. But do these deviations also meet the publicity check on exception making? The most serious moral complaints against this use of violence come from the objects of violent means themselves, individuals who charge that their agency and well-being interests were not properly considered in a determination of justification. Admittedly, there is one sense in which leaders who resort to violence plainly present their exception-making behavior to others with whom they disagree. By forcing the objects of violence to answer questions about what costs they are willing to tolerate, the use of violent means sometimes goes directly to people's views about the importance of the privileged status that they are guaranteed through maintenance of the status quo. Like most civil disobedience, then, violence can be an impetus to a public determination of justification. Yet using violence to get answers to these questions hardly constitutes a good faith appeal to the judgment of others. Since it does not use rational persuasion to focus the attention of the objects of violence on costs that are morally central to the injustice, the unwillingness of these individuals to tolerate the costs that violence attaches to the current system often tells us very little about their view of the justice or injustice of that system. In many cases, such a response will be primarily a result of the fear and terror that violence brings with it. Generally speaking, given that violence and its threat invariably have this characteristic, using such means generally jeopardizes a genuine appeal to others for a determination of justification, thereby risking that this determination will be left to the executors of violence themselves.

A publicity check on appeals to violence is important because moral inclusiveness alone does not determine whether this kind of exception making would be justified. But opposition to moral inclusiveness is also insufficient to undercut the value of this end or prove that violence would not be justified to achieve it. In fact, leaders will sometimes believe that the use of force is justified precisely because they have exhausted all opportunities for rational persuasion, essentially giving up on the capacity of the potential objects of violence to make accurate determinations of justification. At the very least, however, we can expect leaders who resort to violent means on such grounds to check their behavior by submitting it to the judgment of outsiders who are also committed to the cause of moral inclusion. To the extent that there is agreement that violence would be justified in the circumstances, leaders have greater reason than they would otherwise have had to believe that they might be justified in employing violent means. The fact that outsiders see violent means as justified can thus support a leader's exceptions to prohibitions on violence, even in those cases in which his determination of justification is ultimately incorrect. So, not unlike leaders who engage in other forms of non-public exception making, leaders who use violence have a response to epistemic uncertainty that sometimes allows them to avoid attributions of blameworthiness.

One recent example of leadership behavior characterized by a failure to meet this condition on the use of violence was the United States response to Iraqi non-compliance with United Nations directives. Advocating a policy of preemption, President George W. Bush moved forward with military action in Iraq without getting final support from the United Nations Security Council.[85] Again, failure to meet this condition does not imply that the use of force was unjustified in the circumstances as a means to expanding the scope of morality either inside or outside of Iraq. Indeed, a determination that military action was the morally correct course of action would make an attribution of blameworthiness for the use of force out of place, in which case Bush could not be blamed for this behavior. However, if it turns out that these deviations from generally applicable moral requirements against the use of violence were unjustified, then the president cannot avoid an attribution of blameworthiness for his part in the war. By failing to satisfy one of the behavioral checks on exception making, Bush ignored a very strong signal that his means might not be justified. As Robert McNamara, former secretary of defense in the Kennedy and Johnson administrations, put it in an interview after the major campaign in Iraq had ended, "If we can't persuade nations with comparable values of the merits of our case, we better re-examine our reasoning."[86] Still, any blame that comes with a determination that violence was unjustified would be less strong than it would have been

---

[85] Bush ultimately abandoned hopes for a United Nations Security Council resolution co-sponsored by the United States, Britain, and Spain. This resolution would have authorized the use of force in the disarmament of Iraq.

[86] Samantha Power, "War and Never Having To Say You're Sorry," *New York Times* (December 14, 2003).

had Bush been completely without international support.[87] Assuming that blameworthiness can be assessed on a continuum, some appeal to the capacity of others to participate in determinations of justification bodes better for judgments of responsibility than no appeal at all.

As we have seen, the willingness of leaders to accept the penalty for the exceptions they make of themselves sometimes constitutes not self-sacrifice for wrongs done on behalf of followers or outsiders but, rather, respect for the capacity of others to determine whether these exceptions were wrong in the first place. But there must also be limits on this behavioral check on exception making. Not unlike meeting robust versions of the publicity and non-violence conditions, willingness to accept the penalty for exception-making behavior can rule out potentially justifiable means to which leaders might appeal. It would be unreasonable, for example, to expect that leaders such as those in resistance movements against the Nazi regime in World War II or in the Underground Railroad in the United States always be willing to submit their behavior to others for this kind of determination of justification. Simply put, leaders sometimes need to carry out a series of deviations from generally applicable moral requirements, and purposeful evasion can be instrumental to this end. In these cases, willingness to accept the penalty for particular deviations risks sacrificing what leaders rightly see as the ultimate benefits of exception making. Admittedly, strict conformity to this behavioral check does not mean that leaders *will* be penalized for their exception-making behavior, only that they *might* be penalized. Since others may agree with leaders that a particular deviation was justified, submitting exception-making behavior to the judgment of others might advance, not impede, leaders' long-term ends. But the possibility that others will be mistaken in their determinations of justification suggests that leaders can sometimes avoid attributions of blameworthiness for exception

---

[87] In his 2004 State of the Union address, President Bush counters the criticism that "our duties in Iraq must be internationalized. This particular criticism is hard to explain to our partners in Britain, Australia, Japan, South Korea, the Philippines, Thailand, Italy, Spain, Poland, Denmark, Hungary, Bulgaria, Ukraine, Romania, the Netherlands, Norway, El Salvador, and the 17 other countries that have committed troops to Iraq. As we debate at home, we must never ignore the vital contributions of our international partners, or dismiss their sacrifices. From the beginning, America has sought international support for our operations in Afghanistan and Iraq, and we have gained much support. There is a difference, however, between leading a coalition of many nations, and submitting to the objections of a few. America will never seek a permission slip to defend the security of our country."

making despite the fact that they are only later willing to accept the penalty for it.

Whether leaders will be required to accept penalties for deviations from generally applicable moral requirements depends, to some extent at least, on who gets to make the determinations of justification. Hardly ever will all affected parties be convinced that a leader's exception-making behavior was justified, even if the leader actually has justification on his side. Unfortunately, for no parties is this truer than for those individual followers or outsiders who have the greatest cause for complaint. They too can overestimate the normative force of their ends, thereby failing to see the real value of the ends to which leaders are committed. The difficulties involved in making determinations of justification thus generate a further limit on the behavioral check of willingness to accept the penalty for exception making. Although all complaints should be fully heard, decisions about penalties as well as the expectation that leaders be willing to accept them must be reserved for more broadly constituted decision-making bodies. Followers as a collective may be in a position to make these determinations, as when they decline to reelect a leader or otherwise reject his leadership on the grounds that he did not take their interests seriously enough. But in cases in which it is their interests that ostensibly justify the exception making, follower support of a leader's behavior may not be a reliable indicator of whether he was justified in the exceptions he made of himself. Determinations of justification in these cases are better suited to hearings by independent third parties such as those carried out within professional associations, by ethics boards, or at international tribunals.

In the end, it may appear somewhat paradoxical to defend even a refined version of this behavioral check. How can willingness to accept the penalty for exception-making behavior be a necessary condition on avoiding attributions of blameworthiness for the behavior itself? When a leader has satisfied this behavioral check along with the others, what can he be legitimately penalized for? After all, the defense of these checks assumes that lack of justification is not by itself sufficient for an attribution of blameworthiness. In short, if a leader is not to blame for the exceptions he makes of himself, then what is the point of asking him to risk being penalized for what he has done by allowing others to determine whether he had justification for his behavior? What this objection ignores is that the behavioral checks on exception making also assume that leaders who elude attributions of blameworthiness have done the best that can reasonably be expected of them with the beliefs that they had. Put another way, the checks assume that the ignorance of leaders is not itself culpable. Properly limited, willingness to accept the penalty for exception making constitutes submission of leadership behavior to others not only for a determination of justification but also for epistemic assessment. Leaders in a position of epistemic uncertainty can be held responsible for their exception-making behavior, then, either because they did not do better in their own determinations of justification or because, even though they did the best that can be reasonably expected of them with the beliefs that they had, they failed to adopt the normative responses to the epistemic limits of leadership.

Chapter 7

Ignorance, History, and Moral Membership

I. INTRODUCTION

This chapter begins with the assumption that there is little to be said morally in favor of many of the social practices of the past. Here, in particular, I have in mind the United States' shameful connections to the institution of slavery and, especially, the connections between this institution and many of our most revered leaders, leaders such as Thomas Jefferson. Atrocities committed against generations of human beings and the legal framework that made these atrocities possible remain on our collective conscience.[1] But these past ethical failures are not the only ones I have in mind. My argument also draws on other criticizable aspects of our history – for example, our own society's treatment of women. Of course, practices of this moral turpitude are not limited to the United States or, for that matter, even to the West. However, I want to focus on the immoral social practices that will be most familiar to our leaders because my argument is ultimately one about how they ought to draw on these examples to negotiate the difficulties associated with the moral evaluation of present social practices. My claim, then, is that recognizing central features of our historical immorality has important implications for how contemporary leaders should respond to some of the most important moral problems they currently face. The main implication of this argument is that there are strong epistemic reasons against the kind of moral exclusiveness that characterizes leadership as it is ordinarily understood.

---

[1] For President Clinton's statements on African slavery, see, for example, James Bennet, "In Uganda, Clinton Expresses Regret on Slavery in U.S.: Stops Short of Apology," *New York Times* (March 25, 1998).

It is not uncommon to look to the past to support claims about the good fortune of those of us living in the present. Whatever the metaphysical problems associated with comparisons of this kind, there is surely some truth to the claim that contemporary leaders are lucky not to have been born and reared under social institutions such as slavery. For all the obvious reasons, they can certainly consider themselves lucky not to have been born into the position of the enslaved. Additionally, though, contemporary leaders should recognize how lucky they are to have been born in an era in which neither they nor their followers have the legal rights of slaveholders. This second sense in which they are lucky is well captured by what Thomas Nagel, in his seminal discussion of moral luck, calls "luck in one's circumstances." As Nagel tells us,

> What we do is . . . limited by the opportunities and choices with which we are faced, and these are largely determined by factors beyond our control. Someone who was an officer in a concentration camp might have led a quiet and harmless life if the Nazis had never come to power in Germany. And someone who led a quiet and harmless life in Argentina might have become an officer in a concentration camp if he had not left Germany for business reasons in 1930.[2]

Luckily, contemporary leaders will never know what it is like to run up against the moral challenges that infected the opportunities and choices available to the most powerful members of slaveholding societies. Nor will they ever know how they would have responded to these choices and opportunities. The hope, of course, is that our leaders would have used their positions of power in that society to take a moral stand against the practice of slavery, regardless of the consequences for followers and for themselves. We may like to believe, that is, that they would have been moved to act beyond the partiality of leadership, on a broader commitment to humanity, and with the courage needed to act on this commitment. My concern, however, is that for many contemporary leaders the odds are not all that good that they would have done so.[3]

Our inclination may be to believe, then, that contemporary leaders are lucky enough to have eluded moral challenges of the caliber that confronted past leaders. If current society is characterized by no such practices, then, luckily for our leaders, they have simply missed the

---

[2] Thomas Nagel, "Moral Luck," in his *Mortal Questions* (Cambridge: Cambridge University Press, 1979), pp. 25–26.

[3] More poignantly, one of my students expressed his shock to me at the fact that the Forest of the Righteous Gentiles was not larger than it is. Trees are planted in this forest to recognize non-Jews who assisted Jews in the Holocaust.

chance to test the motivational purchase of their moral commitments. But this line of thinking must also assume that their current moral commitments are roughly correct. For, if this assumption is false, then it is possible that, without realizing it, contemporary leaders are actually up against the same kinds of moral challenges that past leaders faced. So, before our leaders can conclude that they have luckily avoided those circumstances in which they might prove *volitionally* lacking, the assumption must first be made that they are in a *cognitive* position to recognize immoral social practices when they see them.[4] In support of this assumption, Susan Wolf tentatively suggests that our contemporaries, unlike some moral agents of the past, are lucky enough "to *have* minimally sufficient abilities cognitively and normatively to recognize and appreciate the world for what it is."[5] But what reason do contemporary leaders have to think that their evaluations of current social practices are roughly correct? Could these leaders not make faulty assessments of current social practices even though they are doing the best that they can with their beliefs about the legitimacy of these practices? Perhaps they are not so lucky after all.

There is a real possibility that the members of future generations will look back on our leaders with the strong sense of moral judgment that we sometimes direct toward past leaders. One explanation of the assumptions behind these intergenerational assessments of blameworthiness points to what Richard Nisbett and Lee Ross call the *"representativeness* heuristic. This heuristic involves the application of relatively simple resemblance or 'goodness of fit' criteria to problems of categorization."[6] Relying on this cognitive shortcut, we attribute "the harmful action . . . to a corresponding harmful intent or malevolent disposition."[7] Assessments of blameworthiness that overutilize the representativeness heuristic thus privilege volitional understandings of ethical failures in leadership. Nowhere is this truer than in our explanations of racial or ethnic prejudice, which is "at the least importantly aided, and perhaps

---

[4] For the argument against the suggestion that our ancestors were in no epistemic position to recognize immoral social practices, see Michele M. Moody-Adams, "Culture, Responsibility, and Affected Ignorance," *Ethics* 104 (1994): 291–309. Her argument is discussed in detail in Section II of this chapter.

[5] Susan Wolf, "Sanity and the Metaphysics of Responsibility," in Ferdinand Schoeman, ed., *Responsibility, Character, and the Emotions: New Essays in Moral Psychology* (Cambridge: Cambridge University Press, 1987), p. 58.

[6] Richard Nisbett and Lee Ross, *Human Inference: Strategies and Shortcomings of Human Judgment* (Englewood Cliffs, NJ: Prentice-Hall, 1980), p. 24.

[7] Nisbett and Ross, *Human Inference*, p. 241.

even largely determined, by cognitive shortcomings."[8] But the readiness of our descendents to make intergenerational attributions of blameworthiness may also be due to the future transparency of our leaders' moral failings. The transparent immorality of our practices, that is, may suggest that the cause of the failings of contemporary leaders must have been volitional, not cognitive. Based on this suggestion, future leaders may consider themselves lucky not to have been put to the motivational test by what are, from their perspectives, our obviously immoral social practices. After all, as they might think to themselves, how hard could it have been for our leaders to recognize that supporting such behavior was wrong, even though it would have been difficult to act against the strong societal currents of their time?

The question for us, then, is this: What should leaders make of the real chance that our current social practices are open to legitimate criticism from future generations, perhaps as a result of our bad epistemic luck? Are there further measures that leaders can take now to avoid these judgments from our moral descendents? One response holds that "our judgments of responsibility can only be made from here, on the basis of the understandings and values that we can develop by exercising the abilities we do possess as well and as fully as possible."[9] Against this view, I propose in this chapter that morality ultimately requires that our leaders do more. Specifically, it requires that they draw on normative prescriptions that accommodate, rather than lament, their epistemic limitations, and that they do so in anticipation of judgments of responsibility from future generations. My reasoning is that contemporary leaders have something that past leaders lacked – a robust awareness of their own fallibility as moral agents and a good sense of the specific inclinations behind immoral social practices. This kind of self-awareness gives leaders good epistemic reasons to adopt a principle of moral inclusiveness at the margins of moral community, even though this principle is in direct conflict with many of our most common presuppositions about leadership. Accordingly, we should fully expect that the judgments of future generations will focus on the extent to which leaders bring this principle to bear on our current social practices. Recognizing their own epistemic limitations, that is, makes leaders more responsible for our practices, not less.

---

[8] Nisbett and Ross, *Human Inference*, p. 229.
[9] Wolf, "Sanity and the Metaphysics of Responsibility," p. 61.

II. RESPONSIBILITY FOR THE PAST: LEADER VOLITION

Any theory of responsibility that leans heavily on the epistemic limits of humans comes up against an important challenge in the writings of Michele Moody-Adams. Moody-Adams takes particular aim at what she calls the inability thesis: "the claim that sometimes one's upbringing in a culture simply renders one unable to know that certain actions are wrong."[10] She thinks that, among its other faults, the appeal to culturally induced moral blind spots "dangerously ignores the common, and culpable, tendency simply to affect ignorance of the possibility that some cultural practice might be morally flawed."[11] Moody-Adams's view thus connects historical immoralities to a kind of ignorance, but the ignorance in question can be traced back to non-epistemic failings for which people in the past were culpable. Our historical connection to slavery, for instance, reflects individual choices "to perpetuate an institution that benefited non-slaves in various ways."[12] One way to put Moody-Adams's point, then, is to say that the explanation of historical immorality does not end with an appeal to the cognitive predicament of past leaders. Rather, the explanation is ultimately a volitional one. Even if past leaders believed that some individuals were outside of the moral community and therefore that enslaving these individuals was justified, such leaders were not doing the best that they could with respect to their beliefs about the legitimacy of this practice. Since these leaders were responsible for their own epistemic predicament, an appeal to ignorance does not undermine their responsibility for perpetuating the practice of slavery.

According to Moody-Adams, "perhaps the most common form of affected ignorance is the tendency to avoid acknowledging our human fallibility: as finite and fallible beings, even our most deeply held convictions may be wrong."[13] Leaders who supported slavery are thus subject to blame for "avoiding the *possibility* that the assumptions underlying [slavery] might be wrong."[14] Here, of course, a lot turns on how we understand the claims about human nature underlying Moody-Adams's charge. In fact, at least one understanding of the claim that humans

---

[10] Moody-Adams, "Culture, Responsibility, and Affected Ignorance," p. 293.
[11] Moody-Adams, "Culture, Responsibility, and Affected Ignorance," p. 298.
[12] Moody-Adams, "Culture, Responsibility, and Affected Ignorance," p. 296.
[13] Moody-Adams, "Culture, Responsibility, and Affected Ignorance," p. 301.
[14] Moody-Adams, "Culture, Responsibility, and Affected Ignorance," p. 302, emphasis added.

are "finite and fallible" creates internal problems for her analysis. This claim cannot be taken to imply, for example, that leaders, being human, sometimes get things wrong even though they are doing their epistemic best. For if we see this as a possible outcome of chronic human fallibility, then an acknowledgment of this possibility would not preclude leaders from faultlessly getting things badly wrong. Instead, mistakes are just what we should expect on this interpretation. We should expect, that is, that leaders will sometimes get things badly wrong through no fault of their own. So, understanding our finitude and fallibility in this way actually undermines the argument for the centrality of affected ignorance in analysis of ethical failures in leadership.

The advocate of the volitional account must have in mind some other sense in which leaders are fallible and finite beings. Perhaps Moody-Adams's charge draws attention to the sense in which fallibility and finitude are rooted not in fundamental epistemic limits but rather in the more general ways in which humans are motivated. Clearly, this understanding of human fallibility and finitude is more consistent with a volitional account of slavery and, specifically, with a volitional account of the beliefs on which this practice rested. Simply put, the beliefs of those who supported the institution of slavery can be traced to egoistic origins. For example, pro-slavery leaders were motivated by, among other things, their own interests in sustaining an immoral social practice. Had these leaders only set aside self-interest and examined the assumptions on which slavery rested, they would have seen this practice for the moral monstrosity that it was. This interpretation also comports well with Moody-Adams's Aristotelian urgings that "ignorance of what one ought to do can generally be traced to some personal failure, whether a culpable omission or commission."[15] Again, the specific personal failing to which she appeals must ultimately be one of volition: the "*unwillingness* to consider that some practice might be wrong."[16] Applied to ethical failures in leadership, then, these motivational weaknesses incline leaders

---

[15] Moody-Adams, "Culture, Responsibility, and Affected Ignorance," p. 293. Aristotle says of the morally mistaken individual, "[H]e is himself responsible for having [his] character, by living carelessly, and similarly for being unjust by cheating, or being intemperate by passing his time in drinking and the like; for each type of activity produces the corresponding character" (*Nicomachean Ethics*, trans. Terence Irwin [Indianapolis: Hackett Publishing Company, 1985], p. 67 [1114a4–7]).

[16] Moody-Adams, "Culture, Responsibility, and Affected Ignorance," p. 294, emphasis added.

to immorality by preventing them from making the kind of effort needed to get things right.

Could leaders get things badly wrong even though they are perfectly willing to consider the immorality of a practice? Alternatively put, does the volitional understanding of their fallibility and finitude lend itself to a wholesale explanation of historical immorality? I want to suggest that this account of ethical failure ignores two important ways in which an appeal to the "unwillingness to consider that some practice might be wrong" will be insufficient to explain the immorality of past leaders. First, there is a straightforward sense in which these leaders might have been able to consider the wrongness of a practice and yet failed to do so for fundamentally epistemic reasons, reasons not reducible to criticizable aspects of human motivation. The defense of this claim works from the distinction between what past leaders were able to do by way of consideration of the wrongness of their practices and what we can reasonably expect them to have done on this score. When it comes to cases of historical immorality, Moody-Adams infers from the fact that people did less than they were able to do that they must have been unwilling to do more. But this inference assumes that they knew they should do more. Without this assumption, we are in no position to conclude that past ethical failures in leadership were grounded in the unwillingness of leaders to consider the wrongness of their practices as opposed to ignorance of the fact that more should be done by way of consideration of these practices.

An attribution of responsibility to past leaders for "refusing to consider whether some practice ... might be wrong"[17] needs to show not only that they were able to consider this possibility but also that they did not fail to consider this possibility because they were ignorant of the moral importance of doing so. Unless this latter claim can be established, it would expect too much of them to say that they are at fault for not having considered the possibility and, moreover, that they are blameworthy on these grounds for perpetuating the practice. In effect, the inference from ability to unwillingness assumes away what is perhaps the strongest case for understanding historical immorality in terms of the epistemic limits of leadership – namely, that it is sometimes unreasonable to expect leaders to do all that they are able to do. The distinction between what leaders are able to do and what can be reasonably expected of them ultimately turns on an epistemic matter. Expectations

---

[17] Moody-Adams, "Culture, Responsibility, and Affected Ignorance," p. 296.

can be unreasonable when perfectly able leaders are ignorant of the fact that they should draw on their abilities.[18] Of course, expectations that leaders do more can be reasonable when their ignorance of what they should do is itself affected. Can the volitional account sustain a commitment to the claim that if past leaders did not know that they should do more, then they should have known this?

The charge of epistemic negligence stands up only on the condition that our past leaders were aware, at some earlier point, of the need to take better care in the acquisition and maintenance of their beliefs, especially those that came to bear on the evaluation of a particular set of social practices. As Michael Zimmerman makes this point, "[C]ulpability for ignorant behavior must be rooted in culpability that involves no ignorance."[19] It is not enough, then, simply to point to the "tendency . . . to affect ignorance of the possibility that some cultural practice might be morally flawed."[20] If it is on the basis of this tendency that the ignorance of past leaders was affected, then we would also have to establish that they were appropriately cognizant of the general tendency, and, more to the point, of the fact that it might get played out in the context of a particular set of practices. There is a sense, then, in which efforts to undermine the inability thesis are somewhat misplaced. When it comes to assessing the responsibility of past leaders, the first point of inquiry is not what they were able to do but rather what they had reason (perhaps earlier) to think that they should do. That said, it would be a mistake to draw the stronger inference that issues of ability are entirely beside the point. These issues, however, may well cut differently than the volitional account would allow. In some cases, recognizing the possibility that a practice might be wrong has little payoff for the ability of leaders to get things right.

To establish the second way in which "unwillingness to consider that some practice might be wrong"[21] is insufficient to explain historical immorality, let us concede that past leaders were aware both of the general

---

[18] David H. Jones claims, incorrectly I think, that exculpating deficiencies are impossible to overcome, whereas mitigating deficiencies are merely difficult to overcome (*Moral Responsibility in the Holocaust: A Study in the Ethics of Character* [Lanham, MD: Rowman and Littlefield Publishers, 1999], ch. 5).

[19] Michael J. Zimmerman, "Moral Responsibility and Ignorance," *Ethics* 107 (1997): 417. See also, Holly Smith, "Culpable Ignorance," *Philosophical Review* 92 (1983): 543–571.

[20] Moody-Adams, "Culture, Responsibility, and Affected Ignorance," p. 298.

[21] Moody-Adams, "Culture, Responsibility, and Affected Ignorance," p. 294.

phenomenon of affected ignorance and its potential application to a particular social practice. For the sake of argument, that is, we can assume that past leaders recognized "the possibility that the assumptions underlying [some practice] might be wrong."[22] By itself, recognition of this possibility need not get them very far in an evaluation of the practice under consideration. There is a significant gap, for example, between evidence of opposition to slavery, say, in Aristotle's *Politics*, and any conclusions that we might expect ancient Greeks to draw about the morality of this practice.[23] Similarly, the fact that past leaders may have recognized the possibility that some practice might be wrong – for instance, slavery in the eighteenth century – does not necessarily mean that they were in a position to evaluate this practice correctly. In other words, the evaluation of a practice is often underdetermined by recognition of the possibility that it might be wrong.[24] This is especially true when the questions concerning the practice are not about whether there is a general moral prohibition against it but rather about which individuals are protected by this prohibition. Ancient Greeks and people of the seventeenth century alike recognized that not just anyone could be legitimately enslaved, but they believed nevertheless that this was permissible behavior, for instance, toward barbarians and Africans, respectively.

The distinction between recognizing the possibility that some practice might be wrong and getting things right more readily lends itself to explication in the context of contemporary moral disagreements. Again, this is because the obviousness of historical immoralities makes it hard to accept any account on which the relevant impediments are fundamentally cognitive. From our perspective, the transparent immorality of past social practices inclines us to think that awareness of the mere possibility that a particular practice might be wrong was surely epistemically enough for leaders to try to set things aright. When it comes to our own practices, however, moral evaluation is significantly less straightforward than this. Consider, for instance, that in the United States, state-mandated discrimination against homosexuals is

---

[22] Moody-Adams, "Culture, Responsibility, and Affected Ignorance," p. 302.
[23] Moody-Adams cites this example in "Culture, Responsibility, and Affected Ignorance," p. 296.
[24] Here, it will do little good to suggest that we might avoid moral fallout altogether simply by rejecting a practice upon recognition of the possibility that it might be wrong. Clearly, there are potential moral costs associated both with acting and with failing to act on this possibility.

commonly seen as acceptable when it comes to the institution of marriage.[25] To take another example, many Americans have little objection to according fewer rights to terrorist suspects or "enemy combatants" if they are non-citizens as opposed to citizens.[26] Since the morality of both of these practices is nevertheless highly contested, we can assume that leaders who support these practices are not ignorant of "the *possibility* that the assumptions underlying the practices might be wrong."[27] The presence of sustained disagreement in each of these cases is surely

---

[25] Here, I use *discrimination* in its descriptive sense; in other words, I do not assume that this kind of discrimination cannot be justified. According to a poll conducted by the Pew Research Center for People and the Press in November 2003, "59 percent of those polled said they opposed gay marriages, and only 32 percent favored them" (David E. Rosenbaum, "Legal License; Race, Sex and Forbidden Unions," *New York Times* [December 14, 2003]). President George W. Bush advocated a constitutional amendment against same-sex marriage on February 24, 2004 ("Same-Sex Marriage: Bush's Remarks on Marriage Amendment," *New York Times* [February 25, 2004]).

[26] An August 2002 poll "Civil Liberties Update" conducted by National Public Radio, the Henry J. Kaiser Family Foundation, and Harvard University's Kennedy School of Government found that 54 percent of Americans believe that non-citizens arrested for terrorism should have fewer legal rights than citizens arrested for terrorism (National Public Radio, "NPR/Kaiser/Kennedy School Civil Liberties Update," August 2002). The term *enemy combatant* is most often used to refer to Taliban detainees being held by the United States in Guantanamo Bay, Cuba. One controversy regarding these detainees is whether they merit prisoner-of-war status and the protections of the Geneva Conventions. In December 2003, the Ninth Circuit Court of Appeals declared that "the administration's policy of imprisoning the foreigners without access to U.S. legal protections was unconstitutional as well as a violation of international law" ("'Combatant' cases to be reviewed: Supreme Court will look at U.S. citizens being held in Cuba," *Richmond Times Dispatch* [February 21, 2004]). But the term *enemy combatant* is not exclusively reserved for non-citizens: "Two American citizens – [Jose] Padilla and Yaser Hamdi – [were] being held indefinitely as enemy combatants in military brigs in Charleston, S.C., and Norfolk, Va., respectively" (Warren Richey, "Detainee cases hit court," *Christian Science Monitor* [January 23, 2004]). In the summer of 2004, the United States Supreme Court, "[d]eclaring that 'a state of war is not a blank check for the president,' . . . ruled . . . that those deemed enemy combatants by the Bush administration, both in the United States and at Guantanamo Bay, Cuba, must be given the ability to challenge their detention before a judge or other 'neutral decision-maker'" (Linda Greenhouse, "Access to courts," *New York Times* [June 29, 2004]). We might ask whether the treatment of Padilla, who is a convert to Islam, and Hamdi, who had dual United States and Saudi citizenship, can be attributed – in part at least – to the fact that they are cultural and religious outsiders from the perspective of many citizens of the United States. A similar argument might be applied to the treatment of prisoners in the Abu Ghraib prison scandal in Iraq.

[27] Moody-Adams, "Culture, Responsibility, and Affected Ignorance," p. 302, emphasis added.

sufficient to raise this possibility for our leaders. In fact, taking a position on either side of the issues is often necessary to verify leadership potential. But is it an accurate characterization of the debates over same-sex marriage and the treatment of enemy combatants to say that the parties to the disagreements, regardless of which side the parties take, are simply not trying hard enough to arrive at the correct conclusions about the morality of these practices?

The volitional account would have it that with enough epistemic effort, individuals with incorrect commitments about the rights of homosexuals and enemy combatants would see the error of their ways, whatever the correct conclusion about these rights. This expectation should strike us as unreasonable. It trivializes the moral complexity of the issues involved to say that leaders who incorrectly support or oppose differential treatment of homosexuals and non-citizen terrorist suspects are wrong because their assumptions are "insufficiently examined."[28] Moreover, to the extent that the volitional account is insensitive to the fact of real moral disagreement, it puts leaders at significant risk of becoming overly confident in what they take to be their "sufficiently examined" assumptions about morally controversial issues. A more plausible account of the perpetuation of immoral social practices attributes this kind of ethical failure in leadership to something more than "an unwillingness to consider that some practice might be wrong."[29] Leaders can be badly mistaken about social practices even though they are doing the best that can be reasonably expected of them with the beliefs that they have. There is no reason to think that this was not also true of past leaders.

III. RESPONSIBILITY IN THE PRESENT: LEADER COGNITION

It is not new to point out that the epistemic limits of humans play a fundamental role in the perpetuation of immoral social practices. This view finds its most convincing expression in the work of Susan Wolf. On Wolf's account, "[W]e give less than full responsibility to persons who, though acting badly, act in ways that are strongly encouraged by their societies – the slaveowners of the 1850s, the Nazis of the 1930s, and

---

[28] See, for example, the discussion of communitarian moral theory in Chapter 4. There is a communitarian argument, I take it, for both of these practices. So, we cannot simply assume that they are wrong.
[29] Moody-Adams, "Culture, Responsibility, and Affected Ignorance," p. 294.

many male chauvinists of our fathers' generation, for example."[30] The reasoning, according to her, is that "they are . . . unable cognitively and normatively to recognize and appreciate the world for what it is. In our sense of the term, [they] are not fully *sane*."[31] To make the same point with a leadership example, Wolf creates the following case:

JoJo is the favorite son of Jo the First, an evil and sadistic dictator of a small, underdeveloped country. Because of his father's special feelings for the boy, JoJo is given a special education and is allowed to accompany his father and observe his daily routine. In light of this treatment, it is not surprising that little JoJo takes his father as a role model and develops values very much like Dad's. As an adult, he does many of the same sorts of things his father did, including sending people to prison or to death or to torture chambers on the basis of a whim . . . In light of JoJo's heritage and upbringing – both of which he was powerless to control – it is dubious at best that he should be regarded as responsible for what he does.[32]

With respect to our own sanity, however, Wolf thinks that we can be significantly more optimistic. In this section, I will argue that contemporary leaders cannot justify optimism about their sanity on the grounds that she gives. My argument thus questions whether contemporary leaders can assume they are that much better off than past leaders when it comes to meeting the sanity condition. In the next section, I show how contemporary leaders can be held responsible for the perpetuation of immoral social practices even if they fail to meet this condition on attributions of responsibility.

What reason do contemporary leaders have to think that they are cognitively poised for an accurate evaluation of our social practices? To use Wolf's terminology, how can contemporary leaders ground the assumption that they are sane? Wolf offers the following justification:

What justifies my confidence that, unlike the slaveowners, Nazis, and male chauvinists, . . . we are able to understand and appreciate the world for what it is? The answer to this is that nothing justifies this except widespread intersubjective agreement and the considerable success we have in getting around in the world and satisfying our needs. These are not sufficient grounds for the smug assumption that we are in a position to see the truth about *all* aspects of ethical and social life. Indeed, it seems more reasonable to expect that time will reveal blind spots in our cognitive and normative outlook, just as it has revealed errors

---

[30] Wolf, "Sanity and the Metaphysics of Responsibility," pp. 56–57.
[31] Wolf, "Sanity and the Metaphysics of Responsibility," p. 57.
[32] Wolf, "Sanity and the Metaphysics of Responsibility," pp. 53–54.

in the outlooks of those who have lived before. But our judgments of responsibility can only be made from here, on the basis of the understandings and values that we can develop by exercising the abilities we do possess as well and as fully as possible.[33]

Applied to an analysis of ethical failures in leadership, Wolf's response is encouraging only on the condition that it adequately differentiates the perspective that contemporary leaders might take on our social practices from the comparable perspective of past leaders. For we would not be heartened by her remarks if it turns out that contemporary leaders have no stronger grounds for being confident that they are sane than past leaders had for confidence in their sanity. Presumably, then, contemporary leaders eclipse past leaders on the justificatory criteria that Wolf sets out: (1) widespread intersubjective agreement, and (2) success in getting around in the world and satisfying our needs.[34]

Considering the first justification, it is hard to see how an appeal to intersubjective agreement might separate contemporary leaders from past leaders. To be sure, we now have consensus on many of the issues about which our ancestors disagreed vehemently – for example, the institution of slavery. That said, we have nothing like widespread intersubjective agreement on a host of other moral issues. To return to the examples introduced in Section II, there are quite high levels of disagreement surrounding the issues of same-sex marriage and the treatment of non-citizen terrorist suspects. So even if an appeal to intersubjectivity gives us reason to think that our own evaluations of a historical practice are superior to our ancestors' evaluations of that same practice, such an appeal does little to justify confidence in the assessments we make of current morally controversial practices. With respect to the ethics of same-sex marriage and the treatment of non-citizens, the level of intersubjective agreement to which our leaders might appeal is hardly better than that achieved by past leaders on these same general issues. In fact, relying only on an appeal to consensus, it would seem that past leaders had much stronger grounds for their confidence.

Similar concerns about the comparisons required by Wolf's criteria underwrite a challenge to the second justification that she offers – namely, "the considerable success we have in getting around in the

---

[33] Wolf, "Sanity and the Metaphysics of Responsibility," pp. 60–61.
[34] This use of *justification* refers to its epistemic sense. Are leaders justified in their beliefs about our social practices?

world and satisfying our needs."[35] Admittedly, compared with our moral ancestors, we are able to get around in the world and meet our own needs remarkably well. It is not implausible to say, moreover, that at least some of this success can be attributed to the abilities of our leaders "cognitively and normatively to recognize and appreciate the world for what it is."[36] But if this kind of success is to justify confidence in their sanity, it must distinguish contemporary leaders from past leaders not by a direct comparison of our success with the success of our ancestors but rather by a comparison between the respective perspectives these leaders might take on success. The relevant comparison, that is, is between the perspective contemporary leaders might take on our success and the perspective past leaders might have taken on the success of their contemporaries. Looked at in this way, Wolf's second justificatory criterion fails to differentiate contemporary leaders from past leaders. Making a comparison with the leaders who preceded them, past leaders could also point to the remarkable ability of their contemporaries to get around in the world and to meet their needs. On this reading of the second criterion, then, contemporary leaders are in no better position than were past leaders to justify confidence in their sanity.

There is a deeper problem, however, with Wolf's second justificatory criterion. The most controversial issues in social life raise questions of moral membership. This was true for past leaders with respect to issues such as slavery and women's rights, and it is equally true for us now with respect to such issues as same-sex marriage and the rights of noncitizen terrorist suspects. Given the nature of these issues, an appeal to the success *we* have in getting around in the world and satisfying *our* needs will be set against background assumptions about who counts, and to what extent, for the purposes of morality – in which case many of the central moral problems stand to be assumed away. This is because any assessment of the connection between the success of a practice and its morality would have to assume that we know for whom getting around in the world really matters and for whose needs the presence of dissatisfaction would be worthy of serious moral attention. But these are exactly the issues up for debate. It would therefore be a mistake for leaders to test the accuracy with which they assess the morality of a social practice against *our* ability to negotiate the world in which we live.

[35] Wolf, "Sanity and the Metaphysics of Responsibility," p. 60.
[36] Wolf, "Sanity and the Metaphysics of Responsibility," p. 57.

The distinction between two basic varieties of moral ignorance might help to illuminate this particular line of criticism. In Chapter 1, I suggested that moral ignorance can be based on either *content* mistakes or *scope* mistakes. Mistakes about the content of morality are indexed to beliefs about the moral status of *act-types*. Here, 'act-types' is construed broadly so as to include general ways of acting, believing, choosing, intending, feeling, desiring, or any of their negative correlates such as refraining from acting, believing, choosing, and so on. In their simplest guise, content mistakes are failures to see what act-types are morally impermissible or wrong. For example, an individual might be mistaken about whether sex before marriage is morally impermissible or whether fantasizing about a foe's demise is morally wrong. In contrast, mistakes about the scope of morality are indexed to beliefs about the moral status of *individuals* and, in many cases, to beliefs about which individuals are members of the moral community.[37] As such, these mistakes are over who counts, and to what extent, for the purposes of applying morality's strictures. Corresponding questions of scope thus endeavor to fix the domain of individuals to whom moral duties are owed. These questions ask how far morality's protections should be extended.

One way to put the main point against Wolf's second justificatory criterion is to say that it does not do enough to justify contemporary leaders' confidence that they have correctly answered questions about the scope of morality's requirements. An appeal to our success in getting around in the world is unsuited to this task precisely because of the nature of the ignorance with which we should be most concerned – namely, ignorance about who counts for the purposes of morality. As a matter of history, our most morally reprehensible behavior has been bound up with mistaken views about moral membership. In the United States alone, we can number among these mistakes the "removal and relocation" of Native Americans,[38] the institution of slavery, and the internment of Japanese-Americans in World War II. More generally, we

---

[37] As we have seen, however, an equally important kind of scope mistake, one to which leaders are particularly susceptible, is indexed to questions of which individuals are bound by the requirements of morality.

[38] Vine Deloria, Jr., and Clifford M. Lytle, *American Indians, American Justice* (Austin: University of Texas Press, 1983), p. 6. Documents from the Board of Indian Commissioners make it clear that extermination was also a goal: "[T]he attempt to exterminate them has been carried on at a cost of from three to four millions of dollars per annum, with no appreciable progress made in accomplishing their extermination" (Office of Indian Affairs, *Annual Report of the Commissioner of Indian Affairs to the Secretary for the Year 1871* [Washington, DC: GPO, 1872]).

might think about our historical failure to extend morality's protections to women in our society. In some such cases, moral status is denied altogether on the grounds that these individuals simply do not have the status-conferring characteristics. With greater frequency perhaps, moral status is acknowledged but wildly underestimated because it is mistakenly attributed to derivative characteristics – for example, being mere property – or, alternatively, to insufficiently realized status-conferring properties – for example, having only limited rationality. Whatever the exact grounding of this kind of mistake about the scope of morality, we cannot ignore a history of moral atrocities grounded in failures to acknowledge moral membership. Recognition of this fact should make us suspicious of any leader whose confidence is borne of the success *we* have in getting around in the world and satisfying *our* needs.

In the end, Wolf's justificatory criteria do not demand enough of leaders. The first criterion sanctions inattention to the high levels of disagreement surrounding many of our social practices, and the second criterion promotes a preoccupation with our own needs and interests. Irving Janis's work on *groupthink*, which was discussed in Chapter 6, offers support for the first criticism by showing that leaders of cohesive in-groups are likely to think that they have established genuine intersubjectivity on issues that have serious, negative consequences for out-groups. In fact, the main thesis of Janis's work is that *"[t]he more amiability and esprit de corps among the members of a policy-making in-group, the greater is the danger that independent critical thinking will be replaced by groupthink, which is likely to result in irrational and dehumanizing actions directed against out-groups."*[39] The group dynamics literature also gives us reason to question leaders' appeals to Wolf's second justificatory criterion. For example, as David Messick points out, "The intergroup bias is one of the most frequently replicated effects in social psychology."[40] In these studies, subjects favor the interests of in-group members, even when group categorization is trivially determined.[41] Following Marilynn Brewer, Messick concludes that intergroup bias occurs not because group members want to harm the interests of out-group members but rather because they want to advance the interests of in-group

---

[39] Irving L. Janis, *Groupthink: Psychological Studies of Policy Decisions and Fiascoes*, 2nd edition (Boston: Houghton Mifflin Company, 1982), p. 13.
[40] David M. Messick, "Social Categories and Business Ethics," *Business Ethics Quarterly*, special issue (1998): 156.
[41] Henri Tajfel, "Experiments in Intergroup Discrimination," *Scientific American* 223 (1970): 96–102.

members.[42] In other words, deviations from standards of fairness and equality can be attributed to the preoccupation of in-groups with their own needs and interests.

Here, it is worth noting that "the question of selfishness *per se* is not at issue" in these cases of in-group favoritism.[43] Since the benefits in question go to anonymous members of the in-group and "the allocator gets nothing him or herself,"[44] ethical failures in leadership resulting from this phenomenon will not easily lend themselves to a volitional explanation. In-group interests, not leader self-interest, fuel the bias. Fixation on in-group interests nevertheless impedes the ability of leaders to moderate the justificatory force of leadership, especially if the phenomenon of groupthink makes it unlikely that they will be able to rely on group decision-making processes to overcome this bias. These problems can also be exacerbated by role expectations within groups. Drawing an analogy between business organizations and Philip Zimbardo's famous Stanford prison experiment, in which subjects readily conformed to their roles as "guards" and "prisoners," F. Neil Brady and Jeanne Logsdon remind us, for example, that "[t]he 'loyal agent's' standard for employee behavior demands conformity to organizational norms in order to further the organization's interests."[45]

Applied to the behavior of leaders, then, Wolf's justificatory criteria may actually contribute to ethical failures in leadership. Leaders who lean heavily on these criteria risk misplacing their confidence in the morality of our social practices. Any justification that neglects disagreement and overestimates the importance of our own needs and interests steers us away from recognition of the established social psychological fact that leaders are easily blinded to the immorality of the group. To be sure, cognizance of this fact need not put leaders in a position to overcome their moral ignorance. Still, even if leaders are unable to overcome moral ignorance, there may be room for an attribution of responsibility for how they deal with the epistemic limitations that they face in

---

[42] Messick, "Social Categories and Business Ethics," p. 158. See Marilynn B. Brewer, "In-group Bias in the Minimal Intergroup Situation: A Cognitive-Motivational Analysis," *Psychological Bulletin* 86 (1979): 307–324.

[43] Messick, "Social Categories and Business Ethics," p. 156.

[44] Messick, "Social Categories and Business Ethics," p. 156.

[45] F. Neil Brady and Jeanne M. Logsdon, "Zimbardo's 'Stanford Prison Experiment' and the Relevance of Social Psychology for Teaching Business Ethics," *Journal of Business Ethics* 7 (1988): 707. For the original experiment, see Craig Haney, Curtis Banks, and Philip Zimbardo, "Interpersonal Dynamics in a Simulated Prison," *International Journal of Criminology and Penology* 1 (1973): 69–97.

the moral appraisal of our social practices. We must therefore return to the question of what more leaders can do when their abilities to assess our social practices run out. The answer to this question calls for an examination of what they should know about their own tendencies to be mistaken.

IV. RESPONSIBILITY FROM THE FUTURE: LEADER RESPONSIVENESS

Wolf's justificatory criteria are not entirely satisfying when applied to leadership behavior because they seem to let leaders off the moral hook too easily. The difficulty, however, is in articulating the basis on which leaders might be legitimately held responsible for perpetuating social practices when they are ignorant of the immorality of these practices. The argument I want to develop in this section draws a distinction between the moral circumstances faced by contemporary leaders and those faced by past leaders. What makes our leaders responsible is that they are in a position to understand moral fallibility in a way that past leaders were not. On this argument, contemporary leaders can be expected to recognize the disposition to make a particular kind of mistake in response to a basic moral question. As a consequence, blameworthiness for the perpetuation of social practices that prove to be immoral can be attributed to failures to respond to this feature of their own moral psychology.

The historical asymmetry of my argument rests on a claim about differential access to evidence of moral fallibility in leadership. Contemporary leaders have access to the moral outcomes of the very cases over which past leaders struggled. Our leaders can be quite confident, for example, in the belief that past leaders were wrong in their treatment of Native Americans, African slaves, and women. The fact that this treatment was at the core of severely flawed, yet widely accepted, social practices should remind contemporary leaders that they too could be mistaken in their assessments of our own institutions. On the basis of this recollection, our leaders cannot maintain in good faith that they do not recognize the possibility that our practices might be wrong. Again, a general sense of fallibility is not nearly enough to ground an attribution of responsibility to contemporary leaders for failing to consider this possibility in every particular case. Given the myriad moral possibilities, there are surely limits to the epistemic demands that morality can make on people. But the historical cases to which our leaders have access also imply something specific about the nature of moral fallibility. These cases give contemporary leaders reason to believe that they are particularly liable to error when it comes to questions of who counts, and to what extent, for the purposes of applying morality's strictures. In effect, our historical immorality highlights the set of social practices for which our leaders should seriously consider the possibility that they are mistaken.

Understanding the nature of past wrongs focuses the reflective capacities of contemporary leaders on those social practices that give rise to questions of membership in the moral community. When it comes to exclusive moral practices, then, our leaders cannot avoid an attribution of responsibility simply on the grounds that they were ignorant of the possibility that these particular practices might be wrong. It is a different matter, of course, as to what contemporary leaders might be expected to make of the possibility that they are mistaken about issues of moral membership. For one thing, leaders cannot be expected to move with ease from recognition of this possibility to the conclusion that a particular practice is wrong – for example, that a prohibition on same-sex marriage or current treatment of non-citizen terrorist suspects is wrong. Once more, the expectation that leaders come to a conclusive evaluation of these practices would be out of place if it turns out that they are simply not in a position to get things right. So to some extent, what leaders might be expected to make of the possibility that they are mistaken about moral membership will depend on whether they are able "cognitively and normatively to recognize and appreciate the world for what it is."[46] But the expectations on our leaders will depend on more than just whether they can correctly assess our practices. For contemporary leaders can also be held responsible with respect to their *inability* to come to accurate evaluations of these practices.

Here, I do not have in mind the relatively commonplace truth that leaders can be held responsible for an inability because of failures, say, to nurture natural potentialities or, alternatively, to correct the inability itself by exercising other capabilities. Rather, my claim is that even if it is false both that an inability could have been avoided and that it could have been adequately overcome, leaders can nevertheless be held responsible for how they respond to it. This kind of assessment of responsibility looks to how leaders come to terms with the inability in their efforts to work through the moral challenges with which they

[46] Wolf, "Sanity and the Metaphysics of Responsibility," p. 58.

are currently faced. An attribution of responsibility for the way leaders respond to an inability assumes not only that they have good reason to suspect that they are liable to it but also that they know how the inability typically gets played out in moral life. If leaders do not have a sense of the nature of the moral risk posed by the inability, then they cannot very well know how to work out a response. In the absence of this kind of knowledge, leaders might well respond after they have come to the conclusion that a particular practice is wrong, say, with a readiness to do their part to make amends for support of an immoral social institution. Still, we are ultimately concerned that such institutions not be perpetuated, which would require that leaders know something about the moral risks posed by that inability and, moreover, that they have knowledge of these risks well before being made aware of its full moral costs in a particular case.

We can assume that contemporary leaders know a good deal about the moral fallout of their evaluative limits. This assumption is warranted by a further appeal to the differential access our leaders have to historical immorality. Here, too, contemporary leaders are set apart by virtue of their ability to look back on the misjudgments that past leaders made with respect to immoral social practices. From our leaders' perspective on the "bad moralities"[47] of the past, they know more than just that leaders are liable to be mistaken with respect to questions of membership in the moral community. They also know that the very worst historical practices were premised on a particular kind of answer to these questions. For our purposes, the most salient feature of these practices is that past leaders were overly exclusive on the issue of who counts, and to what extent, for the purposes of morality. Simply put, they were not nearly so inclined mistakenly to overextend moral membership as they were wrongly to refuse it. Colonization, slavery, and gender discrimination are all cases of moral exclusion and moral subordination, as was the treatment of Jews and others in Nazi Germany. We also know that, at least in the case of Nazi Germany, leaders who made the right moral choice had a very different answer to questions about membership in the moral community. Drawing on the research of Samuel and Pearl Oliner, David Jones points out that helpers and rescuers "differed markedly from nonrescuers in the degree to which they possessed the characteristic of 'extensivity' . . . Helpers and rescuers saw Jewish victims of the

[47] This phrase is from Jonathan Bennett, "The Conscience of Huckleberry Finn," *Philosophy* 49 (1974): 123–134.

Final Solution as fellow human beings who were as deserving as anyone else of their benevolent concern and conscientious fulfillment of basic moral duties."[48]

The epistemic limits of leadership, then, get played out in current social practices against the backdrop of an awful tendency to deny and underestimate the position of individuals at the margins of moral community.[49] Warrant Officer Hugh Thompson, a United States aeroscout helicopter pilot in the Vietnam War, recognized this tendency simply by comparing the behavior of fellow soldiers in the massacre at My Lai to the mass shootings of Jews carried out by Nazi Einsatzgruppen and police battalions in World War II.[50] Thompson responded by threatening to open fire on United States soldiers if the massacre continued, thereby challenging one of the central assumptions of leadership – namely, that leaders should always put the interests of in-group members first.[51] Should contemporary leaders also be willing to challenge this assumption? If it turns out that our leaders are committed to overly exclusive social practices, future generations will be right to point to what these leaders currently have reason to believe about their own epistemic limitations and the ways in which other leaders have been inclined to come to terms with such limitations. On this view, an attribution of responsibility to contemporary leaders turns on the inclusiveness of the response they make upon recognition of their liability to a particular kind of mistake about who counts, and to what extent, for the purposes of morality.

---

[48] Jones, *Moral Responsibility in the Holocaust*, p. 202. Jones's reference is to Samuel P. Oliner and Pearl M. Oliner, *The Altruistic Personality: Rescuers of Jews in Nazi Germany* (New York: Free Press, 1988), ch. 10. Unfortunately, out of 65 million Germans, there were only approximately 55,000 helpers and rescuers (Jones, *Moral Responsibility in the Holocaust*, p. 200).

[49] This premise distinguishes my argument from the so-called "moral risk" or "moral uncertainty" arguments in the literature. See, for example, Anne Lindsay, "On the Slippery Slope Again," *Analysis* 35 (1974): 32; Graham Oddie, "Moral Uncertainty and Human Embryo Experimentation," in K. W. M. Fulford, Grant R. Gillett, and Janet Martin Soskice, eds., *Medicine and Moral Reasoning* (New York: Cambridge University Press, 1994), pp. 144–161; Tom Regan, *The Case for Animal Rights* (Berkeley: University of California Press, 1983), p. 367; and Peter Singer, *Practical Ethics* (Cambridge: Cambridge University Press, 1979), p. 119.

[50] *Remember My Lai*, PBS Video (Yorkshire Television production for Frontline, 1989).

[51] According to Lawrence Colburn, former helicopter door gunner, "He told us if the Americans were to open fire on these Vietnamese as he was getting them out of the bunker, that we should return fire on the Americans" (*Remember My Lai*).

At the very least, future generations can reasonably expect that our leaders respond by including individuals at the margins of moral community.[52] After all, this is where past leaders went badly wrong, and contemporary leaders are hardly well situated for confidence in the claim that they will come off any better on future evaluations of our practices. In fact, given what our leaders can be reasonably expected to know about the nature of their moral fallibility, they are likely to come off much worse than past leaders in this kind of assessment of responsibility. This is especially true for controversies over questions of membership in the moral community. If contemporary leaders incorrectly come down on the side of exclusion in these cases, an appeal to their epistemic limitations will not be enough to undermine future attributions of responsibility for the perpetuation of immoral social practices. For our descendents might well concede the difficulty of the moral challenges we face and yet hold our leaders responsible for a lack of responsiveness to their inabilities and, specifically, to what they have reason to believe about the way this inability gets played out in moral life. In effect, future generations will be in a position to blame contemporary leaders for falling back on traditionally failed ways of responding to moral ignorance. Perhaps the best our leaders can do by way of a response is to compensate for inclinations toward exclusivity. One way for leaders to avoid the mistakes of the past is to adopt a principle of inclusiveness at the margins of moral community.

---

[52] The Reverend Warren Hammonds resigned as director of student life at Baptist Theological Seminary in Richmond because his "conscience would not allow him to enforce a policy that excludes practicing homosexuals, including those in committed relationships, from [the] seminary" (Alberta Lindsey, "Director leaves seminary over code on gays," *Richmond Times-Dispatch* [October 2, 2004]). Evan Gerstmann defends same-sex marriage in terms of "legal and constitutional rights that must be applied and protected equally for all people" (*Same-Sex Marriage and the Constitution* [Cambridge: Cambridge University Press, 2004], p. 4).

Works Cited

Ansbro, John J., *Martin Luther King, Jr.: The Making of a Mind* (Maryknoll, NY: Orbis Books, 1982).

Aquinas, Thomas, *On Kingship, To the King of Cyprus*, in Michael L. Morgan (ed.), *Classics of Moral and Political Theory*, 3rd edition (Indianapolis: Hackett Publishing Company, 2001), pp. 397–399.

Aristotle, *The Politics*, translated by T. A. Sinclair, revised and re-presented by Trevor J. Saunders (New York: Penguin Books, 1981).

Aristotle, *Nicomachean Ethics*, translated by Terence Irwin (Indianapolis: Hackett Publishing Company, 1985).

Avolio, Bruce J., and Edwin A. Locke, "Contrasting Different Philosophies of Leader Motivation: Altruism Versus Egoism," *Leadership Quarterly* 13 (2002): 169–191.

Bass, Bernard M., *Leadership and Performance Beyond Expectations* (New York: Free Press, 1985).

Bass, Bernard M., and Paul Steidlmeier, "Ethics, Character, and Authentic Transformational Leadership Behavior," *Leadership Quarterly* 10 (1999): 181–217.

Batson, C. Daniel, Pamela J. Cochran, Marshall F. Biederman, James L. Blosser, Maurice J. Ryan, and Bruce Vogt, "Failure to Help When in a Hurry: Callousness or Conflict?" *Personality and Social Psychology Bulletin* 4 (1978): 97–101.

Bennet, James, "In Uganda, Clinton Expresses Regret on Slavery in U.S.: Stops Short of Apology," *New York Times*, March 25, 1998.

Bennett, Jonathan, "The Conscience of Huckleberry Finn," *Philosophy* 49 (1974): 123–134.

Bennis, Warren G., and Burt Nanus, *Leaders: The Strategies for Taking Charge* (New York: Harper and Row Publishers, 1985).

bin Laden, Osama, "bin Laden's 'letter to America,'" *Observer*, November 24, 2002.

Blake, Robert Rogers, and Jane Srygley Mouton, "The Managerial Dilemma," in their *The Managerial Grid: Key Orientations for Achieving Production Through People* (Houston: Gulf Publishing Company, 1964), pp. 5–17.

Blum, John Morton, *From the Morgenthau Diaries: Years of War 1941–1945* (Boston: Houghton Mifflin Company, 1967).

Bowie, Norman, "A Kantian Theory of Leadership," *Leadership and Organization Development Journal: Special Issue on Ethics and Leadership* 21 (2000): 185–193.

Bowman, Rex, "Not-guilty plea given in D-Day fraud trial," *Richmond Times-Dispatch*, January 31, 2004.

Brady, F. Neil, and Jeanne M. Logsdon, "Zimbardo's 'Stanford Prison Experiment' and the Relevance of Social Psychology for Teaching Business Ethics," *Journal of Business Ethics* 7 (1988): 703–710.

Bratzel, John F., and Leslie B. Rout, Jr., "FDR and the 'Secret Map,'" *Wilson Quarterly* 9, 1 (1985): 167–173.

Brewer, Marilynn B., "In-Group Bias in the Minimal Intergroup Situation: A Cognitive-Motivational Analysis," *Psychological Bulletin* 86 (1979): 307–324.

Brightman, Edgar, *Moral Laws* (New York: Abingdon Press, 1933).

Buchanan, Allen E., "Social Moral Epistemology," *Social Philosophy and Policy* 19 (2002): 126–152.

Burns, James MacGregor, *Leadership* (New York: Harper and Row Publishers, 1978).

Burns, James MacGregor, "Foreword," in Joanne B. Ciulla (ed.), *Ethics, the Heart of Leadership* (Westport, CT: Praeger, 1998), pp. ix–xii.

Burns, James MacGregor, *Transforming Leadership: A New Pursuit of Happiness* (New York: Atlantic Monthly Press, 2003).

Burns, Robert, "Rumsfeld says American forces had no chance of taking Saddam's sons alive," Associated Press, July 24, 2003.

Bush, George W., 2004 State of the Union address.

Butler, Joseph, "Sermon XI: On the Love of our Neighbor," in his *The Analogy of Religion, Natural and Revealed, to the Constitution and Course of Nature; To Which Are Added, Two Brief Dissertations: On Personal Identity, and On the Nature of Virtue; and Fifteen Sermons* (London: Henry G. Bohn, 1852), pp. 361–363.

Carey, Michael R., "Transformational Leadership and the Fundamental Option for Self-Transcendence," *Leadership Quarterly* 3 (1992): 217–236.

Carruthers, Peter, *The Animals Issue* (Cambridge: Cambridge University Press, 1992).

Chemers, Martin M., "Contemporary Leadership Theory," in J. Thomas Wren (ed.), *The Leader's Companion: Insights on Leadership Through the Ages* (New York: Free Press, 1995), pp. 83–99.

Ciulla, Joanne B., "Imagination, Fantasy, Wishful Thinking and Truth," *Business Ethics Quarterly*, special issue (1998): 99–107.

Ciulla, Joanne B., "Leadership Ethics: Mapping the Territory," in Joanne B. Ciulla (ed.), *Ethics, the Heart of Leadership* (Westport, CT: Praeger, 1998), pp. 3–25.

Ciulla, Joanne B. (ed.), *The Ethics of Leadership* (Belmont, CA: Wadsworth/Thomson Learning, 2003).

Ciulla, Joanne B., "Ethics and Leadership Effectiveness," in John Antonakis, Anna T. Cianciolo, and Robert J. Sternberg (eds.), *The Nature of Leadership* (Thousand Oaks, CA: Sage Publications, 2004), pp. 302–327.

Coady, C. A. J., "Politics and the Problem of Dirty Hands," in Peter Singer (ed.), *A Companion to Ethics* (Oxford: Blackwell Publishers, 1993), pp. 373–383.

"'Combatant' cases to be reviewed: Supreme Court will look at U.S. citizens being held in Cuba," *Richmond Times Dispatch*, February 21, 2004.

Crowley, Michael, Stephanie Ebbert, Anthony Flint, Frank Phillips, Michael Rezendes, and Arist Frangules, "Political Capital; Net-Surfing Beacon Hill Watchers Now Able to Read Budgets, Bills Online," *Boston Globe*, April 9, 2000.

Darley, John M., and C. Daniel Batson, "'From Jerusalem to Jericho': A Study of Situational and Dispositional Variables in Helping Behavior," *Journal of Personality and Social Psychology* 27 (1973): 100–108.

Dawes, Robyn M., Alphons J. van de Kragt, and John M. Orbell, "Not Me or Thee but We: The Importance of Group Identity in Eliciting Cooperation in Dilemma Situations: Experimental Manipulations," *Acta Psychologica* 68 (1988): 83–97.

Deloria, Vine, Jr., and Clifford M. Lytle, *American Indians, American Justice* (Austin: University of Texas Press, 1983).

Donovan, Gill, "Ambition, defense of institutional church drove cardinal's career," *National Catholic Reporter*, December 27, 2002.

Doris, John M., "Persons, Situations, and Virtue Ethics," *Noûs* 32 (1998): 504–530.

Duval, Shelley, and Robert A. Wicklund, *A Theory of Objective Self Awareness* (New York: Academic Press, 1972).

Eagly, Alice H., Mary C. Johannesen-Schmidt, and Marloes L. van Engen, "Transformational, Transactional, and Laissez-Faire Leadership Styles: A Meta-Analysis Comparing Women and Men," *Psychological Bulletin* 129 (2003): 569–591.

Eagly, Alice H., and Steven J. Karau, "Role Congruity Theory of Prejudice Toward Female Leaders," *Psychological Review* 109 (2002): 573–598.

Ehrenreich, Barbara, "Two-Tiered Morality," *New York Times*, June 30, 2002.

Erlanger, Steven, "Havel Finds His Role Turning From Czech Hero to Has-Been," *New York Times*, November 4, 1999.

Fairholm, Gilbert W., *Perspectives on Leadership: From the Science of Management to Its Spiritual Heart* (Westport, CT: Quorum Books, 1998).

Feinberg, Joel, "Civil Disobedience in the Modern World," in Joel Feinberg and Russ Shafer-Landau (eds.), *Reason and Responsibility: Readings in Some Basic Problems of Philosophy*, 10th edition (Belmont, CA: Wadsworth Publishing, 1999), pp. 666–680.

Feinberg, Joel, "Psychological Egoism," in Joel Feinberg and Russ Shafer-Landau (eds.), *Reason and Responsibility: Readings in Some Basic Problems of Philosophy*, 10th edition (Belmont, CA: Wadsworth Publishing Company, 1999), pp. 493–505.

Fiedler, Fred Edward, *A Theory of Leadership Effectiveness* (New York: McGraw-Hill, 1967).

Flanagan, Owen, *Varieties of Moral Personality: Ethics and Psychological Realism* (Cambridge, MA: Harvard University Press, 1991).

Fleishman, Edwin A., "The Description of Supervisory Behavior," *Journal of Applied Psychology* 37 (1953): 1–6.

Frankfurt, Harry G., "Freedom of the Will and the Concept of a Person," *Journal of Philosophy* 68 (1971): 5–20.

Works Cited

Frankfurt, Harry G., "Identification and Wholeheartedness," in Ferdinand Schoeman (ed.), *Responsibility, Character, and the Emotions: New Essays in Moral Psychology* (Cambridge: Cambridge University Press, 1987), pp. 27–45.

French, John R. P., Jr., and Bertram Raven, "The Bases of Social Power," in Dorwin Cartwright (ed.), *Studies in Social Power* (Ann Arbor, MI: Institute for Social Research, 1959), pp. 150–167.

Friedman, Thomas L., "Haircut Grounded Clinton While the Price Took Off," *New York Times*, May 21, 1993.

Fulwood, Sam III, "Former Head of United Way is Convicted," *Los Angeles Times*, April 4, 1995.

Gardner, Howard, *Leading Minds: An Anatomy of Leadership*, in collaboration with Emma Laskin (New York: Basic Books, 1995).

Gardner, John W., *On Leadership* (New York: Free Press, 1990).

Garrett, Stephen A., "Political Leadership and the Problem of 'Dirty Hands,'" *Ethics and International Affairs* 8 (1994): 159–175.

Geroux, Bill, "Public picks up the tab, officials spend $410,000 at convention," *Richmond Times-Dispatch*, October 5, 2003.

Gerstmann, Evan, *Same-Sex Marriage and the Constitution* (Cambridge: Cambridge University Press, 2004).

Glater, Jonathan D., "Stewart's Celebrity Created Magnet for Scrutiny," *New York Times*, March 7, 2004.

Glover, Jonathan, *Humanity: A Moral History of the Twentieth Century* (New Haven: Yale University Press, 2000).

Goldhagen, Daniel Jonah, *Hitler's Willing Executioners: Ordinary Germans and the Holocaust* (New York: Knopf, 1996).

Goss, Tracy, Richard Pascale, and Anthony Athos, "The Reinvention Roller Coaster: Risking the Present for a Powerful Future," *Harvard Business Review on Change* (Boston: Harvard Business School Publishing, 1998), pp. 83–112.

Graen, George, "Role-Making Processes Within Complex Organizations," in Marvin D. Dunnette (ed.), *Handbook of Industrial and Organizational Psychology* (Chicago: Rand McNally College Publishing, 1976), pp. 1201–1245.

Graen, George, and James F. Cashman, "A Role-Making Model of Leadership in Formal Organizations: A Developmental Approach," in James G. Hunt and Lars L. Larson (eds.), *Leadership Frontiers* (Kent, OH: The Comparative Administration Research Institute, 1975): pp. 143–165.

Green, Stephen G., and Terence R. Mitchell, "Attributional Processes of Leaders in Leader-Member Interactions," *Organizational Behavior and Human Performance* 23 (1979): 429–458.

Greenhouse, Linda, "Access to Courts," *New York Times*, June 29, 2004.

Greenleaf, Robert K., *Servant Leadership: A Journey into the Nature of Legitimate Power and Greatness* (New York: Paulist Press, 1977).

Hampton, Jean, "The Nature of Immorality," *Social Philosophy and Policy* 7, 1 (1989): 22–44.

Hampton, Jean, "*Mens Rea*," *Social Philosophy and Policy* 7, 2 (1990): 1–28.

Haney, Craig, Curtis Banks, and Philip Zimbardo, "Interpersonal Dynamics in a Simulated Prison," *International Journal of Criminology and Penology* 1 (1973): 69–97.

Harman, Gilbert, "Moral Philosophy Meets Social Psychology: Virtue Ethics and the Fundamental Attribution Error," *Proceedings of the Aristotelian Society* 99 (1999): 315–331.

Harman, Gilbert, "No Character or Personality," *Business Ethics Quarterly* 13 (2003): 87–94.

HarperCollins Study Bible: New Revised Standard Version, edited by Wayne A. Meeks (London: HarperCollins Publishers, 1989).

Hayek, F. A., *Law, Legislation and Liberty: A New Statement of the Liberal Principles of Justice and Political Economy*, Vol. 1 (Chicago: The University of Chicago Press, 1973).

Heifetz, Ronald A., *Leadership Without Easy Answers* (Cambridge, MA: Belknap Press of Harvard University Press, 1994).

Hersey, Paul, and Kenneth H. Blanchard, "Life Cycle Theory of Leadership," *Training and Development Journal* 23, 5 (1969): 26–34.

Hersey, Paul, and Kenneth H. Blanchard, "Situational Leadership," in J. Thomas Wren (ed.), *The Leader's Companion: Insights on Leadership Through the Ages* (New York: Free Press, 1995), pp. 207–211.

Hicks, Douglas A., "Self-Interest, Deprivation, and Agency: Expanding the Capabilities Approach," *Journal of the Society of Christian Ethics* (in press).

Hicks, Douglas A., and Terry L. Price, "An Ethical Challenge for Leaders and Scholars: What Do People Really Need?" in *Selected Proceedings of the 1998 Annual Meeting of the Leaders/Scholars Association* (College Park, MD: James MacGregor Burns Academy of Leadership, 1999), pp. 53–61.

Hilberg, Raul, *The Destruction of the European Jews*, Vol. 3 (New York: Holmes and Meier, 1985).

Hill, Thomas E., Jr., "Servility and Self-Respect," in his *Autonomy and Self-Respect* (Cambridge: Cambridge University Press, 1991), pp. 4–18.

Hobbes, Thomas, *Leviathan*, edited by Richard Tuck (Cambridge: Cambridge University Press, 1991). Originally published in 1651.

Hollander, E. P., *Leaders, Groups, and Influence* (New York: Oxford University Press, 1964).

Homer, *The Odyssey*, translated by Robert Fitzgerald (Garden City, NY: Anchor Books, 1963).

House, Robert J., and Terence R. Mitchell, "Path-Goal Theory of Leadership," *Journal of Contemporary Business* 3, 4 (1974): 81–97.

Howell, Jane M., "Two Faces of Charisma: Socialized and Personalized Leadership in Organizations," in Jay A. Conger, Rabindra N. Kanungo, and Associates (eds.), *Charismatic Leadership: The Elusive Factor in Organizational Effectiveness* (San Francisco: Jossey-Bass Publishers, 1988), pp. 213–236.

Howell, Jane M., and Bruce J. Avolio, "The Ethics of Charismatic Leadership: Submission or Liberation?" *Academy of Management Executive* 6, 2 (1992): 43–54.

Hoyer, Stephen, and Patrice McDaniel, "From Jericho to Jerusalem: The Good Samaritan From a Different Direction," *Journal of Psychology and Theology* 18 (1990): 326–333.

Hu, Winnie, "Bloomberg Says He Has Improved Security at City Hall," *New York Times*, July 26, 2003.

Hume, David, *A Treatise of Human Nature*, 2nd edition, edited by L. A. Selby-Bigge and revised by P. H. Nidditch (Oxford: Clarendon Press of Oxford University Press, 1978).

Janis, Irving L., *Groupthink: Psychological Studies of Policy Decisions and Fiascoes*, 2nd edition (Boston: Houghton Mifflin Company, 1982).

"Janklow stopped 16 times as governor, not ticketed," *Richmond Times-Dispatch*, July 1, 2004.

Jenkins, Brian Michael, "Perspective on Policing; Elite Units Troublesome, but Useful; We Need Them for Tough Assignments, but They Require Skillful Management, Strong Leadership," *Los Angeles Times*, March 27, 2000.

Jones, David H., *Moral Responsibility in the Holocaust: A Study in the Ethics of Character* (Lanham, MD: Rowman and Littlefield Publishers, 1999).

Jones, Edward E., and Richard E. Nisbett, "The Actor and the Observer: Divergent Perceptions of the Causes of Behavior," in Edward E. Jones, David E. Kanouse, Harold H. Kelley, Richard E. Nisbett, Stuart Valins, and Bernard Weiner (eds.), *Attribution: Perceiving the Causes of Behavior* (Morristown, NJ: General Learning Press, 1972), pp. 79–94.

Jordan, Pat, "Bill Walton's Inside Game," *New York Times Magazine*, October 28, 2001.

Kant, Immanuel, "Duties towards Animals and Spirits," in his *Lectures on Ethics*, translated by Louis Infield (New York: Harper and Row Publishers, 1963), pp. 239–241.

Kant, Immanuel, *Groundwork of the Metaphysic of Morals*, translated and analyzed by H. J. Paton (New York: Harper and Row Publishers, 1964). Originally published in 1785.

Kant, Immanuel, "On a supposed right to lie from philanthropy," in his *Practical Philosophy*, translated and edited by Mary J. Gregor (Cambridge: Cambridge University Press, 1996), pp. 605–615. Originally published in 1797.

Kanungo, Rabindra N., and Manuel Mendonca, *Ethical Dimensions of Leadership* (Thousand Oaks, CA: Sage Publications, 1996).

Keeley, Michael, "The Trouble with Transformational Leadership: Toward a Federalist Ethic for Organizations," in Joanne B. Ciulla (ed.), *Ethics, the Heart of Leadership* (Westport, CT: Praeger, 1998), pp. 111–144.

Keller, Tiffany, and Fred Dansereau, "Leadership and Empowerment: A Social Exchange Perspective," *Human Relations* 48 (1995): 127–146.

Kelman, Herbert C., "Manipulation of Human Behavior: An Ethical Dilemma for the Social Scientist," *Journal of Social Issues* 21, 2 (1965): 31–46.

King, Martin Luther, Jr., "Letter from the Birmingham City Jail," in James Melvin Washington (ed.), *A Testament of Hope: The Essential Writings of Martin Luther King, Jr.* (San Francisco: Harper and Row Publishers, 1986), pp. 289–302.

Kirkpatrick, Shelley A., and Edwin A. Locke, "Leadership: Do Traits Matter?" *Academy of Management Executive* 5, 2 (1991): 48–60.

Kotter, John P., "What Leaders Really Do," in J. Thomas Wren (ed.), *The Leader's Companion: Insights on Leadership Through the Ages* (New York: Free Press, 1995), pp. 114–123.

Kotter, John P., "Leading Change: Why Transformation Efforts Fail," *Harvard Business Review on Change* (Boston: Harvard Business School Publishing, 1998), pp. 1–20.

"Kurt Eichenwald discusses the collapse of energy giant Enron," *Fresh Air*, January 17, 2002.

Kymlicka, Will, *Contemporary Political Philosophy: An Introduction* (Oxford: Clarendon Press, 1990).

Leitsinger, Miranda, "Genocide charge denied," *Richmond Times-Dispatch*, January 19, 2004.

Likert, Rensis, *New Patterns of Management* (New York: McGraw-Hill, 1961).

Lindholm, Charles, *Charisma* (Cambridge, MA: Basil Blackwell, 1990).

Lindsay, Anne, "On the Slippery Slope Again," *Analysis* 35 (1974): 32.

Lindsey, Alberta, "Director leaves seminary over code on gays," *Richmond Times-Dispatch*, October 2, 2004.

Lipman-Blumen, Jean, *Connective Leadership: Managing in a Changing World* (Oxford: Oxford University Press, 1996).

Locke, John, *Two Treatises of Government*, edited by Peter Laslett (Cambridge: Cambridge University Press, 1988). Originally published in 1690.

Ludwig, Dean C., and Clinton O. Longenecker, "The Bathsheba Syndrome: The Ethical Failure of Successful Leaders," *Journal of Business Ethics* 12 (1993): 265–273.

Lyons, David, "Moral Judgment, Historical Reality, and Civil Disobedience," *Philosophy and Public Affairs* 27 (1998): 31–49.

Machiavelli, Niccolò, *The Prince*, edited by Quentin Skinner and Russell Price (Cambridge: Cambridge University Press, 1988). Originally published posthumously in 1532.

Machiavelli, Niccolò, *Discourses on the First Ten Books of Titius Livius*, in Michael L. Morgan (ed.), *Classics of Moral and Political Theory*, 3rd edition (Indianapolis: Hackett Publishing Company, 2001), pp. 467–487. Originally published posthumously in 1531.

MacIntyre, Alasdair, *After Virtue: A Study in Moral Theory*, 2nd edition (Notre Dame, IN: University of Notre Dame Press, 1981).

MacIntyre, Alasdair, "Is Patriotism a Virtue?" in Markate Daly (ed.), *Communitarianism: A New Public Ethics* (Belmont, CA: Wadsworth Publishing, 1994), pp. 307–318.

Maitland, Alison, "Clearing up after the visionaries," *Financial Times*, January 30, 2003.

Maraniss, David, *First in His Class: The Biography of Bill Clinton* (New York: Simon and Schuster, 1995).

Mayerfeld, Jamie, *Suffering and Moral Responsibility* (New York: Oxford University Press, 1999).

Mayo, Bernard, *Ethics and the Moral Life* (London: Macmillan and Company, 1958).

McClelland, David C., "N achievement and Entrepreneurship: A Longitudinal Study," *Journal of Personality and Social Psychology* 1 (1965): 389–392.

McClelland, David C., *Human Motivation* (Glenview, IL: Scott, Foresman and Company, 1985).

Mendonca, Manuel, "Preparing for Ethical Leadership in Organizations," *Canadian Journal of Administrative Sciences* 18 (2001): 266–276.

Messick, David M., "Social Categories and Business Ethics," *Business Ethics Quarterly*, special issue (1998): 149–172.

Messick, David M., and Max H. Bazerman, "Ethical Leadership and the Psychology of Decision Making," *Sloan Management Review* 37, 2 (1996): 9–22.

Milgram, Stanley, *Obedience to Authority; An Experimental View* (New York: Harper and Row Publishers, 1974).

Mill, John Stuart, *On Liberty*, edited by Elizabeth Rapaport (Indianapolis: Hackett Publishing Company, 1978). Originally published in 1859.

Mill, John Stuart, *Utilitarianism*, edited by George Sher (Indianapolis: Hackett Publishing Company, 1979). Originally published in 1861.

Miller, Dale T., "The Norm of Self-Interest," *American Psychologist* 54 (1999): 1053–1060.

Miller, Dale T., and Rebecca K. Ratner, "The Power of the Myth of Self-Interest," in Leo Montada and Melvin J. Lerner (eds.), *Current Societal Concerns about Justice* (New York: Plenum Press, 1996), pp. 25–48.

Mitchell, Terence R., and Laura S. Kalb, "Effects of Outcome Knowledge and Outcome Valence in Supervisors' Evaluations," *Journal of Applied Psychology* 66 (1981): 604–612.

Mitchell, Terence R., and Robert E. Wood, "Supervisors' Responses to Subordinate Poor Performance: A Test of an Attributional Model," *Organizational Behavior and Human Performance* 25 (1980): 123–138.

Moody-Adams, Michele M., "Culture, Responsibility, and Affected Ignorance," *Ethics* 104 (1994): 291–309.

Moody-Adams, Michele M., *Fieldwork in Familiar Places: Morality, Culture, and Philosophy* (Cambridge, MA: Harvard University Press, 1997).

"Ms Swift's dilemma," *Economist*, January 29, 2000.

Murphy, Jeffrie G., "Jean Hampton on Immorality, Self-Hatred, and Self-Forgiveness," *Philosophical Studies* 89 (1998): 215–236.

Nagel, Thomas, "Moral Luck," in his *Mortal Questions* (Cambridge: Cambridge University Press, 1979), pp. 24–38.

National Institute for Occupational Safety and Health, United States Department of Health and Human Services, "Stress at Work," Publication No. 99-101, January 7, 1999.

National Public Radio, "NPR/Kaiser/Kennedy School Civil Liberties Update," August 2002.

New Oxford Annotated Bible with the Apocrypha: Revised Standard Version, edited by Herbert G. May and Bruce M. Metzger (New York: Oxford University Press, 1977).

Nisbett, Richard, and Lee Ross, *Human Inference: Strategies and Shortcomings of Social Judgment* (Englewood Cliffs, NJ: Prentice Hall, 1980).

Norris, Floyd, "If Ebbers Masterminded the Fraud, Why Didn't He Sell More Stock?" *New York Times*, March 5, 2004.

Oddie, Graham, "Moral Uncertainty and Human Embryo Experimentation," in K. W. M. Fulford, Grant R. Gillett, and Janet Martin Soskice (eds.), *Medicine and Moral Reasoning* (New York: Cambridge University Press, 1994), pp. 144–161.

Office of Indian Affairs, *Annual Report of the Commissioner of Indian Affairs to the Secretary for the Year 1871* (Washington, DC: GPO, 1872).

Oldenquist, Andrew, "Group Egoism," in Markate Daly (ed.), *Communitarianism: A New Public Ethics* (Belmont, CA: Wadsworth Publishing, 1994), pp. 255–267.

Oliner, Samuel P., and Pearl M. Oliner, *The Altruistic Personality: Rescuers of Jews in Nazi Germany* (New York: Free Press, 1988).

O'Toole, James, *Leading Change: The Argument for Values-Based Leadership* (New York: Ballantine Books, 1996).

Plato, *Republic*, translated by G. M. A. Grube and revised by C. D. C. Reeve (Indianapolis: Hackett Publishing Company, 1992).

Power, Samantha, *"A Problem from Hell": America and the Age of Genocide* (New York: Perennial, 2003).

Power, Samantha, "War and Never Having To Say You're Sorry," *New York Times*, December 14, 2003.

Price, Terry L., "Faultless Mistake of Fact: Justification or Excuse?" *Criminal Justice Ethics* 12, 2 (1993): 14–28.

Price, Terry L., "Explaining Ethical Failures of Leadership," *Leadership and Organization Development Journal: Special Issue on Ethics and Leadership* 21 (2000): 177–184.

Price, Terry L., "Character, Conscientiousness, and Conformity to Will," *Journal of Value Inquiry* 35 (2001): 151–163.

Price, Terry L., "The Ethics of Authentic Transformational Leadership," *Leadership Quarterly* 14 (2003): 67–81.

Price, Terry L., "Ethics," in George R. Goethals, Georgia Sorenson, and James MacGregor Burns (eds.), *Encyclopedia of Leadership* (Thousand Oaks, CA: Sage Publications, 2004), pp. 462–470.

Radant, Nancy, Richard Blackford, Tamara Porch, Paul Shahbaz, and Richard E. Butman, "From Jerusalem to Jericho Revisited: A Study in Helping Behavior," *Journal of Psychology and Christianity* 4 (1985): 48–55.

Rand, Ayn, "The 'Conflicts' of Men's Interests," *Objectivist Newsletter* 1, 8 (1962).

Rauch, Charles F., Jr., and Orlando Behling, "Functionalism: Basis for an Alternate Approach to the Study of Leadership," in James G. Hunt, Dian-Marie Hosking, Chester A. Schriesheim, and Rosemary Stewart (eds.), *Leaders and Managers: International Perspectives on Managerial Behavior and Leadership* (New York: Pergamon Press, 1984), pp. 45–62.

Rawls, John, "Legal Obligation and the Duty of Fair Play," in Sidney Hook (ed.), *Law and Philosophy; A Symposium* (New York: New York University Press, 1964), pp. 3–18.

Rawls, John, *A Theory of Justice* (Cambridge, MA: Belknap Press of Harvard University Press, 1971).

Raz, Joseph, *Engaging Reason: On the Theory of Value and Action* (Oxford: Oxford University Press, 1999).

Regan, Tom, *The Case for Animal Rights* (Berkeley: University of California Press, 1983).

Remember My Lai, PBS Video (Yorkshire Television production for *Frontline*, 1989).

Reuters News Service, "WorldCom CEO pay plan 'excessive,'" *Houston Chronicle*, December 11, 2002.

Rezendes, Michael, "Swift Defends Aides' Help in Personal Life," *Boston Globe*, January 6, 2000.

Richey, Warren, "Detainee cases hit court," *Christian Science Monitor*, January 23, 2004.

Rosebury, Brian, "Moral Responsibility and 'Moral Luck,'" *Philosophical Review* 104 (1995): 499–524.

Rosenbaum, David E., "Legal License; Race, Sex and Forbidden Unions," *New York Times*, December 14, 2003.

Rosener, Judy B., "Ways Women Lead," *Harvard Business Review* 68 (November–December 1990): 119–125.

Ross, W. D., *The Right and the Good* (Oxford: Clarendon Press, 1930).

Rost, Joseph C., *Leadership for the Twenty-First Century* (New York: Praeger, 1991).

Rousseau, Jean-Jacques, *A Discourse on the Origin of Inequality*, in his *The Social Contract and Discourses*, translated by G. D. H. Cole, revised and augmented by J. H. Brumfitt and John C. Hall (London: J. M. Dent Ltd., 1973), pp. 31–126. Originally published in 1755.

Sachs, Susan, "The Capture of Hussein: Ex-Dictator; Hussein Caught in Makeshift Hide-Out; Bush Says 'Dark Era' for Iraqis Is Over," *New York Times*, December 15, 2003.

"Same-Sex Marriage: Bush's Remarks on Marriage Amendment," *New York Times*, February 25, 2004.

Sandel, Michael J., *Liberalism and the Limits of Justice* (Cambridge: Cambridge University Press, 1982).

Sandel, Michael J., "Morality and the Liberal Ideal," *New Republic*, May 7, 1984.

Sartre, Jean-Paul, *Being and Nothingness: An Essay on Phenomenological Ontology*, translated by Hazel E. Barnes (New York: Philosophical Library, 1956). Originally published in 1943.

Schmidtz, David, *The Limits of Government: An Essay on the Public Goods Argument* (Boulder, CO: Westview Press, 1991).

Sears, David O., and Carolyn L. Funk, "Self-Interest in Americans' Political Opinions," in Jane J. Mansbridge (ed.), *Beyond Self-Interest* (Chicago: University of Chicago Press: 1990), pp. 147–170.

Shakespeare, William, *The Complete Works of William Shakespeare* (Cambridge: Cambridge University Press, 1987).

Simmons, A. John, "Tacit Consent and Political Obligation," *Philosophy and Public Affairs* 5 (1976): 274–291.

Simmons, A. John, "Too Much Patriotism?" Keynote Address, 2002 Meeting of the Virginia Philosophical Association.

Simons, Marlise, "Still Defiant, Milosevic Hears the Atrocities Read Out," *New York Times*, October 30, 2001.

Singer, Peter, "Famine, Affluence, and Morality," *Philosophy and Public Affairs* 1 (1972): 229–243.

Singer, Peter, *Practical Ethics* (Cambridge: Cambridge University Press, 1979).

Smith, Adam, *The Theory of Moral Sentiments*, edited by D. D. Raphael and A. L. Macfie (Oxford: Clarendon Press, 1976).

Smith, Holly, "Culpable Ignorance," *Philosophical Review* 92 (1983): 543–571.

Smith, Taylor C., "The Parable of the Samaritan," *Review and Expositor* 47 (1950): 434–441.

Solomon, Robert C., "Ethical Leadership, Emotions, and Trust: Beyond 'Charisma,'" in Joanne B. Ciulla (ed.), *Ethics, the Heart of Leadership* (Westport, CT: Praeger, 1998), pp. 87–107.

Solomon, Robert C., "Victims of Circumstances? A Defense of Virtue Ethics in Business," *Business Ethics Quarterly* 13 (2003): 43–62.

Sorkin, Andrew Ross, and Jonathan D. Glater, "Some Tyco Board Members Knew of Pay Packages, Records Show," *New York Times*, September 23, 2002.

Stogdill, Ralph Melvin, "Personal Factors Associated with Leadership: A Survey of the Literature," *Journal of Psychology* 25 (1948): 35–71.

Stogdill, Ralph Melvin, *Handbook of Leadership: A Survey of Theory and Research* (New York: Free Press, 1974).

Storms, Michael D., "Videotape and the Attribution Process: Reversing Actors' and Observers' Points of View," *Journal of Personality and Social Psychology* 27 (1973): 165–175.

Strawson, Peter, "Freedom and Resentment," in John Martin Fischer and Mark Ravizza (eds.), *Perspectives on Moral Responsibility* (Ithaca: Cornell University Press, 1993), pp. 45–66.

Tajfel, Henri, "Experiments in Intergroup Discrimination," *Scientific American* 223 (1970): 96–102.

Taylor, Shelley E., and Susan T. Fiske, "Point of View and Perceptions of Causality," *Journal of Personality and Social Psychology* 32 (1975): 439–445.

Thomas, Evan, and Andrew Murr, "The Gambler Who Blew It All: The bland smile concealed an epic arrogance. The fall of a preacher's kid who thought he had it all figured out," *Newsweek*, February 4, 2002.

Thoreau, Henry David, "A Plea for Captain John Brown," *Thoreau: People, Principles, and Politics*, edited by Milton Meltzer (New York: Hill and Wang, 1963), pp. 169–191.

The Trial of Adolf Eichmann, PBS Home Video (ABC News Productions and Great Projects Film Company, 1997).

Trilling, Lionel, "Huckleberry Finn," in his *The Liberal Imagination: Essays in Literature and Society* (Harmondsworth, Middlesex, England: Penguin Books, 1970).

Vecsey, George, "At Salad Bar with Knight, Praise Only the Cherry Tomatoes," *New York Times*, February 8, 2004.

Vroom, Victor Harold, and Philip W. Yetton, *Leadership and Decision-Making* (Pittsburgh: University of Pittsburgh Press, 1973).

Walker, Carson, "Former congressman gets jail time for traffic crash," Associated Press State and Local Wire, January 22, 2004.

Walzer, Michael, "Political Action: The Problem of Dirty Hands," *Philosophy and Public Affairs* 2 (1973): 160–180.

Watson, Gary, "Free Agency," *Journal of Philosophy* 72 (1975): 205–220.

Weber, Max, "Politics as a Vocation," in H. H. Gerth and C. Wright Mills (eds.), *From Max Weber: Essays in Sociology* (New York: Oxford University Press, 1946), pp. 77–128.

Werhane, Patricia, "Moral Imagination and the Search for Ethical Decision-Making in Management," *Business Ethics Quarterly*, special issue (1998): 75–98.

Werhane, Patricia H., *Moral Imagination and Management Decision-Making* (Oxford: Oxford University Press, 1999).

White, Ben, "Stock Options Becoming Pay-Plan Dinosaurs?; Image-Sensitive Firms Get Creative With Perks," *Washington Post*, January 31, 2003.

Wicklund, Robert A., and Shelley Duval, "Opinion Change and Performance Facilitation as a Result of Objective Self-Awareness," *Journal of Experimental Social Psychology* 7 (1971): 319–342.

Wiesel, Elie, public lecture, University of Richmond, December 1999.

Williams, Bernard, "Politics and Moral Character," in his *Moral Luck: Philosophical Papers 1973–1980* (Cambridge: Cambridge University Press, 1981), pp. 54–70.

Williams, Jack, "Double standard for pols lives," *Boston Herald*, May 19, 2000.

Winston, Kenneth I., "Necessity and Choice in Political Ethics: Varieties of Dirty Hands," in Daniel E. Wueste (ed.), *Professional Ethics and Social Responsibility* (Lanham, MD: Rowman and Littlefield, 1994), pp. 37–66.

Wolf, Susan, "Moral Saints," *Journal of Philosophy* 79 (1982): 419–439.

Wolf, Susan, "Sanity and the Metaphysics of Responsibility," in Ferdinand Schoeman (ed.), *Responsibility, Character, and the Emotions: New Essays in Moral Psychology* (Cambridge: Cambridge University Press, 1987), pp. 46–62.

Wolf, Susan, *Freedom Within Reason* (Oxford: Oxford University Press, 1990).

Yukl, Gary, *Leadership in Organizations*, 5th edition (Upper Saddle River, NJ: Prentice Hall, 2002).

Zimmerman, Michael J., "Moral Responsibility and Ignorance," *Ethics* 107 (1997): 410–426.

Index

absolutism; *see*: moral theory,
    deontological
Acheson, Dean, 92
actor-observer divergence, 77–82
    causes, 78–81, 82
affected ignorance; *see*: ignorance,
    culpable
Afghanistan, 176
    Taliban, 188
alcohol, 184
    addiction, 41
altruism, 3, 6, 9, 46, 53, 103, 125, 131,
    132, 133, 134, 135, 136, 137, 138,
    144, 146
animals, 154
Ansbro, John, 164
Antonakis, John, 44
Aquinas, Thomas, 5
Aramony, William, 12
Aristotle, 5, 65, 66, 132, 133, 184
    baseness vs. incontinence, 13,
        132
    human flourishing, 31
    Politics, 187
atheism, 34
Athos, Anthony, 147
attribution theory, 77, 78
audits, 17
autonomy, 36, 102, 103, 104, 108
Avolio, Bruce, 6, 46–47, 50, 51, 52–54,
    93, 112, 130

Bakker, Jim, 133
Banks, Curtis, 195
Barnes, Hazel, 130
Bass, Bernard, 9, 98, 127, 128, 129, 130,
    131–132, 133, 134, 135, 136, 137,
    138, 140, 143, 144; *see also*:
    leadership, transforming or
    transformational
Batson, C. Daniel, 62, 71, 81, 136
Bazerman, Max, 73
Behling, Orlando, 95
beliefs, 118, 123
    about costs and benefits of
        immorality, 7, 14, 15, 29, 30,
        31–42, 51, 137
    that exception making is justified,
        1, 6, 7, 8, 9, 26, 29, 32, 41, 50, 51,
        55, 57, 60–90, 114, 125, 136, 137,
        142, 149, 164, 171; *see also*:
        moral mistakes, of scope,
        about who is bound by
        morality
    that excluding outsiders is
        justified, 1, 6, 7, 58, 151, 152,
        154, 156, 165, 174, 183, 192, 197,
        198, 200; *see also*: moral
        mistakes, of scope; about who
        is protected by morality
    about importance of ends, 1, 25, 48,
        55, 56, 58, 62, 67, 68, 81, 136,
        149, 160, 164, 167, 170

beliefs (*cont.*)
about justified legal disobedience, 159, 160
nature of, 80
that one can get away with immorality, 7, 14, 16, 23, 30, 31, 32, 35, 36, 38, 39, 41, 42, 43, 48, 49, 50, 171
that one is special, 1, 30, 38, 41, 42, 43, 45, 49, 62, 63, 65, 74, 84, 88, 141
two senses, 38, 39
Bennet, James, 179
Bennett, Jonathan, 150–152, 153, 155–156, 157, 198
Bennis, Warren, 123
Bey, Djelal Munif, 172
Biederman, Marshall, 81, 136
bin Laden, Osama, 173
Blackford, Richard, 81
Blake, Robert Rogers, 75
Blanchard, Kenneth, 76
Blosser, James, 81, 136
Blum, John Morton, 170
boards of directors, 17, 45, 49
Bosnia, 173
Bowie, Norman, 57
Bowman, Rex, 141
Brady, F. Neil, 195
Bratzel, John, 169
Brewer, Marilynn, 194, 195
Brightman, Edgar: *Moral Laws*, 164
Brown, John: Harpers Ferry, 172
Buber, Martin, 157
Buchanan, Allen, 2
Bukharin, Nikolay, 56
Burns, James MacGregor, 3, 4, 5, 9, 84, 93, 95, 96, 99, 102–103, 104, 105, 106–110, 124, 128–129, 146, 147; *see also*: leadership, transforming or transformational
ethical values, 103
Leadership, 102, 124
value of equality, 108, 109
value of liberty, 107–108, 109
Burns, Robert, 26

Burrow, Richard, 141
Bush, George W., 26, 140, 175, 176, 188
business, 12, 19, 51, 52, 59, 65, 67, 73, 84, 96, 114, 140, 145, 147, 170, 195
Butler, Joseph, 34
"On the Love of our Neighbor," 33
Butman, Richard, 81

Carey, Michael, 128, 130
Carruthers, Peter, 154
Cartwright, Dorwin, 87
Cashman, James, 88
change, 147–149, 154, 156, 157, 163, 165, 166
character; *see*: leadership, trait approaches to; virtue theory
Chemers, Martin, 77
children,
cognitive predicaments of, 22
cover-ups of, 22
rearing of, 34, 183, 190
Cianciolo, Anna, 44
Ciulla, Joanne, 4, 5, 44, 70, 76, 95, 103, 105, 106, 128, 139–140, 153
civil disobedience, 157–168, 174
as exception making, 158, 159, 160, 162, 163
direct vs. indirect, 158, 159
civil rights movement, 157, 166
Clinton, Bill, 25, 48, 132, 179
Coady, C. A. J., 113
Cochran, Pamela, 81, 136
coercion, 4, 114
Colburn, Lawrence, 199
Cole, G. D. H., 85
collective action problems, 55
Colson, Charles, 171
common good, 5, 33, 130, 143, 144
communism, 170
Conger, Jay, 131
conscience, 33, 34, 150, 152, 161, 163
conscientiousness, 33, 151, 164, 199
consensus, 68, 144, 190, 191
lack of, 191, 194, 195

consent, 68, 83, 86, 115, 116, 144
contractualism, 84
courage, 14, 180
Crowley, Michael, 26
Cuban missile crisis, 92
customers, 19, 67

Daly, Markate, 112, 117
Dansereau, Fred, 87
Darley, John, 62, 71, 81, 136
David, King, 15, 26
    and Bathsheba, 15, 22
    and Nathan's parable, 20–23, 26
    and Uriah, 15, 22
    "Bathsheba Syndrome," 15
    cover-up of, 20, 22, 23
    God's indulgence of, 26
    moral knowledge of, 16, 20
Davis, James, 24
Dawes, Robyn, 135
deception, 3, 18, 19, 23, 59, 93, 94, 100,
    114, 169, 170
Declaration of Independence, 107
Deloria, Vine, Jr., 193
democracy, 160, 167
desires, 1, 28, 30, 34, 36, 37, 38, 41,
    42, 43, 46, 47, 66, 67, 104,
    124, 125–127, 134, 135, 137,
    155
    connection to beliefs about value, 7,
        36, 39, 41, 43, 44, 45, 56
    to lead, 66, 67
dirty hands, 8, 110–122, 162
    and moral idealism, 111
Donne, John, 89
Donovan, Gill, 73
Doris, John, 70, 72, 136
drugs
    addiction, 41
    marijuana, 88
Dunnette, Marvin, 88
Duval, Shelley, 79, 142

Eagly, Alice, 144–145
Ebbers, Bernard, 45
Ebbert, Stephanie, 26
Edwards, Jonathan, 155, 156

effectiveness, 3, 4, 5, 6, 7, 60, 64, 66,
    74, 75, 76, 90, 95, 97, 103, 139,
    140
    normative element of, 139, 141
egoism, 14, 15, 17, 18, 32, 33, 46, 47,
    49, 50, 51, 53, 93, 114, 125, 130,
    132, 133, 134, 184; *see also*:
    self-interest
    vs. self-sacrifice, 51, 54
Ehrenreich, Barbara, 73
Eichenwald, Kurt, 22
Eichmann, Adolf, 56
Eisenhower, Dwight, 172
emotions, 70
employees, 19, 24, 46, 75, 88, 98, 133,
    140
    compensation, 46
Enron, 12, 22, 45, 67, 73, 133
Erlanger, Steven, 25
ethical failures
    cognitive account of, 1, 3, 6, 12–14,
        18–27, 28, 39, 41, 42, 49, 128,
        134, 138, 142, 168, 169, 181, 182,
        183, 185, 186, 187
    of cover-ups, 23, 48
    of exception making, 7, 39, 42, 58
ethical failures, volitional account of,
    1, 3, 6, 9, 12–18, 19, 21, 23, 28,
    29–36, 39, 41, 43, 49, 53, 57, 128,
    169, 181, 183, 184, 185, 186, 189,
    195
    of exception making, 7, 29, 39, 42
    and leadership, transformational,
        124, 132, 134
ethics boards, 177
exception making
    behavioral checks on, 9, 149, 156,
        164, 165, 166–178
    against violence, 150, 161, 172, 175,
        176
    and defense of third parties, 172,
        173
    and self-defense, 172, 173
    to accept the penalty, 150, 161, 162,
        163, 176, 177
    epistemic argument for, 164, 165,
        166, 167, 175, 178, 179, 182

exception making (*cont.*)
  principle of inclusiveness, 2, 10,
    150, 156–157, 166, 167, 179, 182,
    199, 200
  publicity condition, 2, 27, 150, 161,
    169, 171, 174, 176
explanation, 17
  vs. moral analysis, 12

Fairholm, Gilbert, 123
fame, 44
family, 89, 151
Feinberg, Joel, 34, 158, 160–161
Fiedler, Fred, 75
Fischer, John Martin, 121
Fiske, Susan, 79
Fitzgerald, Joseph, 50
Fitzgerald, Robert, 17
Flanagan, Owen, 70, 71
Fleishman, Edwin, 75
Flint, Anthony, 26
followers, 1, 2, 76, 90, 97, 99, 100, 116,
    124, 128, 129, 130, 138, 139, 140,
    141, 142, 144, 170, 172, 173, 176,
    177, 180
  agency, 3, 4, 55, 99, 103, 104, 115,
    149, 168, 169
  characteristics of, 70, 76, 79, 80, 82
  exception-making behavior, 79, 82,
    88
  interests of, 1, 3, 4, 5, 29, 43, 44, 46,
    47, 49, 52, 53, 54, 55, 56, 84, 98,
    99, 106, 111, 114, 115, 119, 130,
    140, 141, 142, 145, 146, 149,
    155, 167, 190, 192, 194, 195,
    199
  resistance to change, 148
Frangules, Arist, 26
Frankfurt, Harry, 34, 126, 127
  first-order vs. second-order desires,
    126–127
French, John, Jr., 87
Friedman, Thomas, 48
Fulford, K. W. M., 199
Fulwood, Sam III, 12
Funk, Carolyn, 135
future generations, 181, 182, 199, 200

gambling: addiction, 41
Gandhi, Mahatma, 163
Gardner, Howard, 2
Gardner, John, 4, 5, 123, 130
  On Leadership, 123
Garrett, Stephen, 92, 114
Gates, Bill, 51
Geneva Conventions, 188
Geroux, Bill, 50
Gerstmann, Evan, 200
Gerth, H. H., 113
Gillett, Grant, 199
Glater, Jonathan, 49, 145
Glover, Jonathan, 22, 56, 57, 137, 138,
    151, 154
goal achievement; *see*: effectiveness
God, 5, 23, 26, 157, 173
Goethals, George, 4
Goldhagen, Daniel, 153
Good Samaritan: parable of, 61–63,
    71, 72, 90
Goss, Tracy, 147
Graen, George, 88
Green, Stephen, 78
Greenhouse, Linda, 188
Greenleaf, Robert, 6, 57, 99, 103; *see
    also*: leadership, servant
Gregor, Mary, 94
Grube, G. M. A., 3, 15, 48
guilt, 33, 34, 35, 119
  as a psychological response to the
    epistemic realities of
    leadership, 119–121

Hamdi, Yaser, 188
Hammonds, Warren, 200
Hampton, Jean, 20, 29–31, 32, 35,
    38–39, 135
Haney, Craig, 195
Harman, Gilbert, 70, 71, 72
Havel, Vaclav, 25
Hayek, F. A., 68
Heidegger, Martin, 129
Heifetz, Ronald, 123
helping behavior, 62, 81
Hersey, Paul, 76
Hicks, Douglas, 57, 61, 125, 173

Hilberg, Raul, 154
Hill, Thomas, Jr., 57
Himmler, Heinrich, 153–155
Hiroshima, 136
historical asymmetry, 196, 198
historical immorality, 10, 19, 179–200
  apartheid, 20
  British Colonial rule, 162, 198
  Holocaust, 19, 56, 153, 154, 155, 157,
    180, 189, 192, 198
    cover-up, 22
    Einsatzgruppen, 199
  internment of Japanese-Americans
    in World War II, 193
  segregation, 12, 157, 158, 159, 160,
    161, 165, 166, 173
    Jim Crow, 162, 165
    White Citizens Council, 164
  slavery, 19, 150, 151, 152, 153, 156,
    162, 179, 180, 183, 184, 187, 189,
    191, 193, 196, 198
  treatment of Armenians, 172
  treatment of Native Americans,
    193, 196
  treatment of women, 20, 179, 190,
    192, 194, 196, 198
Hitler, Adolf, 4, 5, 144, 169
  "Hitler problem," 3–5, 6
Hobbes, Thomas, 82, 83, 114, 115
  Leviathan, 82
Hollander, E. P., 84–87, 88, 89, 90, 141,
  142, 145
  idiosyncrasy credits, 84, 85, 86,
    141
Homer, 17
homosexuality, 189, 200
  discrimination, 187, 188
  same-sex marriage, 188, 191, 192,
    197, 200
Hook, Sidney, 160
Hosking, Dian-Marie, 95
House, Robert, 79, 80
Howell, Jane, 6, 130, 131
Hoyer, Stephen, 62, 63
Hu, Winnie, 24
Hume, David, 3
Hunt, James, 88, 95

Hussein, Saddam, 56, 173
  sons, 26
Hutcheson, Frances, 33

ignorance, culpable, 22, 183, 186, 187,
  197
immorality, nature of, 10, 30
Infield, Louis, 154
international community, 19
international criminal court, 140
international tribunals, 177
invisibility, 15, 48
Iran, 173
Iraq, 173, 175, 176
  Abu Ghraib prison scandal, 188
Irwin, Terence, 65, 132, 184

Janis, Irving, 149, 170–171, 194
  groupthink, 170, 194, 195
Janklow, Bill, 25
Jefferson, Thomas, 179
Jenkins, Brian Michael, 74
Jesus, 62
Johannesen-Schmidt, Mary, 145
Johnson, Lyndon, 175
Jones, David, 154, 156, 186, 198, 199
Jones, Edward, 77, 78, 80
Jones, Jim, 143
Jordan, Pat, 88
justification, 1, 2, 7, 8, 9, 23, 24–27, 50,
  91–122, 138, 141, 143, 145, 148,
  149, 150, 156, 157, 159, 160, 161,
  163, 165, 166, 168, 169, 171, 173,
  174, 175, 176, 177, 191
  and behavioral distinctiveness,
    60–65
  vs. excuse, 24, 25, 186
  vs. mitigation, 186

Kahan, Dan, 145
Kalb, Laura, 78
Kanouse, David, 77
Kant, Immanuel, 3, 40, 94, 100–101,
  102, 104, 107, 108, 154, 156,
  158
  broad or meritorious duties vs.
    strict or narrow duties, 102

Kant, Immanuel (*cont.*)
  categorical imperative, 40, 94, 104, 158
  commitment to volitional account, 40
  contradiction in conception, 100
  contradiction in will, 40, 101, 104
  on exception making, 39–40
  impartiality, 116
  on sympathy, 156
Kanungo, Rabindra, 6, 131
Karau, Steven, 144–145
Keeley, Michael, 128, 130
Keller, Tiffany, 87
Kelley, Harold, 77
Kelman, Herbert, 103
Kennedy, Joe, 105
Kennedy, John, 175
King, Martin Luther, Jr., 157–159, 161–162, 163, 165, 166
  epistemic concerns, 164
  "Letter from Birmingham City Jail," 166
  Montgomery boycott, 164
  Playboy Interviews, 164
King, William, 50
Kirkpatrick, Shelley, 66–67, 68, 69, 73
Knight, Bobby, 73
Kotter, John, 147, 148
Kozlowski, Dennis, 49
kulaks, 56
Kymlicka, Will, 108

Larson, Lars, 88
Laslett, Peter, 87
law, 135, 157–165
  just vs. unjust, 159, 161, 163
  respect for, 162, 163
Law, Bernard, 73
Lay, Kenneth, 73
leader agency, 57
leader-follower relationship, 3, 4, 44, 83–90, 104, 141, 170
  and role responsibilities, 63, 64, 195; *see also*: leadership, transactional approaches to

inequality between leaders and followers, 26
instrumental connection to goal achievement, 97
internal goods of, 96
leader well-being, 56
leaders, reasonable expectations on, 185, 189, 196, 197
  vs. what leaders are able to do, 185
leadership, charismatic, 6, 130
leadership, ends of, 6, 29, 45, 46, 48, 67, 68, 85, 96–102, 105, 106, 139, 140, 141, 142, 144, 145, 159, 165, 166, 167, 168, 174, 175, 176
  collective nature of, 1, 2, 138, 146
  and consequentialist moral theory, 97–100, 102
  and costs of immorality, 29
  instrumental connection to leader self-interest, 43, 44, 45, 47, 48, 49, 50, 53, 57, 133
  intrinsic value of, 29, 44, 50–58
  moral weight of, 93, 95, 96, 164, 177
  and preference satisfaction, 98
  variability in, 97–102
leadership, "Great Man" view of; *see*: leadership, trait approaches to
leadership, justificatory force of, 8, 26, 27, 111, 138–143, 149, 167, 168, 169, 171, 195
leadership, means of, 3, 101, 102, 105, 144, 159, 160, 164, 165, 166, 168, 176
leadership, nature of, 2, 10, 182
  and change, 147, 148
  consequentialism, 2, 95, 97–99, 111
  minimal agency, 4
  normative force, 7; *see also*: leadership, justificatory force of
  partiality, 2, 111, 114, 116–119, 140, 141, 143, 180
leadership, privileges of, 14, 16, 27, 46, 48, 49, 84
leadership, servant, 6, 57, 99
  and servility, 57
  test of, 99

leadership, situational approaches to, 7, 63, 64, 74–82, 83, 90
  Contingency Theory, 75
  path-goal theory, 79
  Situational Leadership, 76
leadership, trait approaches to, 7, 63, 64, 65–75, 77, 83, 90, 141, 144, 184
  knowledge, 63, 66, 68–69, 73
    business vs. moral, 69
  motivation, 63, 66–68, 73
  self-confidence, 66, 73–74, 128, 145
    vs. overconfidence, 73, 81, 144, 189, 195
  virtue, 63, 66, 69–74, 144, 146
leadership, transactional approaches to, 7, 63, 64, 82–90, 102, 103, 124, 125, 141
  Leader-Member Exchange Theory (LMX), 88, 170
leadership, transforming or transformational, 9, 10, 95, 102–110, 124, 125, 127, 128, 138, 143–146
  assumptions about knowledge, 128, 134, 143
  authentic, 9, 123–139
    vs. pseudo-transformational or inauthentic, 129–134, 138, 143, 144
  consequentialist elements of, 105–110
  deontological elements of, 104, 105
  end-values vs. modal values, 102–110, 143
  test of, 105, 106, 124
  and women, 145
leadership, women in, 10, 26, 144, 145, 146
  expectations on, 144
leadership ethics, 64, 94, 96, 146
  alleged obviousness of, 13, 18, 182, 187
  challenges to, 2, 5, 9, 13, 15, 19, 26, 27, 59, 89, 90, 96, 102, 103, 125, 144, 200

  definitional approach to, 3–5, 139, 189
  distinctiveness of, 1, 8, 14, 18, 21, 23, 25, 60, 64
  and moral fallibility, 8, 9, 10, 69, 70, 168, 182, 183, 184, 185, 196–200
leadership practice, 2, 9, 10, 14, 17–18, 27, 66, 75, 92, 99, 109, 140, 150, 163, 166, 169, 171, 175, 178, 179, 182, 184, 186, 187, 189, 196, 197, 199, 200
leadership studies, 3, 4, 10, 83, 123
leadership styles, 75, 80
  task vs. relationship, 75, 76, 80
Leitsinger, Miranda, 56
Lerner, Melvin, 135
Lewis, John, 105
liberalism, 167
  impartiality, 117, 118
Likert, Rensis, 75
Lincoln, Abraham, 137
Lindholm, Charles, 143
Lindsay, Anne, 199
Lindsey, Alberta, 200
Lipman-Blumen, Jean, 130
Locke, Edwin, 46–47, 50, 51, 54, 66–67, 68, 69, 73, 93, 112
Locke, John, 87, 115, 116, 167
  express vs. tacit consent, 87
  leader discretion or prerogative, 115
Logsdon, Jeanne, 195
Long, Huey, 105
Longenecker, Clinton, 12, 13–14, 15–17, 18, 20, 23, 133
Los Angeles Police Department, 74
Lott, Trent, 12, 20
loyalty, 15, 117, 118, 170
  loyal agent's standard, 195
Ludwig, Dean, 12, 13–14, 15–17, 18, 20, 23, 133
lying; *see*: deception
Lyons, David, 161, 162–163
Lytle, Clifford, 193

Macfie, A. L., 33
Machiavelli, Niccolò, 5, 74, 75, 76, 113,
        114
    Discourses, 5
    The Prince, 74
    amoralism of, 5
MacIntyre, Alasdair, 71, 117–118
Maitland, Alison, 45
management, 17
    vs. leadership, 148
manipulation, 3, 18, 93, 94, 103, 108,
        114, 169, 170
Mao Zedong, 138
    Cultural Revolution, 56
Mansbridge, Jane, 135
Maraniss, David, 25
Marx, Karl, 129
master-slave relationship, 4
May, Herbert, 21, 61
Mayerfeld, Jamie, 68
Mayo, Bernard, 72
McClelland, David, 6, 68
McDaniel, Patrice, 62, 63
McNamara, Robert, 175
Meeks, Wayne, 61
Meltzer, Milton, 172
men in leadership, 145
Mendonca, Manuel, 6, 46
Messick, David, 73, 194, 195
Metzger, Bruce, 21, 61
Milgram, Stanley, 71, 136
military, 51, 53, 73, 141, 151, 157, 169,
        170, 176
    West Point, 52
Mill, John Stuart, 5, 99, 107, 148
Miller, Dale, 51, 135
Mills, C. Wright, 113
Milosevic, Slobodan, 172
mistakes, factual, 7, 16, 28, 31, 41
Mitchell, Terence, 78, 79, 80
Montada, Leo, 135
Moody-Adams, Michele, 152,
        181, 183–185, 186–187, 188,
        189
    inability thesis, 183, 186
moral conservatism, 149, 150
moral correction, 150–157

moral imagination, 142
moral luck, 120, 180, 182
moral membership, 10, 19, 179–200
moral mistakes, 1, 6, 28, 67, 69, 72,
        106, 119, 149, 171, 179–200
    of content, 7, 14, 18, 19, 20, 21, 23,
        193
    about the importance of morality,
        7, 36, 37, 39, 41, 43, 49, 55, 67,
        68, 81, 136, 137, 140, 142, 143,
        144, 146, 149, 200
    of scope, 7, 8, 14, 19, 20, 21, 23, 25,
        28, 31–36, 43, 102, 138, 144, 145,
        193
    about who is bound by morality,
        7, 9, 13, 20, 22, 26, 28, 37, 42, 59,
        168, 193
    about who is protected by
        morality, 7, 10, 20, 28, 168, 173,
        187, 193, 198, 199
moral motivation, 29–43, 49, 51, 55
    external constraints on behavior,
        31, 35, 46, 49
    internal constraints on behavior,
        32, 33, 35, 36, 49
moral problems, contemporary, 10,
        179, 180, 182, 187, 190, 191, 196,
        199, 200
moral psychology, 7, 9, 13, 18, 24,
        27, 29, 35, 36, 41, 43, 60, 61,
        71, 112, 124, 138, 140, 151,
        196
moral requirements, 2, 6, 12, 13, 14,
        30, 31, 37, 49, 53, 58, 68, 71, 72,
        78, 89, 90, 93, 109, 111, 118, 128,
        137, 142, 146, 150, 167, 171,
        176
    against deception, manipulation,
        and coercion, 93, 94, 107, 115,
        125, 169
    against harming innocent civilians,
        125, 136, 138
    against killing, 157
    against slavery, 187
    against taking advantage of less
        privileged, 21
    against use of violence, 174, 175

application of, 1, 8, 19, 22, 23, 24,
25, 27, 28, 37, 39, 40, 41, 42, 56,
59–65, 67, 73, 81, 82, 86, 91, 92,
106, 108, 109, 117–118, 141, 142,
155, 157; *see also*: moral
mistakes, of scope
competing norms, 135, 136, 140, 143
epistemic reasons to adhere to, 8,
110, 112, 119–121, 148, 160, 168
to help those in need, 20, 81, 101,
104
to keep promises, 37, 59, 100, 151,
152
to respect property rights, 150, 152,
194
to save a life, 37, 95
on treatment of followers, 77, 113,
114, 115, 117, 138
on treatment of other leaders, 113,
116
on treatment of outsiders, 113, 116,
118
variable authority of, 8, 32, 37, 38,
39, 41, 59, 64, 76, 82, 83, 90, 93
moral theory, 2, 27, 50, 60, 70, 93, 112
communitarian, 116–119, 189
moral particularity, 117
role differentiation, 117
consequentialist, 94, 96, 97–100,
105, 106, 110, 116
deontological, 94, 95, 96, 100–102,
103, 105, 106, 110, 111, 116, 168
morality, nature of, 22, 60, 104, 110
authoritativeness, 23, 30, 31, 38, 42,
135, 136, 137
morality, public, 153, 154, 155, 156,
165
Morgan, Michael, 5, 75
Morgenthau, Henry, Jr., 170
Mother Teresa, 51
Mouton, Jane Srygley, 75
Murphy, Jeffrie, 39
Murr, Andrew, 73
My Lai, 199

Nagasaki, 136
Nagel, Thomas, 180

Nanus, Burt, 123
narcissism, 133
Nisbett, Richard, 18, 77, 78, 80,
181–182
Nixon, Richard, 170
non-profit sector, 12, 59, 133
Norris, Floyd, 45
Nuon Chea, 56

obligation, political, 162, 163
Oddie, Graham, 199
Odysseus, 17
Oldenquist, Andrew, 112
Oliner, Pearl, 198, 199
Oliner, Samuel, 198, 199
ombudsmen, 17
Orbell, John M., 135
O'Toole, James, 4, 76, 147, 148, 171
outsiders, 89, 90, 97, 99, 113, 116, 149,
150, 156, 172, 173, 175, 176, 177,
188
conflicts of interests between
groups, 52, 53, 55, 118
interests of, 3, 29, 55, 99, 111, 116,
118, 140, 143, 168, 174, 194

Pachachi, Adnan, 56
pacificism, 157
Padilla, Jose, 188
Paige, Glen, 170
Pascale, Richard, 147
Paton, H. J., 40, 94, 156
patriotism, 118
Phillips, Frank, 26
Plato, 3, 15, 48, 50, 65, 66
Republic, 15, 65
philosopher king, 65
ring of Gyges, 15, 48
Thrasymachus, 50
Pol Pot, 56
politics, 12, 45, 59, 65, 77, 84, 89, 92,
96, 105, 106, 108, 111, 113, 114,
116, 121, 137, 141, 147, 161, 162,
167, 169, 170, 171, 172, 173
bureaucrats, 148
Porch, Tamara, 81
poverty, 99

power, 4, 5, 6, 15, 16, 27, 38, 44, 46, 48, 49, 68, 82, 83, 87, 95, 113, 130, 170, 180
  coercive, 87
  legitimate, 87
  personalized vs. socialized power motives, 6, 68, 69, 130
Power, Samantha, 172, 173
Price, Russell, 5, 74, 113
Price, Terry, 4, 12, 24, 120, 123, 125, 166
pride, 33
professions, 167, 177
profit, 97, 98
psychology, cognitive, 2, 18

racism, 20, 22, 143, 162, 165, 181
Radant, Nancy, 81, 82
Rand, Ayn, 47, 51
Rapaport, Elizabeth, 148
Raphael, D. D., 33
rationality, 23, 28, 30, 32, 38, 46, 47, 61, 67, 102, 112, 121, 135, 136, 141, 194
  application of, 39
  authoritativeness of, 38
Ratner, Rebecca K., 135
Rauch, Charles, Jr., 95
Raven, Bertram, 87
Ravizza, Mark, 121
Rawls, John, 84, 100, 160
  "duty of fair play," 160, 161, 163
Raz, Joseph, 7, 36–37
realist view, 8, 92, 110–122
  and amoralism, 92, 113
reconciliation view, 8, 92, 93, 96, 102, 103, 106, 108, 110, 111, 112, 118
rectitude, 33
Regan, Tom, 199
regicide, 15
regret, 35, 118, 119
  as psychological response to epistemic realities of leadership, 119–121
religion, 61, 73, 133, 136, 154, 158, 164, 173, 200
remorse, 33, 34, 35

representativeness heuristic, 181
respect, 36
responsibility, 9, 10, 22, 24, 25, 125, 131, 147, 149, 150, 162, 166, 167–178, 181, 182, 183–200
  assessed on continuum, 176
revenge, 19
Rezendes, Michael, 26
Richey, Warren, 188
rights, 107, 134, 143, 144, 146, 188, 189
role congruity theory, 145
Roosevelt, Franklin, 105, 106, 108, 137, 169, 170
  "secret map," 169
Rosebury, Brian, 120
Rosenbaum, David, 188
Rosener, Judy, 145
Ross, Lee, 18, 181–182
Ross W. D.: prima facie duties, 38
Rost, Joseph, 128
Rousseau, Jean-Jacques, 84, 129
Rout, Leslie, Jr., 169
Rumsfeld, Donald, 26
Rwanda, 173
Ryan, Maurice, 81, 136

Sachs, Susan, 56
Sandel, Michael, 117
Sartre, Jean-Paul, 129
Schmidtz, David, 115
Schoeman, Ferdinand, 42, 127, 181
Schriesheim, Chester, 95
Sears, David, 135
Selby-Bigge, L. A., 3
self-interest, 1, 3, 5, 9, 14, 16, 28, 29, 30, 31, 32, 36, 43–58, 61, 93, 114, 125, 128, 129, 130, 132, 133, 134, 135, 137, 140, 145, 184
  of morality, 15, 17, 31, 46, 47
  as part of human nature, 13
  as socially acceptable, 51
selfishness, 1, 33, 34, 49, 50, 52–55, 129, 135, 195
September 11, 136, 173
sex, 12, 15, 34, 135, 193
  addiction, 41

Shafer-Landau, Russ, 34, 158
Shahbaz, Paul, 81
Shakespeare, William, 123
　Hamlet, 123
　　Laertes, 123
　　Polonius, 123
shame, 33, 34
　vs. embarrassment, 34
shepherd analogy, 5
Sher, George, 99
Simmons, A. John, 87, 88, 116
Simons, Marlise, 172
Sinclair, T. A., 5, 65
Singer, Peter, 99, 113, 199
Sisyphus, 57
Skinner, Quentin, 5, 74, 113
Smith, Adam, 33
　The Theory of Moral Sentiments, 33
Smith, Holly, 22, 186
Smith, Taylor, 63
social contract theory, 83, 115
social Darwinism, 143
social psychology, 70, 71, 77, 194,
　195
　in-group vs. out-group, 194
　intergroup bias, 194, 195
social sciences, 3, 10, 50, 74, 134
Socrates, 31
Solomon, Robert, 70, 71, 72
Sorenson, Georgia, 4
Sorkin, Andrew, 49
Soskice, Janet Martin, 199
Sponseller, Richard, 50
sports, 73, 88, 96
state of nature, 83–89, 114, 167
Stalin, Joseph, 56
　purges, 57
Steidlmeier, Paul, 9, 98, 129, 130,
　　131–132, 133, 134, 135, 136, 137,
　　138, 140, 143, 144
Stephanopoulos, George, 48
Sternberg, Robert, 44
Stewart, Martha, 145
Stewart, Rosemary, 95
stockholders, 19, 133
Stogdill, Ralph, 75, 95
Storms, Michael, 79

Strawson, Peter, 121
success: by-products of, 15, 16,
　133
suffering, 36
Supreme Court, 159, 188
Swift, Jane, 26
sympathy, 61, 101, 125, 136, 155
　vs. belief, 151
　as check on morality, 150–157

Tajfel, Henri, 194
Taylor, Shelley, 79
temptation, 16, 17, 18, 137
Ten Commandments, 103
terrorism, 59
terrorist suspects, 188, 189, 191, 192,
　197
　enemy combatants, 188, 189
Thomas, Evan, 73
Thompson, Hugh, 199
Thoreau, Henry David, 163, 172
torture, 138
Trilling, Lionel, 152
Truman, Harry, 136, 138, 170
trust, 70, 95
truth to self, 123–130, 132, 133
Tuck, Richard, 83, 115
Twain, Mark, 150
　Huckleberry Finn, 150–153, 154, 155,
　　156
　　Jim, 150, 151, 152, 153,
　　156
　　Miss Watson, 152, 153, 154, 156
Tyco, 49

Underground Railroad, 176
United Nations, 175
United Way, 12
utilitarianism, 94, 98, 99, 100, 106, 107,
　110, 111, 112
　impartiality, 98, 111, 116, 140
　rule utilitarianism, 95

Valins, Stuart, 77
van de Kragt, Alphons, 135
van Engen, Marloes, 145
Vecsey, George, 73

virtue theory, 65, 71, 74, 89
  critique of, 70–72
Vogt, Bruce, 81, 136
volenti non fit injuria, 86
Vroom, Victor, 169

Walker, Carson, 25
Wal-Mart, 19, 73
Walton, Bill, 88
Walzer, Michael, 105, 110–111, 115,
    120, 121, 122, 141, 162
Washington, James, 158
Watson, Gary, 34, 126–127
  values-based account of the self,
    127
wealth, 6, 44
  executive compensation, 45, 49
    as desert, 45
    as incentives, 45
    "golden handcuffs," 45
    "golden parachutes," 45
Weber, Max, 113
Weiner, Bernard, 77
Welch, Jack, 140

Werhane, Patricia, 54, 142
whistle-blowing, 20, 21
White, Ben, 45
Wicklund, Robert, 79, 142
Wiesel, Elie, 157
Williams, Bernard, 112, 119, 120, 122
Williams, Jack, 45
Winston, Kenneth, 112, 114, 121
Wolf, Susan, 42, 69, 102, 181, 182,
    189–197
  sanity, 190, 192
Wood, Robert, 78
Wooden, John, 88
WorldCom, 45
Wren, J. Thomas, 76, 77, 148
Wueste, Daniel, 112

Yetton, Philip, 169
Yukl, Gary, 97–98, 170

Zimbardo, Philip, 195
  Stanford Prison experiment,
    195
Zimmerman, Michael, 186